Everyman, I will g[o with thee]
and be thy guide

WOMEN ROMANTICS
1785–1832:
WRITING IN PROSE

Edited by
JENNIFER BREEN
University of North London

EVERYMAN
J. M. DENT · LONDON
CHARLES E. TUTTLE
VERMONT

This edition first published by Everyman Paperbacks in 1996

Selection, introduction and other critical apparatus
© Jennifer Breen, 1996

J. M. Dent
Orion Publishing Group
Orion House
5 Upper St Martin's Lane
London WC2H 9EA
and
Charles E. Tuttle Co. Inc.
28 South Main Street
Rutland, Vermont 05701, USA

Typeset by CentraCet Ltd, Cambridge
Printed in Great Britain by
The Guernsey Press Co. Ltd, Guernsey, C. I.

British Library Cataloguing-in-Publication Data
is available upon request.

ISBN 0 460 87793 3

CONTENTS

Note on the Editor   ix
Chronology of the Authors' Times   xi
Introduction   xix
Note on the Texts   xli

WOMEN ROMANTICS 1735–1832:
  WRITING IN PROSE   1

MARY WOLLSTONECRAFT   3
From *Thoughts on the Education of Daughters*:
  Reading   5
From the *Analytical Review*:
  Article XXV (1789)   7
  Article XVII (1791)   8
From *A Vindication of the Rights of Woman*:
  Chapter 9   8
To Joseph Johnson:
  Letter 16   19
From *Letters Written during a Short Residence in Sweden,
    Norway, and Denmark*:
  Letter 4   20
  Letter 7   22
Letter:
  Introductory to a Series of Letters on the Present Character
    of the French Nation   31
Letters to Gilbert Imlay:
  Letter 69   35
  Letter 70   36

Letter 71   37
Letter 73   37
Letter 74   38
Letter 75   38
Letter 76   40
Letter 77   41
Letter 78   42

ANNA SEWARD   45
Letter 5: To Josiah Wedgwood   46
Letter 61: To Helen Maria Williams   49
Letter 66: To Sir Walter Scott   50

CATHERINE MACAULAY   55
From *Letters on Education*:
    Letter 14   56
    Letter 15   61
    Letter 22   64

HELEN MARIA WILLIAMS   69
From *Letters from France*:
    Letter 4   71

MARY HAYS   75
From *Letters and Essays*:
    No. 3   76
From the *Monthly Magazine*: Improvements Suggested in
    Female Education   81

ANNA BARBAULD   87
Letter to Mrs Carr   89
From 'On the Origin and Progress of Novel-Writing'   90

JOANNA BAILLIE   97
Plays on the Passions:
    From 'Introductory Discourse'   99

HANNAH MORE   105
From *Strictures on the Modern System of Female Education*:
   Chapter 8   106
From *Moral Sketches of Prevailing Opinions and Manners*:
   Unprofitable Reading   115

MARY ROBINSON   121
From *Letter to the Women of England on the Injustice
of Subordination*   122
From *Memoirs of Mary Robinson*   128

FANNY BURNEY   137
From *Diary and Letters*:
   1802   138
   1815   145

JANE TAYLOR   149
From Letter to Miss S. L. C.   150
The Troublesome Friend   152
A Letter to Whomsoever It May Concern   155

DOROTHY WORDSWORTH   161
From *Letters of William and Dorothy Wordsworth*:
   Letter to Lady Beaumont, April 1806   163
   Letter to Lady Beaumont, September 1806   165
From *A Journal of a Tour on the Continent* (1820)   167

MARY LAMB   191
On Needlework   193

MARY RUSSELL MITFORD   199
Letter to Sir William Elford   200
Our Village   202

MARY SHELLEY   213
From *History of a Six Weeks' Tour*:
   Letter 1: 17 May 1816   214
   Letter 2: 1 June 1816   217
On Ghosts   220
Letter to Maria Gisborne, 15 August 1822   226

CLAIRE CLAIRMONT   237
From *Journal*   239

FRANCES TROLLOPE   241
From *The Domestic Manners of the Americans*:
   Chapter 22, 'Small Landed Proprietors – Slavery'   242

Notes   251
The Authors and Their Critics   271
Suggestions for Further Reading   285
Acknowledgements   290
Index of Authors' Names   292

NOTE ON THE EDITOR

JENNIFER BREEN has lectured in the UK and abroad on Romantic Poetry and Twentieth-Century Literature. Dr Breen has edited *Wilfred Owen: Selected Poetry and Prose* (1988), *Women Romantic Poets, 1785–1832: An Anthology* (new edn 1994), *Victorian Women Poets, 1830–1901: An Anthology* (1994), and is author of *In Her Own Write: Twentieth-Century Women's Fiction* (1990).

Year	Artistic Context	Historical Events
1785	Boswell, *Journal of a Tour of the Hebrides* Cowper, *Poems* Gainsborough, *Mrs Siddons* (portrait) Ann Yearsley, *Poems on Several Occasions*	Bill for Parliamentary Reform collapses; Edmund Cartwright patents the power loom; first Channel crossing made by balloon
1786	Burns, *Poems* Reynolds, *The Duchess of Devonshire and her Small Daughter* (portrait)	Financial reforms; commercial treaty with France
1787	Mary Wollstonecraft, *Thoughts on the Education of Daughters* Charlotte Smith, *Elegiac Sonnets*	American Constitution signed
1788	Hannah More, *Slavery: A Poem* Mary Wollstonecraft, *Original Stories from Real Life* Helen Leigh, *Miscellaneous Poetry* Charlotte Smith, *Emmeline*	Australia settled by British; *Times* founded; trial of Warren Hastings begins; William Wilberforce's first motion to abolish slave trade
1789	Blake, *Songs of Innocence*; *Book of Thel* Phillip, *The Voyage of Governor Phillip to Botany Bay* Elizabeth Hands, *The Death of Amnon*	French Revolution, Fall of Bastille (July); Declaration of Rights of Man and the Citizen (August); Washington is US President; first cotton textiles factory in Manchester

Year	Artistic Context	Historical Events
1790	Joanna Baillie, *Poems* Burke, *Reflections on the French Revolution* Helen Maria Williams, *Julia*; *Letters Written from France* Blake, *Marriage of Heaven and Hell* C. Macaulay, *Letters on Education*	Lavoisier publishes a table of chemical elements
1791	Burns, *Tam o' Shanter* Paine, *The Rights of Man* Anna Barbauld, *Epistle to William Wilberforce*	
1792	Robert Anderson, ed., *Poets of Great Britain* Mary Wollstonecraft, *A Vindication of the Rights of Woman*	Pitt's attack on slave trade; September Massacres in Paris; Republic proclaimed in France; first successful use of coal-gas in lighting
1793	Burns, *Songs* Wordsworth, *An Evening Walk* Godwin, *Political Justice* Mary Hays, *Letters and Essays* Mary Robinson, *Poems, 1791–3*	Washington's second term as President; execution of Louis XVI (June); execution of Marie-Antoinette (October); France at war with Britain
1794	Blake, *Songs of Experience* Ann Radcliffe, *Mysteries of Udolpho*	Execution of Lavoisier in France; Habeas Corpus Act suspended in Britain until 1801
1795	Southey, *Poems*	Treason & Sedition Acts; acquittal of Warren Hastings; first settlement of New Zealand
1796	Wordsworth, *The Borderers* Ann Yearsley, *The Rural Lyre* Mary Wollstonecraft, *Letters Written . . . Sweden, Norway, and Denmark*	War between Spain and Britain; Royal Technical College founded in Glasgow
1797	Matilda Bethem, *Elegies and Other Small Poems* S. T. Coleridge, *The Ancient Mariner* Charlotte Smith, *Elegiac Sonnets*, Vol. 2	*Journal of Natural Philosophy, Chemistry & other Arts* founded

Year	Artistic Context	Historical Events
1798	Joanna Baillie, *Plays on the Passions*, Vol. 1 Malthus, *Principles of Population* Elizabeth Moody, *Poetic Trifles* Wordsworth & S. T. Coleridge, *Lyrical Ballads*	
1799	Blake, *The Adoration of the Magi* (tempera) Hannah More, *Strictures on the Modern System of Female Education*	Napoleon is First Consul; Religious Tract Society is founded; Treason & Sedition Acts
1800	Maria Edgeworth, *Castle Rackrent* Wordsworth, *Michael*	Jefferson is US President; Royal Institution of Science founded
1801	Maria Edgeworth, *Belinda* Amelia Opie, *The Father and Daughter* *Memoirs of Mary Robinson*	First Census (Pop. 9,168,000); General Enclosure Act
1802	Joanna Baillie, *Plays on the Passions*, Vol. 2 Anna Dodsworth, *Fugitive Pieces* *Edinburgh Review* founded Anne Hunter, *Poems* Eliza Kirkham Mathews, *Poems* Amelia Opie, *Poems*	Peace of Amiens; Health & Morals of Apprentices Act; beginnings of photography
1803	Mme de Staël, *Delphine* Turner, *Calais Pier* (painting)	War with France renewed; John Dalton establishes atomic theory
1804	Joanna Baillie, *Miscellaneous Plays* Matilda Bethem, *Biographical Dictionary of Celebrated Women* Blake, *Jerusalem*; *Milton*	Thomas Telford commences construction of Caledonian Canal
1805	Milne, *Simple Poems on Simple Subjects* Scott, *Lay of the Last Minstrel* Jane & Ann Taylor, *Original Poems for Infant Minds* Wordsworth completes *The Prelude* (published in 1850) Turner, *Shipwreck* (painting)	Battle of Trafalgar; London Docks opened; first factory lit by gas at Manchester

Year	Artistic Context	Historical Events
1806	Byron, *Fugitive Pieces* Charlotte Richardson, *Poems Written on Different Occasions* Mary Robinson, *Poetical Works* Charlotte Smith, *Beachy Head and other Poems* Scott, *Ballads*	Bill for the Abolition of the slave trade passed in Parliament; East India Docks open in London
1807	Byron, *Hours of Idleness* Charles & Mary Lamb, *Tales from Shakespeare* Mme de Staël, *Corinne* Turner, *The Sun Rising through Vapour* (painting) Wordsworth, *Poems in Two Volumes*	Air pump for mines introduced
1808	Anne Grant, *The Highlanders* Felicia Hemans, *Poems* Amelia Opie, *The Warrior's Return* Leigh Hunt founds *Examiner*	Peninsular War beings
1809	Charles & Mary Lamb, *Poetry for Children* *Quarterly Review* founded	
1810	Alexander Chalmers, *English Poets* S. T. Coleridge lectures on Shakespeare Anna Seward, *Poetical Works*	Durham Miners' Strike; method of preserving food in cans discovered
1811	Jane Austen, *Sense and Sensibility* Scott, *The Lady of the Lake* Shelley, *The Necessity of Atheism* *Letters of Anna Seward*	Princes of Wales is Regent; Shelley expelled from Oxford
1812	Joanna Baillie, *Plays on the Passions*, Vol. 3 Byron, *Childe Harold* (Cantos 1 & 2) Maria Edgeworth, *The Absentee* Felicia Hemans, *The Domestic Affections*	French retreat from Moscow; Elgin Marbles brought to England; 'Luddite Riots' commence; John Common invents a reaping-machine

Year	Artistic Context	Historical Events
1813	Jane Austen, *Pride and Preduduce* Byron, *The Bride of Abydas* Shelley, *Queen Mab* Blake, *Day of Judgement* (drawings)	
1814	Jane Austen, *Mansfield Park* Byron, *The Corsair* Anne Grant, *Eighteen Hundred and Thirteen* Wordsworth, *The Excursion* Turner, *The Frosty Morning* (painting)	Napoleon abdicates; first Treaty of Paris between Allies and France; invention of cylinder-press printing; Corn Law passed by Parliament
1815	Constable, *Boat Building* (painting)	Battle of Waterloo; Stephenson patents the steam engine
1816	Jane Austen, *Emma* Matilda Bethem, *The Lays of Marie* Byron, *Poems on His Domestic Circumstances* S. T. Coleridge, *Christabel*; *Kubla Khan*; *Pains of Sleep* Hannah More, *Poems* Peacock, *Headlong Hall* Jane Taylor, *Essays in Rhyme on Morals and Manners* *Blackwood's Magazine* founded	End of Twenty Years War leaves acute distress in England; Robert Owen opens school at cotton mill
1817	S. T. Coleridge, *Biographia Literaria* Keats, *Poems* Constable, *Flatford Mill* (painting) M. & P. Shelley, *History of a Six Weeks' Tour*	Habeas Corpus suspended
1818	Jane Austen, *Northanger Abbey* Matilda Bethem, *Vignettes in Verse* Peacock, *Nightmare Abbey* Charlotte Richardson, *Harvest: A Poem* Mary Shelley, *Frankenstein*	First passenger ship made of iron; Institute of Civil Engineers founded

Year	Artistic Context	Historical Events
1819	Byron, *Don Juan* (two cantos) Shelley, *The Cenci*	Peterloo Massacre; first macadam roads laid
1820	Clare, *Poems* Anna Barbauld, *The British Novelists* Keats, *La Belle Dame Sans Merci*; *Lamia*; *Isabella*; *Eve of St Agnes*; *Hyperion and Other Poems* Lamb, *Essays of Elia* Shelley, *Prometheus Unbound* Southey, *Vision of Judgment*	Accession of George IV; Royal Astronomical Society founded; opening of Regent's Canal, London
1821	Joanna Baillie, *Metrical Legends* Elizabeth Bentley, *Poems* Clare, *The Village Minstrel* De Quincey, *Confessions of an Opium Eater* Letitia E. Landon, *The Fate of Adelaide* Constable, *The Hay Wain* (painting) Shelley, *Adonais*	London Co-operative Society founded; Michael Faraday expounds the principle of electric motor
1822	Byron, *The Vision of Judgment*	Royal Academy of Music founded in London
1823	Helen Maria Williams, *Poems on Various Subjects* Felicia Hemans, *The Siege of Valencia* Lamb, *The Essays of Elia*	Peel's penal reforms begin; Birkbeck College founded; Charles Babbage works on a calculating machine; *The Lancet* founded; Mechanics Institutes founded
1824	Letitia E. Landon, *The Improvisatrice* M. R. Mitford, *Our Village*	Repeal of 1662 Poor Law Act; Repeal of Combination Laws of 1799 and 1801; establishment of National Gallery
1825	Anna Barbauld, *Works* Felicia Hemans, *The Forest Sanctuary* Letitia E. Landon, *The Troubador*	First passenger train in Britain (Stockton–Darlington railway); commercial crisis in England
1826	Elizabeth Barrett, *Essay on Mind* Mary Shelley, *The Last Man*	Anti-Power Loom Riots in Lancashire

Year	Artistic Context	Historical Events
1827	Clare, *The Shepherd's Calendar* Fenimore Cooper, *The Prairie* Letitia E. Landon, *The Golden Violet* Keble, *The Christian Year*	University of London founded
1828	Felicia Hemans, *Records of Women* Constable, *Salisbury Cathedral* (painting)	Wellington is Prime Minister; repeal of Test & Corporation Acts
1829	Letitia E. Landon, *The Venetian Bracelet*	Catholic Emancipation Act; Metropolitan Police Force established by Peel
1830	Cobbett, *Rural Rides* Felicia Hemans, *Songs of the Affections* Mary Shelley, *Perkin Warbeck*	Accession of William IV; resignation of Wellington; Earl Grey is Prime Minister; agricultural labourers' riots in South England; Royal Geographical Society founded

INTRODUCTION

During the 'Romantic' period (1785–1832), the genre of the
novel was favoured by the majority of women readers and
writers.[1] The non-fiction prose written by women in this period
is nevertheless important and this selection reflects the main
themes of women essayists and thinkers in that era: the edu-
cation and conduct of girls and women; women's reading and
social criticism; women's rights *vis-à-vis* men's; France, the
Revolution and war; slavery; the 'uncanny'. These women's
prose forms were also wide-ranging: personal letters and formal
public letters; moral sermons and philosophical pamphlets;
literary prefaces and journalistic articles; private diaries and
public memoirs; literary reviews and political tracts. In order to
give the reader a wide variety of this non-fiction prose from the
period, I have reprinted some selections from works that are
already available, such as the letters of Dorothy Wordsworth
and Mary Wollstonecraft Shelley, and the seven-volume edition
of Mary Wollstonecraft's writings. My main purpose, however,
is to provide substantial passages from interesting works that
are difficult to obtain: Catherine Macaulay's *Letters on Edu-
cation* (1790) and Mary Robinson's *Letter to the Women of
England* (1799), for example, which are available only in
depository libraries such as the British Library.

Only some of these women authors are 'Romantic' in the
sense of writing on the topics that form part of one or other
narrow view of 'Romanticism'. Yet 'Romanticism', as David
Simpson has recently pointed out, can be said to encompass all
'the writings of the late eighteenth and early nineteenth centur-
ies, sharing a general historical situation but not necessarily held
together by any essential or prescriptive characteristics. Literary
critics and historians have traditionally posited such character-
istics in a manner allowing them to distinguish between what is
more or less "romantic", early and late romantic, pre- and post-
romantic, highly or anti-romantic. Such usages are seldom

consistent, and have mostly been employed to justify one set of preferences over others according to some standard or other of exemplary historicality.'[2] A broad 'period' definition allows the inclusion in this 'Romantic' anthology of any woman prose writer whose works were printed between 1785 and 1832, whether they have the characteristics of a conventional 'romanticism' or not.

Nevertheless, Mary Wollstonecraft's heightened account of the execution of Louis XVI, Helen Maria Williams's evocation of the storming of the Bastille and Anna Letitia Barbauld's atmospheric re-creation of a death by drowning connect with the late-eighteenth-century male poets' frequent interest in what has come to be known as the 'uncanny'. Similarly, the letters of Dorothy Wordsworth and Mary Shelley share the preoccupations of the male Romantics in, for example, their precise detailing of natural phenomena. On the other hand, the fabricated 'letters' of Mary Hays and Mary Robinson are concerned with the status of women, a subject which has not often been seen as central to past theories about Romanticism.

Male Romantics, such as Coleridge and Shelley, were concerned with questions of knowledge and how knowledge is acquired. David Simpson suggests that 'in the late eighteenth century there is an unusually widespread preoccupation with the problem of knowledge. There is a concern about whether objectivity and accuracy are possible in perception and description, about whether we can ever know anything wholly.'[3] But theoreticians of Romanticism must also query their own 'credibility' if they continue to omit women prose writers from the canon, apart from the usual three: Dorothy Wordsworth, Mary Wollstonecraft and Mary Shelley.[4]

For women writers of the Romantic period, questions about how to acquire and deal with knowledge differed from men's, since upper- and middle-class men had more opportunity to be educated fully in logical discourse. A few women writers thus posed the question, 'How are we to obtain access to knowledge?' Or, in other words, 'How are we women to be educated?' These questions form part of that general Enlightenment for which the eighteenth century is noted. But, as Marshall Brown demonstrates, the traditional notion that 'Romantic' writers of 1785–1832 were in revolt against the Enlightenment is faulty:

'Far from being a repudiation of Enlightenment, Romanticism was its fulfilling summation.'[5]

As part of eighteenth-century Enlightenment, those women who had acquired a classical education through their fathers' or their brothers' assistance, or through their own seizing of opportunities, began to question the status quo in regard to women's education generally. Marshall Brown suggests that male Romantic writers were bringing about change or 'revolution' in the sense of a cyclical movement 'toward the future'.[6] That women's questions about their education are part of a process of cyclical change is shown by the fact that, as early as 1697, Mary Astell, in *A Serious Proposal to the Ladies for the Advancement of their True and Greatest Interest*, suggested that upper- and middle-class women should be educated at a live-in academy in order to prepare themselves to deal better afterwards with the problems of their social worlds. But Astell's aims were religious in orientation rather than secular.

In the 1790s, women who wrote on education defined their subject broadly, including under this heading subjects such as procedures for nurturing infants satisfactorily, methods of moral training and questions about the co-education of boys and girls. Catherine Macaulay, in *Letters on Education* (1790), gave education for women a secular interpretation in her 'letters' to Hortensia. This mode of writing moral or philosophical essays by means of imagined letters was popular with women at that time, perhaps because this form allowed them a certain informality of register that suited their aims in attracting as wide an audience as possible. In her letters, Macaulay discusses how to bring up babies as well as how to educate children in the elements of formal knowledge. These letters were addressed to aristocratic women rather than to the middle classes, perhaps because aristocratic women were deemed to have more money to spend on their children's education.

Macaulay suggests, for example, that aristocratic women should not feel obliged to breastfeed their infants, despite the fact that the practice of 'wet-nursing' as a substitute was already considered undesirable.[7] Macaulay asserted rhetorically: 'Can you expect that a fine lady should forego all her amusements and enter into the sober habits of domestic life, in order to enable her to nourish her offspring with wholesome food?' Twentieth-century readers might think that this rhetorical question is satiric, but Macaulay subsequently advocated that infants of the upper classes should be handed over to be brought up by 'an active young wench' or 'where people can afford it, two or three of them'.[8] *Plus ça change* ...

Macaulay, however, was the first woman writer to advocate the education of girls in a similar way to boys, arguing that girls should be taught sports and boys needlework, and that both sexes should be taught classical and modern languages, mathematics and philosophy (Letter 15). In this way, she believed, society would be reformed in that marriages would be based on both partners having equal advantages in learning. Women would not be regarded, in relation to their thinking capacities, as being inferior to men.

Both Astell's and Macaulay's treatises on education were, *inter alia*, concerned with the well-being of upper-class women, whereas Wollstonecraft made it clear, in *A Vindication of the Rights of Woman* (1792), that she was addressing the middle classes:

> ... the instruction which has hitherto been addressed to women has rather been applicable to *ladies* ... but, addressing my sex in a firmer tone, I pay particular attention to those in the middle class, because they appear to be in the most natural state. [...] Discussing then those pretty feminine phrases, which the men condescendingly use to soften our slavish dependence, and despising that weak elegancy of mind, exquisite sensibility, and sweet docility of manners, supposed to be the sexual characteristics of the weaker vessel, I wish to show that elegance is inferior to virtue, that the first object of laudable ambition is to obtain a character as a human being, regardless of the distinction of sex; and that secondary views should be brought to this simple touchstone.[9]

Both Wollstonecraft and Macaulay argued that it was necessary to educate women so that they might become better companions in marriage. Wollstonecraft also idealistically thought that everyone, regardless of gender, should 'obtain a character as a human being', that is, develop the inner self to its fullest capacity through education and experience. But how is this to be done? She noted that 'the power of generalizing ideas, of drawing comprehensive conclusions from individual observations' is the true purpose of education, but that in her time this 'power' of generalizing 'has not only been denied to women; but writers have insisted that it is inconsistent, with a few exceptions, with their sexual character'. In other words, women cannot be educated to generalize from particular instances because the characteristics of their sex make such education impossible to achieve.

Wollstonecraft nevertheless drew up a plan of education for post-revolutionary France that took into account differences in ability which she imputed to be the result of class differences, not gender differences:

> ... day schools, for particular ages, should be established by government, in which boys and girls might be educated together. The schools for younger children, from five to nine years of age ought to be absolutely free and open to all classes.[10]

At the age of nine, according to Wollstonecraft, children from different social strata should be separated, the less clever learning a suitable trade, and the more advanced taking on higher intellectual studies. Although Wollstonecraft appeared to be addressing only the more democratic and therefore more enlightened Republic of France, her ideas about education were intended to be applicable to England.

In this proposed plan for universal education, Wollstonecraft envisaged that co-education would ensure friendly relations between the sexes and encourage early beneficial marriages between intellectual equals, and that education for women would make them better companions for their male partners as well as better mothers for their children. In Chapter 9, which is reprinted here, she allows, however, that educated women might remain single and lead fulfilling lives.

Hannah More's writings also formed part of that revolutionary cycle of change brought in by the Enlightenment in that her later work was directed towards the working classes and their education. But her political aim was to keep working-class people to their station in life through the inculcation of a religious morality, rather than to encourage democracy. She also addressed the subject of the education of middle-class women, but her work, *Strictures on the Modern System of Female Education* (1799), and her essays, including 'Unprofitable Reading', are written from a stronger religious perspective than Wollstonecraft's are. More believed in the concept of 'original sin' whereas Wollstonecraft did not. Wollstonecraft commented on the French Revolution, 'We must get entirely clear of all the notions drawn from the wild traditions of original sin ... [that] persuade us that we are naturally inclined to evil: we shall then leave room for the expansion of the human heart, and, I trust, find that men will insensibly render each other happier as they grow wiser.'[11] Sin for Wollstonecraft is immoral behaviour induced by poor social arrangements, including bad laws, whereas, like William Blake, she sees the free expression of the imagination as overcoming the attractions of evil. Thus she sees good education as essentially helping human beings to develop their faculties as much as they can in the realms of art, science and morality.

More, on the other hand, believes that children are 'beings who bring into the world a corrupt nature and evil disposition, which it should be the great end of education to rectify'. From this viewpoint she argues that 'the prevailing system of education' is failing to 'counteract' the 'corruption of our nature'.[12] Because of this belief, More's adumbrations on education tend to emphasize the formation of the child's moral character, whereas Wollstonecraft's theories of education are geared towards bringing out a child's intellect and imagination in order to develop her generalizing powers as well as her character.

Like Wollstonecraft, however, More does not differentiate between the male and female sexes in her plans for improving their moral education. To More, for example, vanity is a sin that is as pernicious in men as in women, even if vanity might be thought to flourish more in women than in men. For More, differences in the behaviour of men and women are brought about by their legal and social status, not by any inherently different characteristics. But, in contrast with Wollstonecraft, More's comments on women's education are not founded on the idea that women suffer from the oppression of men, but rather that women themselves are their own worst enemies, because they become addicted to fashions in conduct and dress rather than being desirous of acquiring the virtues of self-denial and modesty in the pursuit of 'mental and moral excellence'.

Despite their different philosophical and religious stances, Wollstonecraft and More are in agreement about the superficiality of most women's habits of thought. But More is satisfied with her identification of the problems without seeking practical solutions, whereas Wollstonecraft advocates that boys and girls should be educated in the same subjects in the same rational manner. They agree that a smattering of 'accomplishments' in art, music and dancing are a waste of a female's time. More writes satirically about the number of dancing instructors that are needed to teach a girl to dance.[13]

Wollstonecraft comments:

> the instruction which women have hitherto received has tended only, with the constitution of civil society, to render them insignificant objects of desire – mere propagators of fools! – if it can be proved that in aiming to accomplish them, without cultivating their understandings, they are taken out of their sphere of duties and made ridiculous and useless when the short-lived bloom of beauty is over, I presume that *rational* men will excuse me for endeavouring to persuade them [women] to become more masculine and respectable.[14]

Wollstonecraft is indirectly asserting that women should be fully educated rather than given a few accomplishments which might aid them in catching a husband. Both More and Wollstonecraft speak from the viewpoint of experienced educators, since Wollstonecraft ran a school at Stoke Newington before she took up writing professionally, and More had taught girls at her sisters' school in Bristol.

The main difference between More's and Wollstonecraft's ideas on education lies in their emphases. In *Strictures on Female Education*, More is concerned with moral training rather than with education in rational modes of thought that Wollstonecraft favours. Despite the fact that More had taught girls, her writing concentrates not on intellectual skills but on fostering in women the virtues of humility, sobriety, industry and economy rather than advocating, as Wollstonecraft does, that women be taught sciences such as anatomy, medicine, botany and astronomy, as well as engineering, history, philosophy, politics and languages. But on one matter both More and Wollstonecraft concur fully: that voracious reading of second-rate novels has a pernicious effect on the minds of young women. More writes in her essay 'Unprofitable Reading':

> *all* these books are not wicked . . . Many works of fiction may be read with safety, some even with profit . . . Among the overflowing number of fictitious writings, not a few are there in the English,

and still more and worse in the French and German schools, in
which the intrigue between the already married hero and heroine
is opened by means so apparently innocent, and conducted so
gradually, and with so much plausibility, as, for a time, to escape
detection. Vicious scenes are artfully kept out of sight, while
virtuous principles are silently, but systematically, undermined, till
the imagination, that notorious corrupter of the heart, has had
time to prepare the work of destruction. Such fascinating qualities
are lavished on the seducer, and such attractive graces on the
seduced, that the images indulged with delight by the fancy, carry
on the reader imperceptibly to a point which is not so far from
their indulgence in the act as some imagine. (pp. 116, 117)

More suggests that literature should be a repository of moral
standards which affects the reader for good. Even when reading
novels that are now canonized, such as Fielding's *Tom Jones* or
Rousseau's *Heloise*, More thinks that the reader's imagination
is probably corrupted. In other words, she thinks that the
reading of sensational novels actually perverts the morality of
the reader so that she becomes indifferent to aspects of right and
wrong; for example, in such novels, the breaking of the seventh
commandment, which condemns adultery, is represented as
attractive – even natural – to the reader. More's views here are
somewhat akin to twentieth-century social critics who think that
the reading and viewing of scenes of violence and pornography
predispose the reader and viewer to commit similar acts.

Conversely, Wollstonecraft's objections to the reading of
second-rate novels are made primarily on aesthetic grounds and
only secondarily on moral ones:

... stupid novelists, who, knowing little of human nature, work
up stale tales, and describe meretricious scenes, all retailed in a
sentimental jargon, which equally tend to corrupt the taste, and
draw the heart aside from its daily duties... when I exclaim
against novels, I mean when contrasted with those works which
exercise the understanding and regulate the imagination. For any
kind of reading I think better than leaving a blank still a blank,
because the mind must receive a degree of enlargement and obtain
a little strength by a slight exertion of its thinking powers; besides,
even the productions that are only addressed to the imagination,
raise the reader a little above the gross gratification of appetite, to
which the mind has not given a shade of delicacy.[15]

Wollstonecraft deplores trite 'sentimental' novels mainly because she thinks that women who read such ill-written works are not developing common sense nor the ability to generalize. Thus her comments, although verging on moral disgust, are nevertheless mainly concerned with matters of taste and aesthetic value.

Anna Barbauld, who, like More and Wollstonecraft, mixed and worked with dissenting religious groups, nevertheless distinguishes between literary and social criticism when discussing the novels of the period. In 'On the Origin and Progress of Novel-Writing' – her introduction to an edition of major novels, which included Richardson's *Clarissa* – Barbauld asserts that the main purpose of the novel is to entertain rather than to educate. She concludes that if a novel fails to entertain the reader, then it fails as a work of art:

> ... when I take up a novel, my end and object is entertainment; and as I suspect that to be the case with most readers, I hesitate not to say that entertainment is their legitimate end and object ... It is pleasant to the mind to sport in the boundless regions of possibility; to find relief from the sameness of everyday occurrences by expatiating amidst bright skies and fairer fields; to exhibit love that is always happy, valour that is always successful; to feed the appetite for wonder by a quick succession of marvellous events; and to distribute, like a ruling providence, rewards and punishments which fall just where they ought to fall ... The unpardonable sin in a novel is dullness: however grave or wise it may be, if its author possesses no powers of amusing, he has no business to write novels, he should employ his pen in some more serious part of literature.

At first Barbauld seems to oppose the views of both More and Wollstonecraft because, unlike them, she regards novels purely as a form of entertainment and suggests that reading need not always be seen as a means of education and instruction. Nevertheless, Barbauld also thinks that novels might have a moral effect on the reader. With regard to English novels she finds, somewhat chauvinistically, that the effects are usually beneficial: 'It is impossible to deny that the most glowing and impressive sentiments of virtue are to be found in many of these compositions [novels], and have been deeply imbibed by their youthful readers' (p. 91). Thus, although Barbauld shows awareness that a novel is a fabrication and not a representation of actual lived experience, at the same time she thinks that a novel is 'a mirror of life', and, even when evil behaviour is represented, the reader can learn about evil without actually encountering evil in real life. But she subsequently adds that, even if the 'trash ... poured out upon the public from the English presses' is 'not vicious', French novelists such as Crébillon and Louvet might 'contaminate' the minds of female readers. One might think that Barbauld's views in her introduction are partly dictated by the necessities of *real politik*, because she could scarcely criticize severely those works which she introduced in reprints to the public.

One view to which all three critics subscribe is that the vogue in young women for reading the sentimental novels of the day promoted vacuity of thought and an exaggerated sentimentalism that was injurious to sensible relationships between men and women, whether married or unmarried. Barbauld writes, 'Least of all will a course of novels prepare a young lady for the neglect and tedium of life which she is perhaps doomed to encounter' (p. 94). More condemns such reading even more virulently: 'the habitual indulgence in such reading [of novels] is a silent, mining mischief ... The constant habit performs the work of a mental atrophy; it produces all the symptoms of decay, and the danger is not less for being more gradual, and, therefore, less suspected' (p. 116). Wollstonecraft's insistence that women should eschew trashy novels and take up serious reading is a constant theme in her reviews for Joseph Johnson's periodical, the *Analytical Review* (1788–97). In *A Vindication of the Rights of Woman*, she adds criticism of the social behaviour of women:

> Novels, music, poetry, and gallantry, all tend to make women the creatures of sensation, and their character is thus formed in the mould of folly during the time they are acquiring accomplishments, the only improvement they are excited, by their station in society to acquire. This overstretched sensibility naturally relaxes the other powers of the mind, and prevents intellect from attaining the sovereignty which it ought to attain to render a rational creature useful to others, and content with its own station: for the exercise of the understanding, as life advances, is the only method pointed out by nature to calm the passions.[16]

Wollstonecraft herself wrote two novels: *Mary* (1787) and *The Wrongs of Woman* (1798), the latter of which was published posthumously. Both these novels are didactic and thus not 'in the mould of folly'. Yet, Hannah More is censorious of *The Wrongs of Woman* because she claims that in it Wollstonecraft 'asserts ... that adultery is justifiable, and that the restrictions placed on it by the laws of England constitute one of the *Wrongs of Women*'.[17] Wollstonecraft, however, merely represented in fictional form how the laws of England in regard to divorce were stricter for women then than they were for men.

For More, Wollstonecraft and Barbauld, social and moral criticism form part of the work of literary criticism. Joanna Baillie, on the other hand, in her introduction to her first series of plays, confines herself to her own practice as a dramatist. Her introduction predates William Wordsworth's similar 'Preface' to the second edition of his and S. T. Coleridge's *Lyrical Ballads* (1800). Baillie assesses the worth of novels on the grounds of whether they reveal 'human nature' to the reader:

> After all the wonderful incidents, dark mysteries, and secrets revealed, which eventful novel so liberally presents to us; after the beautiful fairy ground, and even the grand and sublime scenes of nature with which descriptive novel so often enchants us; those works which most strongly characterize human nature in the middling and lower classes of society, where it is to be discovered by stronger and more unequivocal marks, will ever be the most popular. For though great pains have been taken in our higher sentimental novels to interest us in the delicacies, embarrass-ments, and artificial distresses of the more refined part of society, they have never been able to cope in the public opinion with these. The one is a dressed and beautiful pleasure-ground, in which we are enchanted for a while, amongst the delicate and unknown plants of artful cultivation; the other is a rough forest of our native land; the oak, the elm, the hazel, and the bramble are there; and amidst the endless varieties of its paths we can wander for ever. Into whatever scenes the novelist may conduct us, what objects soever he may present to our view, still is our attention most sensibly awake to every touch faithful to nature; still are we upon the watch for everything that speaks to us of ourselves. (pp. 99–100)

Baillie implies that works of art should be concerned with the feelings and behaviour of the common man and woman rather than with the 'artificial', cultivated feelings 'of the more refined part of society'. Subsequently, she discusses the work of the dramatist in devising dialogue that is both convincing and natural.

Other women prose writers of the Romantic period show more concern with the problems of social existence as women than in trying to represent life in art. Mary Hays – whose development as a writer was influenced by her friendship with Mary Wollstonecraft, William Godwin and their circle – sets out, in her *Letters and Essays* (1793), an impassioned argument against the subordination of women: she describes 'the absurd despotism which has hitherto, with more than gothic barbarity, enslaved the female mind, the enervating and degrading system of manners by which the understandings of women have been chained down to frivolity and trifles, have increased the general tide of effeminacy and corruption'. She suggests that women are encouraged to 'conform to the perpetual fluctuation of fashion', not for their own good, but for commercial reasons in order to foster 'a brisk circulation of money' (p. 76). Writers such as Mary Wollstonecraft, according to Hays, 'are endeavouring to dispel the magical illusion of custom' so as to 'restore women to the glory of rationality'. In other words, if men enjoy the fruits of rational thought, why should women not do so as well?

Hays then proposes the ideal of an equal intellectual partnership: 'Similarity of mind and principle is the only true basis of harmony.' Hays admitted that she owed much to Wollstonecraft's work and, in fact, she asked Wollstonecraft to advise her on the content of *Letters and Essays* prior to publication. Hays supposes that 'authority' and vested interests aim to suppress women's assertion of their 'rights to rationality' in the same way that an hereditary king or queen will 'with paternal solicitude endeavour to guard his people from light and knowledge'. Here Hays alludes to the French Revolutin of 1789, implying that the arbitrary use of power in England, whether private or public, will lead to a similar rebellion on the part of the oppressed:

> every infringement of right weakens duty, every stretch of prerogative gives a mortal wound to monarchy, and every weak sense of proscription prepares the way for their utter demolition . . . The love of arbitrary power, with morbid influence, corrupts the human mind; and after the factitious strength of delirium, exhausted by the unnatural exertion, sinks into helpless effeminacy

and cowardly despondence, the usurper must sooner or later be
the victim of his usurpation. (p. 77)

Hays, like Wollstonecraft, also compares women to siren-like
creatures who try to attain power over men, as well as to slaves.
When men exert blind authority over women as husbands and
fathers, they are able to enforce 'sullen acquiescence, gloomy
resignation, fretful impatience or degrading servility', but their
womenfolk seek methods of defecting from such rule. Thus
Hays warns men that despotism in the family leads to insubor-
dination in the ranks at home. She also asserts that if women
were educated in a similar way to men, then women would be
better able to assess the quality of men's thought.

Hays attempts to quash the idea that both she and Wollstone-
craft might be seen 'by some sagacious married men to be
incompetent to form any just opinion of the cares and duties of
a conjugal state, from never having entered the matrimonial lists
. . .' She suggests that 'the cool impartial looker on' – as she and
Wollstonecraft both are – is in fact much better qualified to
make an objective assessment of the problems of married life
than are those who are actively engaged in marriage. She makes
an analogy here between married men and West Indian planta-
tion owners whom she sees, just like husbands in regard to their
wives, as being incapable of taking just action in relation to the
abolition of slavery because of their vested interests.

Mary Robinson's pamphlet, *Letter to the Women of England
on the Injustice of Subordination* (1799), published two years
after Wollstonecraft's death, bears some comparison with *A
Vindication of the Rights of Woman* and Hays's *Letters and
Essays.* Under the pseudonym Anne Frances Randall, Robinson
firmly links herself with Wollstonecraft just as Hays had done
earlier, by referring to the fact that 'an illustrious British female,
(whose death has not been sufficiently lamented, but to whose
genius posterity will render justice) has already written volumes
in vindication of "The Rights of Woman"'. In a footnote,
Robinson comments that 'it requires a *legion of Wollstonecrafts*
to undermine the poisons of prejudice and malevolence' in
relation to justice for women.

Robinson's fundamental claim is that women should have
access to public and private power, and that society operates by
double standards in preventing women from engaging in any

social activity in which men desire to maintain power. She cites drunkenness and gambling as vices that are kept in the province of men, and suggests ironically that these supposed pleasures are forbidden to women as part of women's general subordination:

> Man may enjoy the convivial board, indulge the caprices of his nature; he may desert his home, violate his marriage vows, scoff at the moral laws that unite society, and set even religion at defiance, by oppressing the defenceless; while woman is condemned to bear the drudgery of domestic life, to vegetate in obscurity, to *love* where she abhors, to *honour* where she despises, and to *obey*, while she shudders at subordination. (pp. 125–6)

By writing under a pseudonym, Robinson probably thought that she could prevent male critics from making personal attacks such as suggesting, because her own marriage had failed, that she could know nothing about marriage. Robinson's main argument is that men have a vested interest in keeping women ignorant in order that women can be more easily suppressed as potential rivals in any sphere: '[men] continue to debilitate the female mind, for the sole purpose of enforcing subordination'. But, according to Robinson, the fact that stupidity is not inherent in the female gender is shown by the genius of Mary Wollstonecraft, Catherine Macaulay and Mme de Sévigné. In fact, for Robinson, the mind and soul are without gender, and women are as capable of rational thought as men.

As Stuart Curran points out, at the time that Wollstonecraft, Hays and Robinson were writing, other women authors demonstrated their intellectual and philosophical abilities in a 'flood of writing by women': 'The 1790s in Britain form the arena for the first concerted expression of feminist thought in modern European culture ... a wholly new sense of empowerment impels women writers, whatever the individual's political professions.'[18] The individual's 'political profession' seemed, however, to have a bearing on what she wrote. Both Hays and Wollstonecraft moved in dissenting circles which included the Presbyterian minister, philosopher and chemist, Joseph Priestley, who discovered oxygen; William Godwin, the philosopher; Joseph Johnson, the radical publisher; William Blake, poet and engraver; and members of Nonconformist religious groups such as Robert Robinson. Marlon B. Ross describes the position of the dissenting woman in these groups:

Her status of double dissent – as a political female and as a female within a nonconforming community deprived of civil liberties – presented obstacles equal to the opportunities it afforded, for it required her to articulate the insight peculiar to her dual position without having any access to sanctioned political forms (academic oratory, parliamentary debate, legal pleading, court and minister- ial intrigue, and so forth). More tellingly, her access to formal political participation was limited even within her own noncon- forming communities. Among the conventional modes of politics practiced by the dissenters in their fight for civil rights (the petition, the political sermon, the political association, the corre- sponding society, and so on), the only formal avenue open to the political female was the periodical, which welcomed her literary contributions, even though these contributions were easy targets for controversy and could be dismissed as the presumptions of a political female.[19]

But, as Hays, Wollstonecraft and Robinson demonstrate, sym- pathetic publishers were also willing to bring out in book form their contentious political theorizing about the status of women.

In their political views, Nonconformist dissenting women writers ranged from the conservative Hannah More to the radical Mary Wollstonecraft. But their common ground was that, from their position on the double margins of dissent and gender, they could sympathize with the slave who had no civil liberty whatsoever. More wrote her long political poem, 'Slav- ery',[20] at the behest of the Society for the Abolition of the Slave Trade in support of one of William Wilberforce's attempts to get an Abolition Bill through Parliament. Thus, although More could not herself put forward a Bill in Parliament, she could express her dissenting voice through one of the avenues open to women at that time.

What is interesting, however, apart from the general spate of women's writing at that time against slavery,[21] is the way in which both Hays and Wollstonecraft employ concepts of enslavement as metaphors for the position of women. Wollstone- craft refers, in a general attack on established politics, to the 'abominable traffic' of the slave trade, adding, in relation to the legal status of women, that a 'more specious slavery . . . chains the very soul of woman, keeping her forever under the bondage of ignorance'. Moreover, in an extension of this metaphor of slavery, she adds, 'they [women] are made slaves to their persons, and must render them alluring that man may lend them his reason to guide their tottering steps aright. Or should they be ambitious, they must govern their tyrants with sinister tricks, for without rights there cannot be any incumbent duties. The laws respecting woman ... make an absurd unit of a man and his wife; and then, by the easy transition of only considering him as responsible, she is reduced to a mere cypher.'[22] If, for a woman in marriage, her 'very being or legal existence ... is suspended during the marriage',[23] then she is dependent on her husband's goodwill for her food, lodging and general maintenance, and, like a child, she is not legally responsible for any of her actions in society. Her position is that of a slave, without the incumbency to perform menial tasks or heavy physical labour for long hours, and without the imposition of chains.

Anna Seward, in a letter to the abolitionist Josiah Wedgwood, gives both sides of the argument for and against slavery: 'I have had long acquaintance with a Mr Newton ... who made a large fortune in the East, where slavery pervades every opulent establishment. He constantly assured me, that the purchase, employment, and strict discipline of the negroes were absolutely necessary to maintain our empire, and our commerce, in the Indies.' Elsewhere, Wedgwood's 'letter, and the tracts which accompanied it, have changed my ideas on the subject. They have given me indignant convictions, decided principles, and better hopes that the floodgates of this overwhelming cruelty may be let down without ruin to our national interests' (Letter 5, pp. 46, 47). But Seward's conversion does not extend to the composition of poetry on the evils of the slave trade, because she does not wish to compete with Hannah More nor with More's protégée, the working-class poet Ann Yearsley, in the publication of poems on the subject of slavery.

The slave trade was abolished in the British Empire in 1834, but, as the historian Kathryn Castle states, slavery was not constitutionally outlawed in the USA until the end of the American Civil War in 1865. Fanny Trollope in *Domestic Manners of the Americans* (1832) describes the inhumanity of slave-owners in Virginia and Maryland:

I had, indeed, frequent opportunities of observing this habitual indifference to the presence of their slaves. They talk of them, of their condition, of their faculties, of their conduct, exactly as if they were incapable of hearing. I once saw a young lady, who, when seated at table between a male and a female, was induced by her modesty to intrude on the chair of her female neighbour to avoid the indelicacy of touching the elbow of *a man*. I once saw this very [same] young lady lacing her stays with the most perfect composure before a negro footman. A Virginian gentleman told me that ever since he had married, he had been accustomed to have a negro girl sleep in the same chamber with himself and his wife. I asked for what purpose this nocturnal attendance was necessary? 'Good heavens!' was the reply, 'if I wanted a glass of water during the night, what would become of me?' (p. 249)

Trollope's account made entertaining reading for British readers who were probably not aware of British plantation-owners' similar behaviour to slaves in the West Indies.[24]

Dorothy Wordsworth also kept travel journals, which remained unpublished until after her death. In fact, Wordsworth did not publish any of her journals. Instead, she seems to have written many of them for her brother William to read and draw upon for his own writing. Because these diaries are now already available in various editions, two letters by Dorothy to Lady Beaumont are printed here as well as an excerpt from a travel book in order to demonstrate her talent for formal writing, as compared to the informality of some of her diaries.[25] Jane Taylor, on the other hand, fabricated letters in order to give moral instruction to, as well as to entertain, her youthful audience. And Helen Maria Williams's *Letters From France* (1790) resemble a book of reportage in the form of letters that give vivid accounts of Paris just after the French Revolution. These letters, however, have the hallmark, not of social realism, which readers might expect, but of 'Gothic' melodrama of the kind that occurs in this description of the Bastille just after its fall into the hands of insurgents:

We drove under the porch which so many wretches have entered never to repass, and, alighting from the carriage, descended with difficulty into the dungeons, which were too low to admit of our standing upright, and so dark that we were obliged at noon-day to visit them with the light of a candle. We saw the hooks of those chains by which the prisoners were fastened round the neck to the walls of their cells; many of which, being below the level of the

> water, are in a constant state of humidity; and a noxious vapour
> issued from them, which more than once extinguished the candle,
> and was so insufferable that it required a strong spirit of curiosity
> to tempt one to enter. Good God! – and to these regions of horror
> were human creatures dragged at the caprice of despotic power. (p. 71)

The 'noxious vapour' which 'extinguishes the candle' symbol-
ically suggests the deaths of prisoners as well as the fact that
Williams thinks that she is risking her own life by entering the
dungeons in order to report on them for the reader.

As well as writing letters and journals about their travels,
Romantic women authors attempted straightforward autobiog-
raphy. But this genre was problematic for women in that they
could not afford – as male writers such as De Quincey could –
to lose their reputations by being frank about their sexual
misdemeanours. Mary Robinson's *Memoirs* is a carefully con-
structed work that appears to represent a portrait of the
emergent artist or poet, but without the sexual peccadilloes that
readers find fascinating, especially in women. Her memoir,
unfinished at her death, was added to and posthumously pub-
lished by her daughter. Robinson paints a picture of herself as a
'Romantic' poet along the lines of Wordsworth's *The Prelude*
and Coleridge's *Biographia Literaria*. Her description of her
birth, for example, is quintessentially 'Romantic':

> In this awe-inspiring habitation, which I shall henceforth denomi-
> nate the Minster House, during a tempestuous night, on the 27th
> of November, 1758, I first opened my eyes to this world of
> duplicity and sorrow. I have often heard my mother say that a
> more stormy hour she never remembered. The wind whistled
> round the dark pinnacles of the minster tower and the rain beat in
> torrents against the casements of her chamber. Through life the
> tempest has followed my footsteps, and I have in vain looked for
> a short interval of repose from the perseverance of sorrow. (p. 129)

She portrays the storm that raged at the hour of her birth as a
metaphor for the 'tempest' of life, as if she were somehow fated
from birth to face a difficult existence, rather than bringing
destructive events on herself through her own behaviour.

Her childhood epitomizes that of a genius: during her infancy
and childhood, the church services in the nearby minster made
a 'sublime impression' on her, as did the reading of the lessons;

she took a morbid interest in epitaphs and inscriptions in the nearby churchyard; she memorized lines by Pope and other poets from the age of seven; she also learnt to play the harpsichord and to sing melancholy ballads by Gay and Lyttelton. Even though she might be seen to have merely acquired a smattering of the accomplishments that both More and Wollstonecraft thought to be an ineffectual method of educating young women, Robinson presents them as a kind of inauguration into the life of a poet. Probably Robinson received the basis of her education at More's sisters' school at Bristol, but Robinson passes the period over in one paragraph, preferring to concentrate on the details of her first experience of drama, for which she also proved to have a talent as an actress.

At the age of ten, Robinson's parents separated, and she boarded with Meribah Lorrington, a governess who had received 'a masculine education', but who also showed a then masculine propensity for the excessive consumption of alcohol. Nevertheless, Robinson claims that she acquired from her 'all that I ever learned'. It was to Mrs Lorrington that Robinson showed her early poems about 'love', poems which 'the governess never failed to applaud'. Thus the dominant interests of Robinson's future – writing, acting and sexual love – are introduced early in her life. In fact, according to Robinson, she received her first proposal when she was only thirteen. But her memoir peters out just at the time when she began to make the acquaintance of the Prince of Wales. Thus she does not re-create the period in which she became notorious as his mistress and lost her reputation in such a way as to prevent her contemporary readership taking her work seriously. Robinson's *modus operandi* in her *Memoirs* is described by Linda H. Petersen as that of an attempt 'to recall and illustrate her natural genius' which, at that time, was considered the prerequisite to becoming a poet. Petersen also accepts Robinson's daughter's representation of her later life: 'In the daughter's account, maternal devotion pays off in literary production ... As Maria states it, "the silence of the sick chamber prove[d] favourable to the muse."'[26] This comment might be accurate about Robinson's poetry, but her unfinished *Memoirs* seem, in their contrivance, clichéd.

Other women writers of the period favoured the private journal as a means of self-expression. Claire Clairmont, who seemed to relinquish quite early her desire for publication, nevertheless in her *Journal* cleverly satirized the follies of Byron and Shelley in a series of brief caricatures. In these draft 'Caricatures', intended to be accompanied by cartoons, both poets are represented as having abhorred children. Byron had insisted on taking over the care of his and Claire's illegitimate daughter, Allegra, who died from illness at the age of twelve, in a convent. Byron also rejected Clairmont's first attempt at a novel, which she never published. Unlike Robinson, Clairmont never found domestic happiness with her daughter, and her later life was spent in working as a governess throughout Europe. Even her brief caricatures, which might have amused readers in her own day, were not published until 1968.

Fanny Burney's *Diary and Letters* are a mixture of genres in which she turned her letters into a type of journal. The two excerpts printed in this anthology are from letters to her father, Charles Burney, in which she describes her journey to France to meet her husband, General d'Arblay. In the first, written in 1802, she describes the reaction among the French to the end of the Anglo-French war. In the 1815 letter, she dwells on the 'sights of wretchedness' in Brussels that formed the aftermath of Wellington's victory at Waterloo. Fanny Burney herself worked to assist the wounded, and her account consists of excellent first-hand reportage.

Mary Shelley used two of her 1816 letters – that were possibly addressed to her half-sister, Fanny Imlay – in her travel book, *History of a Six Weeks' Tour*, published with Percy Bysshe Shelley. These dual-purpose letters to an educated recipient allow her to comment philosophically on the effects of the French Revolution, for example, in the following passage: 'Here [in Geneva] a small obelisk is erected to the glory of Rousseau, and here (such is the mutability of human life) the magistrates, the successors of those who exiled him from his native country, were shot by the populace during that revolution, which his writings mainly contributed to mature, and which, notwithstanding the temporary bloodshed and injustice with which it was polluted, has produced enduring benefits to mankind, which all the chicanery of statesmen, nor even the great conspiracy of kings, can entirely render vain' (p. 218). These letters are comparable with those written by her mother, Mary Wollstonecraft, about her own travels in Sweden, Norway and Denmark twenty years earlier (1796). But during those same travels,

Wollstonecraft also wrote personal letters to her lover, Gilbert Imlay, by whom she had her first child, Fanny. Whether Wollstonecraft wished to have these letters published or not, they are a record of her private struggle to accommodate her sex life to her political espousal of woman's right to free herself from the enslavement of sexual love.

Women Romantics 1785–1832: Writing in Prose will help readers to understand better women's status in society two hundred years ago. This selection illustrates the varied ways in which women overcame the obstacles to becoming practitioners of a kind of philosophical and political prose considered to belong to the realm of men.

JENNIFER BREEN

References

1 Stuart Curran, 'Women readers, women writers', in *The Cambridge Companion to British Romanticism*, ed. Stuart Curran (Cambridge: Cambridge University Press, 1993), pp. 177–95.

2 David Simpson, 'Romanticism, Criticism and Theory', in *The Cambridge Companion to British Romanticism*, ed. Stuart Curran (Cambridge: Cambridge University Press, 1993), p. 1.

3 *ibid.*, pp. 21–2.

4 See, for example, Meena Alexander, *Women in Romanticism: Mary Wollstonecraft, Dorothy Wordsworth and Mary Shelley* (London: Macmillan, 1989).

5 Marshall Brown, 'Romanticism and Enlightenment', in *The Cambridge Companion to British Romanticism*, ed. Stuart Curran (Cambridge: Cambridge University Press, 1993), p. 38.

6 *ibid.*, p. 47.

7 See, for example, Benjamin Lara, *An Essay on the Injurious Custom of Mothers Not Suckling Their Own Children* (London: Moore, 1791).

8 Catherine Macaulay, *Letters on Education* (1790), pp. 33–4.

9 Mary Wollstonecraft, *A Vindication of the Rights of Woman*, vol. 5, in *The Works of Mary Wollstonecraft*, ed. Marilyn Butler and Janet Todd (London: Pickering & Chatto, 1989), pp. 74–5.

10 *ibid.*, p. 230.

11 *ibid.*, pp. 21–2.

12 *The Works of Hannah More*, vol. V, new edn, 1830, p. 44.

13 *ibid.*, pp. 45–54.

14 *A Vindication of the Rights of Woman*, vol. V, p. 76.

15 *ibid.*, p. 256.

16 *ibid.*, p. 130.

17 *The Works of Hannah More*, vol. V, p. 32.

18 Curran, 'Women readers, women writers', pp. 184–5.

19 Marlon B. Ross, 'The Woman Writer and the Tradition of Dissent', in *Re-visioning Romanticism: British Women Writers, 1776–1837*, ed. Carol Shiner Wilson and Joel Haefner (Philadelphia: University of Pennsylvania Press, 1994), pp. 93–4.

20 See my *Women Romantic Poets, 1785–1832: An Anthology*, new edn (London: Everyman, 1994), pp. 10–20.

21 Moira Ferguson puts forward the idea that writing about slavery from a sentimental point of view, as More did, was seen as a 'woman's thing' by male writers (*Subject to Others: British Women Writers and Colonial Slavery, 1670–1834* (London & New York: Routledge, 1992), p. 153).

22 *A Vindication of the Rights of Woman*, vol. V, pp. 214–15.

23 William Blackstone, *Commentaries on the Laws of England*, 3rd edn (1768), I, 15, iii, p. 442.

24 Mary Prince's oral account, *The History of Mary Prince, a West Indian Slave; related by herself* (1831), was apparently bowdlerized by her amanuensis, the daughter of the secretary for the Society for the Abolition of the Slave Trade. This written account gives details of her physical abuse by her owners, but skates over the theme of sexual abuse. It is impossible to know how much Prince's amanuensis contributed to her representation of her protégée's life of slavery.

25 Dorothy Wordsworth's *Grasmere Journal* has recently been re-edited by Pamela Woof, who has restored it to its exact form as left by Dorothy Wordsworth, without editorial tidying-up, and can now be read in the informal style in which it was first written.

26 Linda H. Petersen, 'Becoming an Author: Mary Robinson's *Memoirs* and the Origins of Woman's Autobiography', in *Re-visioning Romanticism: British Women Writers, 1776–1837*, eds Carol Shiner Wilson and Joel Haefner (Philadelphia: University of Pennsylvania Press, 1994), pp. 37, 44.

NOTE ON THE TEXTS

In cases of works for which recent scholarly editions are available, I have used these. In all other cases, I have used the earliest best edition available. Spelling and punctuation have been modernized when necessary. Any footnotes are the authors' own notes. Asterisks refer to the editor's explanatory notes found at the back of the anthology, pp. 251–70. The works of these women authors are introduced in order of the date of the first piece by each author, and their prose passages are printed in chronological order of the date of first publication. This date appears at the end of each passage. The source for each passage is given at the end of the Note on the Author with which each section opens.

WOMEN ROMANTICS
1785–1832:
WRITING IN PROSE

MARY WOLLSTONECRAFT

MARY WOLLSTONECRAFT (1759–97), essayist, novelist, transla-
tor, anthologist, children's writer, travel writer and reviewer, is
probably best known for her *A Vindication of the Rights of
Woman* (1792). She lived away from her parents from the age
of nineteen, earning her living as a governess and teacher. After
the school she had set up at Newington Green failed in 1786,
she became a governess for Lord Kingsborough's family in
Ireland. In 1788, Joseph Johnson published her first novel,
Mary, and employed her as a reviewer and translator at his
publishing house, where she met leading authors and radicals of
the day. In 1790, Johnson published her *Vindication of the
Rights of Man*, which was a direct response to Edmund Burke's
Reflections on the French Revolution. She had a fruitless obses-
sion with the artist, Henry Fuseli, who was already married and
refused to live in a *ménage à trois* with her. In 1792, she
travelled to Paris in order to write about the aftermath of the
1789 Revolution. The first volume of her *View of the French
Revolution* was published in 1784. When in Paris, she met
Gilbert Imlay, an American businessman and writer, who
became her lover, and by whom she had a daughter, Fanny. She
undertook a business commission on his behalf in Scandinavia,
writing at the same time her travel book, *Letters Written During
a Short Residence in Sweden, Norway and Denmark* (1796).
Subsequently, after discovering that Imlay was involved with
another woman, Wollstonecraft tried unsuccessfully to drown
herself in the Thames. She married William Godwin
(1756–1836) in 1797 after she became pregnant by him. She
died from complications just after the birth of her second
daughter, Mary (later Shelley). 'Reading' comes from *Thoughts
on the Education of Daughters* (1787), pp. 48–56; Article XXV
from the *Analytical Review*, December 1789, vol. 5, pp. 488–9;
Article XVII from the *Analytical Review*, August 1791, vol. 10,
p. 528; the chapter from *A Vindication of the Rights of Woman*,

Chapter 9, is reprinted from a new edition, ed. Mrs Henry Fawcett (1891), pp. 212–24; the texts of Letters 4 and 7 in *Letters Written during a Short Residence in Sweden, Norway, and Denmark* are from the 1796 edition, pp. 37–41 and 74–92; 'The Present Character of the French Nation', Letter 16 to Joseph Johnson, and Letters 69 to 78 to Gilbert Imlay are from *Posthumous Works* (1798), ed. William Godwin, vol. 4, pp. 39–51, 92–5, 100–36.

Reading

It is an old, but a very true observation, that the human mind
must ever be employed. A relish for reading, or any of the fine
arts, should be cultivated very early in life; and those who reflect
can tell, of what importance it is for the mind to have some
resource in itself, and not to be entirely dependent on the senses
for employment and amusement. If it unfortunately is so, it must
submit to meanness, and often to vice, in order to gratify them.
The wisest and best are too much under their influence; and the
endeavouring to conquer them, when reason and virtue will not
give their sanction, constitutes a great part of the warfare of life.
What support, then, have they who are all senses, and who are
full of schemes, which terminate in temporal objects?

   Reading is the most rational employment, if people seek food
for the understanding, and do not read merely to remember
words; or with a view to quote celebrated authors, and retail
sentiments they do not understand or feel. Judicious books
enlarge the mind and improve the heart, though some, by them,
'are made coxcombs whom nature meant for fools'.*

   Those productions which give a wrong account of the human
passions, and the various accidents of life, ought not to be read
before the judgment is formed, or at least exercised. Such
accounts are one great cause of the affectation of young women.
Sensibility is described and praised, and the effects of it repre-
sented in a way so different from nature, that those who imitate
it must make themselves very ridiculous. A false taste is
acquired, and sensible books appear dull and insipid after those
superficial performances, which obtain their full end if they can
keep the mind in a continual ferment. Gallantry is made the
only interesting subject with the novelist; reading, therefore, will
often co-operate to make his fair admirers insignificant.

   I do not mean to recommend books of an abstract or grave
cast. There are in our language many, in which instruction and
amusement are blended; the *Adventurer** is of this kind. I
mention this book on account of its beautiful allegories and

affecting tales, and similar ones may easily be selected. Reason
strikes most forcibly when illustrated by the brilliancy of fancy.
The sentiments which are scattered may be observed, and when
they are relished, and the mind is set to work, it may be allowed
to choose books for itself, for everything will then instruct.

I would have everyone try to form an opinion of an author
themselves, though modesty may restrain them from mentioning
it. Many are so anxious to have the reputation of taste, that they
only praise the authors whose merit is indisputable. I am sick of
hearing of the sublimity of Milton, the elegance and harmony of
Pope, and the original, untaught genius of Shakespeare. These
cursory remarks are made by some who know nothing of nature,
and could not enter into the spirit of those authors, or under-
stand them.

A florid style mostly passes with the ignorant for fine writing;
many sentences are admired that have no meaning in them,
though they contain 'words of thundering sound',* and others
that have nothing to recommend them but sweet and musical
terminations.

Books of theology are not calculated for young persons;
religion is best taught by example. The Bible should be read
with particular respect, and they should not be taught reading
by so sacred a book; lest they might consider that as a task,
which ought to be a source of the most exalted satisfaction.

It may be observed, that I recommend the mind's being put
into a proper train, and then left to itself. Fixed rules cannot be
given, it must depend on the nature and strength of the
understanding; and those who observe it can best tell what kind
of cultivation will improve it. The mind is not, cannot be created
by the teacher, though it may be cultivated, and its real powers
found out.

The active spirits of youth may make time glide away without
intellectual enjoyments; but when the novelty of the scene is
worn off, the want of them will be felt, and nothing else can fill
up the void. The mind is confined to the body, and must sink
into sensuality; for it has nothing to do but to provide for it,
'how it shall eat and drink, and wherewithal it shall be clothed'.*

All kinds of refinements have been found fault with for
increasing our cares and sorrows; yet surely the contrary effect
also arises from them. Taste and thought open many sources of
pleasure, which do not depend on fortune.

No employment of the mind is a sufficient excuse for neglecting domestic duties, and I cannot conceive that they are incompatible. A woman may fit herself to be the companion and friend of a man of sense, and yet know how to take care of his family.*

1787

FROM THE *ANALYTICAL REVIEW*

Article XXV, November 1789

Almeria Belmore, A Novel, in a Series of Letters. Written by a Lady. 12 mo. 267 p. Price 3s. sewed. Robinsons. 1789.

Miss O'Connor complains, in her address to the public, of a celebrated clergyman, who approved of her novel when *she* read it to him, and afterwards was a little inclined to recant, and not repeat the praise the eyes of a young, fair *authoress* – for we will, to heighten the scene, suppose her fair – extorted from him: but we wish the gentleman had not been under undue influence, he would then have spoken out, and spared us some trouble. Yet, on further consideration, we must add, that we do not think that he would have had power, with all his eloquence, to prevail on her to throw her bantling into the fire. She has not sufficient judgment – we had almost said modesty – to follow such sound advice, or she could never have written, and afterwards read (to a *man*) the unnatural tragi-comic tale we have just been laughing at; in which there is no discrimination of character, no acquaintance with life, nor – do not start, fair lady! – any passion: but, perhaps, we are not able to discover such an elegant sensation. This kind of trash, these whipped syllabubs, overload young, weak stomachs, and render them squeamish, unable to relish the simple food nature prepares.

M.

Article XVII, August 1791

Advice to Unmarried Women: To recover and reclaim the Fallen; and to prevent the Fall of others, into the Snares and Consequences of Seduction. 12 mo. 44 pp. Price 4p. sewed. Rivingtons. 1791.

This well-meant advice, addressed to uneducated females, deserves praise, and we recommend it to those considerate mistresses of families who furnish their servants with books.

M.

FROM *A VINDICATION OF THE RIGHTS OF WOMAN*

Chapter 9

Of the Pernicious Effects Which Arise from the Unnatural Distinction Established in Society

From the respect paid to property flow, as from a poisoned fountain, most of the evils and vices which render this world such a dreary scene to the contemplative mind. For it is in the most polished society that noisesome reptiles and venomous serpents lurk under the rank herbage; and there is voluptuousness pampered by the still sultry air, which relaxes every good disposition before it ripens into virtue.

One class presses on another; for all are aiming to procure respect on account of their property: and property, once gained, will procure the respect due only to talents and virtue. Men neglect the duties incumbent on man, yet are treated like demigods; religion is also separated from morality by a ceremonial veil, yet men wonder that the world is almost, literally speaking, a den of sharpers or oppressors.

There is a homely proverb, which speaks a shrewd truth, that whoever the devil finds idle he will employ. And what but habitual idleness can hereditary wealth and titles produce? For man is so constituted that he can only attain a proper use of his faculties by exercising them, and will not exercise them unless necessity of some kind first set the wheels in motion. Virtue likewise can only be acquired by the discharge of relative duties;

but the importance of these sacred duties will scarcely be felt by the being who is cajoled out of his humanity by the flattery of sycophants. There must be more equality established in society, or more morality will never gain ground, and this virtuous equality will not rest firmly even when founded on a rock, if one half of mankind be chained to its bottom by fate, for they will be continually undermining it through ignorance or pride.

It is vain to expect virtue from women till they are in some degree independent of men; nay, it is vain to expect that strength of natural affection which would make them good wives and mothers. Whilst they are absolutely dependent on their husbands they will be cunning, mean, and selfish, and the men who can be gratified by the fawning fondness of spaniel-like affection have not much delicacy, for love is not to be bought, in any sense of the words; its silken wings are instantly shrivelled up when anything beside a return in kind is sought. Yet whilst wealth enervates men, and women live, as it were, by their personal charms, how can we expect them to discharge those ennobling duties which equally require exertion and self-denial? Hereditary property sophisticates the mind, and the unfortunate victims to it, if I may so express myself, swathed from their birth, seldom exert the locomotive faculty of body or mind; and, thus viewing everything through one medium, and that a false one, they are unable to discern in what true merit and happiness consist. False, indeed, must be the light when the drapery of situation hides the man, and makes him stalk in masquerade, dragging from one scene of dissipation to another the nerveless limbs that hang with stupid listlessness, and rolling round the vacant eye which plainly tells us that there is no mind at home.

I mean, therefore, to infer that the society is not properly organized which does not compel men and women to discharge their respective duties, by making it the only way to acquire that countenance from their fellow-creatures which every human being wishes some way to attain. The respect, consequently, which is paid to wealth and mere personal charms, is a true north-east blast that blights the tender blossoms of affection and virtue. Nature has wisely attached affections to duties to sweeten toil, and to give that vigour to the exertions of reason which only the heart can give. But the affection which is put on merely because it is the appropriated insignia of a certain character, when its duties are not fulfilled, is one of the empty compliments which vice and folly are obliged to pay to virtue and the real nature of things.

To illustrate my opinion, I need only observe that when a woman is admired for her beauty, and suffers herself to be so far intoxicated by the admiration she receives as to neglect to discharge the indispensable duty of a mother, she sins against herself by neglecting to cultivate an affection that would equally tend to make her useful and happy. True happiness, I mean all the contentment and virtuous satisfaction that can be snatched in this imperfect state, must arise from well-regulated affections; and an affection includes a duty. Men are not aware of the misery they cause and the vicious weakness they cherish by only inciting women to render themselves pleasing; they do not consider that they thus make natural and artificial duties clash by sacrificing the comfort and respectability of a woman's life to voluptuous notions of beauty when in nature they all harmonize.

Cold would be the heart of a husband, were he not rendered unnatural by early debauchery, who did not feel more delight at seeing his child suckled by its mother, than the most artful wanton tricks could ever raise; yet this natural way of cementing the matrimonial tie and twisting esteem with fonder recollections, wealth leads women to spurn. To preserve their beauty and wear the flowery crown of the day, which gives them a kind of right to reign for a short time over the sex, they neglect to stamp impressions on their husbands' hearts that would be remembered with more tenderness when the snow on the head began to chill the bosom than even their virgin charms. The maternal solicitude of a reasonable affectionate woman is very interesting, and the chastened dignity with which a mother returns the caresses that she and her child receive from a father who has been fulfilling the serious duties of his station, is not only a respectable but a beautiful sight. So singular indeed are my feelings, and I have endeavoured not to catch factitious ones, that after having been fatigued with the sight of insipid grandeur and the slavish ceremonies that with cumbrous pomp supplied the place of domestic affections, I have turned to some other scene to relieve my eye by resting it on the refreshing green everywhere scattered by nature. I have then viewed with pleasure a woman nursing her children, and discharging the duties of her station with, perhaps, merely a servant maid to take off her hands the servile part of the household business. I have seen her prepare herself and children, with only the luxury of cleanliness, to receive her husband, who returning weary home in the evening found smiling babes and a clean hearth. My heart has loitered in the midst of the group, and has even throbbed with sympathetic emotion, when the scraping of the well-known foot has raised a pleasing tumult.

Whilst my benevolence has been gratified by contemplating this artless picture, I have thought that a couple of this description, equally necessary and independent of each other, because each fulfilled the respective duties of their station, possessed all that life could give. Raised sufficiently above abject poverty not to be obliged to weigh the consequence of every farthing they spend, and having sufficient to prevent their attending to a frigid system of economy, which narrows both heart and mind, I declare, so vulgar are my conceptions, that I know not what is wanted to render this the happiest as well as the most respectable situation in the world, but a taste for literature, to throw a little variety and interest into social converse, and some superfluous money to give to the needy and to buy books. For it is not pleasant when the heart is opened by compassion and the head active in arranging plans of usefulness, to have a prim urchin continually twitching back the elbow to prevent the hand from drawing out an almost empty purse, whispering at the same time some prudential maxim about the priority of justice.

Destructive, however, as riches and inherited honours are to the human character, women are more debased and cramped, if possible, by them than men, because men may still, in some degree, unfold their faculties by becoming soldiers and statesmen.

As soldiers, I grant, they can now only gather, for the most part, vainglorious laurels, whilst they adjust to a hair the European balance, taking especial care that no bleak northern nook or sound incline the beam.* But the days of true heroism are over, when a citizen fought for his country like a Fabricius* or a Washington,* and then returned to his farm to let his virtuous fervour run in a more placid, but not a less salutary, stream. No, our British heroes are oftener sent from the gaming table than from the plough; and their passions have been rather inflamed by hanging with dumb suspense on the turn of a die, than sublimated by panting after the adventurous march of virtue in the historic page.

The statesman, it is true, might with more propriety quit the faro bank, or card table, to guide the helm, for he has still but to shuffle and trick. The whole system of British politics, if system it may courteously be called, consisting in multiplying dependents and contriving taxes which grind the poor to pamper the rich; thus a war, or any wild goose chase, is, as the vulgar use the phrase, a lucky turn-up of patronage for the minister, whose chief merit is the art of keeping himself in place. It is not necessary then that he should have bowels for the poor, so he can secure for his family the odd trick. Or should some show of respect, for what is termed with ignorant ostentation an Englishman's birthright, be expedient to bubble* the gruff mastiff that he has to lead by the nose, he can make an empty show very safely by giving his single voice and suffering his light squadron to file off to the other side. And when a question of humanity is agitated he may dip a sop in the milk of human kindness* to silence Cerberus,* and talk of the interest which his heart takes in an attempt to make the earth no longer cry for vengeance as it sucks in its children's blood, though his cold hand may at the very moment rivet their chains by sanctioning the abominable traffic. A minister is no longer a minister than while he can carry a point which he is determined to carry. Yet it is not necessary that a minister should feel like a man, when a bold push might shake his seat.

But, to have done with these episodical observations, let me return to the more specious slavery which chains the very soul of woman, keeping her for ever under the bondage of ignorance.

The preposterous distinctions of rank, which render civilization a curse by dividing the world between voluptuous tyrants and cunning envious dependents, corrupt, almost equally, every class of people, because respectability is not attached to the discharge of the relative duties of life, but to the station, and when the duties are not fulfilled the affections cannot gain sufficient strength to fortify the virtue of which they are the natural reward. Still there are some loopholes out of which a man may creep, and dare to think and act for himself; but for a woman it is a herculean task, because she has difficulties peculiar to her sex to overcome which require almost superhuman powers.

A truly benevolent legislator endeavours to make it the interest of each individual to be virtuous; and thus private virtue becoming the cement of public happiness, an orderly whole is consolidated by the tendency of all the parts towards a common centre. But, the private or public virtue of woman is very problematical; for Rousseau, and a numerous list of male writers, insist that she should all her life be subjected to a severe restraint, that of propriety. Why subject her to propriety – blind propriety, if she be capable of acting from a nobler spring, if she be an heir of immortality? Is sugar always to be produced by vital blood? Is one-half of the human species, like the poor African slaves, to be subject to prejudices that brutalize them, when principles would be a surer guard, only to sweeten the cup of man? Is not this indirectly to deny woman reason? for a gift is a mockery, if it be unfit for use.

Women are, in common with men, rendered weak and luxurious by the relaxing pleasures which wealth procures; but added to this they are made slaves to their persons, and must render them alluring that man may lend them his reason to guide their tottering steps aright. Or should they be ambitious, they must govern their tyrants by sinister tricks, for without rights there cannot be any incumbent duties. The laws respecting woman, which I mean to discuss in a future part, make an absurd unit of a man and his wife; and then, by the easy transition of only considering him as responsible, she is reduced to a mere cypher.

The being who discharges the duties of its station is independent; and, speaking of women at large, their first duty is to themselves as rational creatures, and the next in point of importance, as citizens, is that which includes so many, of a mother. The rank in life which dispenses with their fulfilling this duty necessarily degrades them by making them mere dolls. Or, should they turn to something more important than merely fitting drapery upon a smooth block, their minds are only occupied by some soft platonic attachment; or, the actual management of an intrigue may keep their thoughts in motion; for when they neglect domestic duties, they have it not in their own power to take the field and march and counter-march like soldiers, or wrangle in the senate to keep their faculties from rusting.

I know that, as a proof of the inferiority of the sex, Rousseau has exultingly exclaimed, 'How can they leave the nursery for the camp!'* And the camp has by some moralists been termed the school of the most heroic virtues; though, I think, it would puzzle a keen casuist to prove the reasonableness of the greater number of wars that have dubbed heroes. I do not mean to consider this question critically; because, having frequently viewed these freaks of ambition as the first natural mode of civilization, when the ground must be torn up, and the woods cleared by fire and sword, I do not choose to call them pests; but surely the present system of war has little connection with virtue of any denomination, being rather the school of *finesse* and effeminacy than of fortitude.

Yet if defensive war, the only justifiable war, in the present advanced state of society, where virtue can show its face and ripen amidst the rigours which purify the air on the mountain's top, were alone to be adopted as just and glorious, the true heroism of antiquity might again animate female bosoms. But fair and softly, gentle reader, male or female, do not alarm thyself, for though I have compared the character of a modern soldier with that of a civilized woman, I am not going to advise them to turn their distaff into a musket, though I sincerely wish to see the bayonet converted into a pruning-hook. I only recreated an imagination, fatigued by contemplating the vices and follies which all proceed from a feculent stream of wealth that has muddied the pure rills of natural affection, by supposing that society will some time or other be so constituted, that man must necessarily fulfil the duties of a citizen or be despised, and that while he was employed in any of the departments of civil life, his wife, also an active citizen, should be equally intent to manage her family, educate her children, and assist her neighbours.

But, to render her really virtuous and useful, she must not, if she discharge her civil duties, want, individually, the protection of civil laws; she must not be dependent on her husband's bounty for her subsistence during his life or support after his death – for how can a being be generous who has nothing of its own? or virtuous, who is not free? The wife, in the present state of things, who is faithful to her husband, and neither suckles nor educates her children, scarcely deserves the name of a wife, and has no right to that of a citizen. But take away natural rights, and duties become null.

Women then must be considered as only the wanton solace of men when they become so weak in mind and body that they cannot exist themselves, unless to pursue some frothy pleasure or to invent some frivolous fashion. What can be a more melancholy sight to a thinking mind than to look into the numerous carriages that drive helter-skelter about this metropolis in a morning full of pale-faced creatures who are flying from themselves! I have often wished, with Dr Johnson, to place some of them in a little shop with half a dozen children looking up to their languid countenances for support. I am much mistaken if some latent vigour would not soon give health and spirit to their eyes, and some lines drawn by the exercise of reason on the blank cheeks, which before were only undulated by dimples, might restore lost dignity to the character, or rather enable it to attain the true dignity of its nature. Virtue is not to be acquired even by speculation, much less by the negative supineness that wealth naturally generates.

Besides, when poverty is more disgraceful than even vice, is not morality cut to the quick? Still to avoid misconstruction, though I consider that women in the common walks of life are called to fulfil the duties of wives and mothers, by religion and reason, I cannot help lamenting that women of a superior cast have not a road open by which they can pursue more extensive plans of usefulness and independence. I may excite laughter by dropping a hint which I mean to pursue some future time, for I really think that women ought to have representatives, instead of being arbitrarily governed without having any direct share allowed them in the deliberations of government.

But, as the whole system of representation is now in this country only a convenient handle for despotism, they need not complain, for they are as well represented as a numerous class of hard-working mechanics, who pay for the support of royalty when they can scarcely stop their children's mouths with bread. How are they represented whose very sweat supports the splendid stud of an heir-apparent, or varnishes the chariot of some female favourite who looks down on shame? Taxes on the very necessaries of life enable an endless tribe of idle princes and princesses to pass with stupid pomp before a gaping crowd, who almost worship the very parade which costs them so dear. This is mere gothic grandeur, something like the barbarous useless parade of having sentinels on horseback at Whitehall, which I could never view without a mixture of contempt and indignation.

How strangely must the mind be sophisticated when this sort of state impresses it! But, till these monuments of folly are levelled by virtue, similar follies will leaven the whole mass. For the same character, in some degree, will prevail in the aggregate of society; and the refinements of luxury, or the vicious repinings of envious poverty, will equally banish virtue from society, considered as the characteristic of that society, or only allow it to appear as one of the stripes of the harlequin coat worn by the civilized man.

In the superior ranks of life every duty is done by deputies, as if duties could ever be waived, and the vain pleasures which consequent idleness forces the rich to pursue appear so enticing to the next rank that the numerous scramblers for wealth sacrifice everything to tread on their heels. The most sacred truths are then considered as sinecures, because they were procured by interest, and only fought to enable a man to keep *good company*. Women, in particular, all want to be ladies. Which is simply to have nothing to do, but listlessly to go they scarcely care where, for they cannot tell what.

But what have women to do in society? I may be asked, but to loiter with easy grace; surely you would not condemn them all to suckle fools and chronicle small beer!* No. Women might certainly study the art of healing, and be physicians as well as nurses. And midwifery, decency seems to allot to them, though I am afraid the word midwife in our dictionaries will soon give place to *accoucheur*,* and one proof of the former delicacy of the sex be effaced from the language.

They might also study politics, and settle their benevolence on the broadest basis; for the reading of history will scarcely be more useful than the perusal of romances, if read as mere biography; if the character of the times, the political improvements, arts, etc., be not observed. In short, if it be not considered as the history of man; and not of particular men, who filled a niche in the temple of fame, and dropped into the black rolling stream of time, that silently sweeps all before it, into the shapeless void called – eternity. For shape, can it be called, 'that shape hath none'?*

Business of various kinds they might likewise pursue, if they were educated in a more orderly manner, which might save many from common and legal prostitution. Women would not then marry for a support, as men accept of places under government, and neglect the implied duties; nor would an attempt to earn their own subsistence – a most laudable one! – sink them almost to the level of those poor abandoned creatures who live by prostitution. For are not milliners and mantua-makers reckoned the next class? The few employments open to women, so far from being liberal, are menial; and when a superior education enables them to take charge of the education of children as governesses, they are not treated like the tutors of sons, though even clerical tutors are not always treated in a manner calculated to render them respectable in the eyes of their pupils, to say nothing of the private comfort of the individual. But as women educated like gentlewomen are never designed for the humiliating situation which necessity sometimes forces them to fill, these situations are considered in the light of a degradation; and they know little of the human heart, who need to be told that nothing so painfully sharpens sensibility as such a fall in life.

Some of these women might be restrained from marrying by a proper spirit of delicacy, and others may not have had it in their power to escape in this pitiful way from servitude; is not that government then very defective, and very unmindful of the happiness of one half of its members, that does not provide for honest, independent women, by encouraging them to fill respectable stations? But in order to render their private virtue a public benefit, they must have a civil existence in the state, married or single; else we shall continually see some worthy woman, whose sensibility has been rendered painfully acute by undeserved contempt, droop like 'the lily broken down by a plow-share'.*

It is a melancholy truth – yet such is the blessed effect of civilization! – the most respectable women are the most oppressed; and, unless they have understandings far superior to the common run of understandings, taking in both sexes, they must, from being treated like contemptible beings, become contemptible. How many women thus waste life away the prey of discontent, who might have practised as physicians, regulated a farm, managed a shop, and stood erect, supported by their own industry, instead of hanging their heads surcharged with the dew of sensibility, that consumes the beauty to which it at first gave lustre: nay, I doubt whether pity and love are so near akin as poets feign, for I have seldom seen much compassion excited by the helplessness of females, unless they were fair; then, perhaps, pity was the soft handmaid of love, or the harbinger of lust.

How much more respectable is the woman who earns her own bread by fulfilling any duty, than the most accomplished beauty! – beauty did I say? – so sensible am I of the beauty of moral loveliness, or the harmonious propriety that attunes the passions of a well-regulated mind, that I blush at making the comparison; yet I sigh to think how few women aim at attaining this respectability by withdrawing from the giddy whirl of pleasure, or the indolent calm that stupefies the good sort of women it sucks in.

Proud of their weakness, however, they must always be protected, guarded from care, and all the rough toils that dignify the mind. If this be the fiat of fate, if they will make themselves insignificant and contemptible, sweetly to waste 'life away', let them not expect to be valued when their beauty fades, for it is the fate of the fairest flowers to be admired and pulled to pieces by the careless hand that plucked them. In how many ways do I wish, from the purest benevolence, to impress this truth on my sex; yet I fear that they will not listen to a truth that dear-bought experience has brought home to many an agitated bosom, nor willingly resign the privileges of rank and sex for the privileges of humanity, to which those have no claim who do not discharge its duties.

Those writers are particularly useful, in my opinion, who make man feel for man, independent of the station he fills; or the drapery of factitious sentiments. I then would fain convince reasonable men of the importance of some of my remarks; and prevail on them to weigh dispassionately the whole tenor of my observations. I appeal to their understandings; and, as a fellow-creature, claim, in the name of my sex, some interest in their hearts. I entreat them to assist to emancipate their companion, to make her a *help meet* for them.

Would men but generously snap our chains, and be content with rational fellowship instead of slavish obedience, they would find us more observant daughters, more affectionate sisters, more faithful wives, more reasonable mothers – in a word, better citizens. We should then love them with true affection, because we should learn to respect ourselves; and the peace of mind of a worthy man would not be interrupted by the idle vanity of his wife, nor the babes sent to nestle in a strange bosom, having never found a home in their mother's.

1792

LETTER TO JOSEPH JOHNSON

Letter 16

Paris, 26 December 1792

I should immediately on the receipt of your letter, my dear friend, have thanked you for your punctuality, for it highly gratified me, had I not wished to wait till I could tell you that this day was not stained with blood. Indeed the prudent precautions taken by the National Convention to prevent a tumult, made me suppose that the dogs of faction would not dare to bark, much less to bite, however true to their scent; and I was not mistaken; for the citizens, who were all called out, are returning home with composed countenances, shouldering their arms. About nine o'clock this morning, the king passed by my window, moving silently along (excepting now and then a few strokes on the drum, which rendered the stillness more awful) through empty streets, surrounded by the national guards, who, clustering round the carriage, seemed to deserve their name. The inhabitants flocked to their windows, but the casements were all shut, not a voice was heard, nor did I see any thing like an insulting gesture. – For the first time since I entered France, I bowed to the majesty of the people, and respected the propriety of behaviour so perfectly in unison with my own feelings. I can scarcely tell you why, but an association of ideas made the tears flow insensibly from my eyes, when I saw Louis sitting, with more dignity than I expected from his character, in a hackney coach, going to meet death, where so many of his race have triumphed. My fancy instantly brought Louis XIV before me, entering the capital with all his pomp, after one of the victories most flattering to his pride, only to see the sunshine of prosperity overshadowed by the sublime gloom of misery. I have been alone ever since; and, though my mind is calm, I cannot dismiss the lively images that have filled my imagination all the day. –

Nay, do not smile, but pity me; for, once or twice, lifting my eyes from the paper, I have seen eyes glare through a glass-door opposite my chair, and bloody hands shook at me. Not the distant sound of a footstep can I hear. – My apartments are remote from those of the servants, the only persons who sleep with me in an immense hotel, one folding door opening after another. – I wish I had even kept the cat with me! – I want to see something alive; death in so many frightful shapes has taken hold of my fancy. – I am going to bed – and, for the first time in my life, I cannot put out the candle.

M. W.

FROM *LETTERS WRITTEN DURING A SHORT RESIDENCE IN SWEDEN, NORWAY, AND DENMARK*

Letter 4

The severity of the long Swedish winter tends to render the people sluggish; for, though this season has its peculiar pleasures, too much time is employed to guard against inclemency. Still, as warm clothing is absolutely necessary, the women spin, and the men weave, and by these exertions get a fence to keep out the cold. I have rarely passed a knot of cottages without seeing cloth laid out to bleach; and when I entered, always found the women spinning or knitting.

A mistaken tenderness, however, for their children, makes them, even in summer, load them with flannels; and, having a sort of natural antipathy to cold water, the squalid appearance of the poor babes, not to speak of the noxious smell which flannel and rugs retain, seems a reply to a question I had often asked – Why I did not see more children in the villages I passed through? Indeed the children appear to be nipped in the bud, having neither the graces nor charms of their age. And this, I am persuaded, is much more owing to the ignorance of the mothers than to the rudeness of the climate. Rendered feeble by the continual perspiration they are kept in, whilst every pore is absorbing unwholesome moisture, they give them even at the breast, brandy, salt fish, and every other crude substance, which air and exercise enables the parent to digest.

The women of fortune here, as well as everywhere else, have nurses to suckle their children; and the total want of chastity in the lower class of women frequently renders them very unfit for the trust.

You* have sometimes remarked to me the difference of the manners of the country girls in England and America; attributing the reserve of the former to the climate – to the absence of genial suns. But it must be their stars, not the zephyrs gently stealing on their senses, which here lead frail women astray. – Who can look at these rocks, and allow the voluptuousness of nature to be an excuse for gratifying the desire it inspires? We must, therefore, find some other cause besides voluptuousness, I believe, to account for the conduct of the Swedish and American country girls; for I am led to conclude, from all the observations I have made, that there is always a mixture of sentiment and imagination in voluptuousness, to which neither of them have much pretension.

The country girls of Ireland and Wales equally feel the first impulse of nature, which restrained in England by fear or delicacy, proves that society is there in a more advanced state. Besides, as the mind is cultivated, and taste gains ground, the passions become stronger, and rest on something more stable than the casual sympathies of the moment. Health and idleness will always account for promiscuous amours; and in some degree I term every person idle, the exercise of whose mind does not bear some proportion to that of the body.

The Swedish ladies exercise neither sufficiently; of course, grow very fat at an early age; and when they have not this downy appearance, a comfortable idea, you will say, in a cold climate, they are not remarkable for fine forms. They have, however, mostly fine complexions, but indolence makes the lily soon displace the rose. The quantity of coffee, spices, and other things of that kind, with want of care, almost universally spoil their teeth, which contrast but ill with their ruby lips.

The manners of Stockholm are refined, I hear, by the introduction of gallantry, but in the country, romping and coarse freedoms, with coarser allusions, keep the spirits awake. In the article of cleanliness, the women, of all descriptions, seem very deficient; and their dress shows that vanity is more inherent in women than taste.

The men appear to have paid still less court to the graces.

They are a robust, healthy race, distinguished for their common-sense and turn for humour, rather than for wit and sentiment. I include not, as you may suppose, in this general character, some of the nobility and officers, who having travelled, are polite and well informed.

I must own to you, that the lower class of people here amuse and interest me much more than the middling, with their apish good breeding and prejudices. The sympathy and frankness of heart conspicuous in the peasantry produces even a simple gracefulness of deportment, which has frequently struck me as very picturesque; I have often also been touched by their extreme desire to oblige me, when I could not explain my wants, and by their earnest manner of expressing that desire. There is such a charm in tenderness! – It is so delightful to love our fellow-creatures, and meet the honest affections as they break forth. Still, my good friend, I begin to think that I should not like to live continually in the country, with people whose minds have such a narrow range. My heart would frequently be interested; but my mind would languish for more companionable society.

The beauties of nature appear to me even more alluring than in my youth, because my intercourse with the world has formed, without vitiating my taste. But, with respect to the inhabitants of the country, my fancy has probably, when disgusted with artificial manners, solaced itself by joining the advantages of cultivation with the interluding sincerity of innocence, forgetting the lassitude that ignorance will naturally produce. I like to see animals sporting, and sympathize in their pains and pleasures. Still I love sometimes to view the human face divine,* and trace the soul, as well as the heart, in its varying lineaments.

A journey to the country, which I must shortly make, will enable me to extend my remarks. – Adieu!

1796

Letter 7

Though the King of Denmark be an absolute monarch, yet the Norwegians appear to enjoy all the blessings of freedom. Norway may be termed a sister kingdom; but the people have no viceroy to lord it over them, and fatten his dependants with the fruit of their labour.*

There are only two counts in the whole country, who have

estates, and exact some feudal observances from their tenantry. All the rest of the country is divided into small farms, which belong to the cultivator. It is true, some few, appertaining to the church, are let; but always on a lease for life, generally renewed in favour of the eldest son, who has this advantage, as well as a right to a double portion of the property. But the value of the farm is estimated; and after his portion is assigned to him, he must be answerable for the residue to the remaining part of the family.

Every farmer, for ten years, is obliged to attend annually about twelve days, to learn the military exercise; but it is always at a small distance from his dwelling, and does not lead him into any new habits of life.

There are about six thousand regulars also, garrisoned at Christiania* and Fredericshall, which are equally reserved, with the militia, for the defence of their own country. So that when the Prince Royal* passed into Sweden, in 1788, he was obliged to request, not command, them to accompany him on this expedition.

These corps are mostly composed of the sons of the cottagers, who being labourers on the farms, are allowed a few acres to cultivate for themselves. These men voluntarily enlist; but it is only for a limited period (six years), at the expiration of which they have the liberty of retiring. The pay is only twopence a day, and bread; still, considering the cheapness of the country, it is more than sixpence in England.

The distribution of landed property into small farms, produces a degree of equality which I have seldom seen elsewhere; and the rich being all merchants, who are obliged to divide their personal fortune amongst their children, the boys always receiving twice as much as the girls, property has had a chance of accumulating till overgrown wealth destroys the balance of liberty.

You will be surprised to hear me talk of liberty; yet the Norwegians appear to me to be the most free community I have ever observed.

The mayor of each town or district, and the judges in the country, exercise an authority almost patriarchal. They can do much good, but little harm, as every individual can appeal from their judgment: and as they may always be forced to give a reason for their conduct, it is generally regulated by prudence.

'They have not time to learn to be tyrants,' said a gentleman to me, with whom I discussed the subject.

The farmers not fearing to be turned out of their farms, should they displease a man in power, and having no vote to be commanded at an election for a mock representative, are a manly race; for not being obliged to submit to any debasing tenure, in order to live, or advance themselves in the world, they act with an independent spirit. I have never yet heard of anything like domineering, or oppression, excepting such as has arisen from natural causes. The freedom the people enjoy may, perhaps, render them a little litigious, and subject them to the impositions of cunning practitioners of the law; but the authority of office is bounded, and the emoluments of it do not destroy its utility.

Last year a man, who had abused his power, was cashiered, on the representation of the people to the bailiff of the district.

There are four in Norway, who might with propriety be termed sheriffs, and, from their sentence, an appeal, by either party, may be made to Copenhagen.

Near most of the towns are commons, on which the cows of all the inhabitants, indiscriminately, are allowed to graze. The poor, to whom a cow is necessary, are almost supported by it. Besides, to render living more easy, they all go out to fish in their own boats; and fish is their principal food.

The lower class of people in the towns are in general sailors; and the industrious have usually little ventures of their own that serve to render the winter comfortable.

With respect to the country at large, the importation is considerably in the favour of Norway.

They are forbidden, at present, to export corn or rye, on account of the advanced price.

The restriction which most resembles the painful subordination of Ireland, is that vessels, trading to the West Indies, are obliged to pass by their own ports, and unload their cargoes at Copenhagen, which they afterwards reship.* The duty is indeed inconsiderable; but the navigation being dangerous, they run a double risk.

There is an excise on all articles of consumption brought to the towns; but the officers are not strict; and it would be reckoned invidious to enter a house to search, as in England.

The Norwegians appear to me a sensible, shrewd people, with

little scientific knowledge, and still less taste for literature: but they are arriving at the epoch which precedes the introduction of the arts and sciences.

Most of the towns are seaports, and seaports are not favourable to improvement. The captains acquire a little superficial knowledge by travelling, which their indefatigable attention to the making of money prevents their digesting; and the fortune that they thus laboriously acquire, is spent, as it usually is in towns of this description, in show and good living. They love their country, but have not much public spirit.[1] Their exertions are, generally speaking, only for their families; which I conceive will always be the case, till politics, becoming a subject of discussion, enlarges the heart by opening the understanding. The French Revolution will have this effect. They sing at present, with great glee, many Republican songs, and seem earnestly to wish that the Republic may stand; yet they appear very much attached to their Prince Royal; and, as far as rumour can give an idea of a character, he appears to merit their attachment. When I am at Copenhagen, I shall be able to ascertain on what foundation their good opinion is built; at present I am only an echo of it.

In the year 1788 he travelled through Norway; and acts of mercy gave dignity to the parade, and interest to the joy his presence inspired. At this town he pardoned a girl condemned to die for murdering an illegitimate child, a crime seldom committed in this country. She is since married, and become the careful mother of a family. This might be given as an instance that a desperate act is not always a proof of an incorrigible depravity of character; the only plausible excuse that has been brought forward to justify the infliction of capital punishments.

I will relate two or three other anecdotes to you; for the truth of which I will not vouch, because the facts were not of sufficient consequence for me to take much pains to ascertain them; and, true or false, they evince that the people like to make a kind of mistress of their prince.

An officer, mortally wounded at the ill-advised battle of Quistram,* desired to speak with the Prince; and, with his dying

---

[1] The grand virtues of the heart, particularly the enlarged humanity which extends to the whole human race, depend more on the understanding, I believe, than is generally imagined. [Author's note]

breath, earnestly recommended to his care a young woman of Christiania, to whom he was engaged. When the prince returned there, a ball was given by the chief inhabitants. He inquired whether this unfortunate girl was invited, and requested that she might be, though of the second class. The girl came; she was pretty; and finding herself amongst her superiors, bashfully sat down as near the door as possible, nobody taking any notice of her. Shortly after, the Prince entering, immediately inquired for her, and asked her to dance, to the mortification of the rich dames. After it was over he handed her to the top of the room, and placing himself beside her, spoke of the loss she had sustained, with tenderness, promising to provide for anyone she should marry – as the story goes. She is since married, and he has not forgotten his promise.

A little girl, during the same expedition, in Sweden, who informed him that the logs of a bridge were cut underneath, was taken by his orders to Christiania, and put to school at his expense.

Before I retail other beneficial effects of his journey, it is necessary to inform you that the laws here are mild, and do not punish capitally for any crime but murder, which seldom occurs. Every other offence merely subjects the delinquent to imprisonment and labour in the castle, or rather arsenal, at Christiania, and the fortress at Fredericshall. The first and second conviction produces a sentence for a limited number of years, – two, three, five, or seven, proportioned to the atrocity of the crime. After the third he is whipped, branded in the forehead, and condemned to perpetual slavery. This is the ordinary march of justice. For some flagrant breaches of trust, or acts of wanton cruelty, criminals have been condemned to slavery for life, the first time of conviction, but not frequently. The number of these slaves do not, I am informed, amount to more than one hundred, which is not considerable, compared with the population, upwards of eight hundred thousand. Should I pass through Christiania, on my return to Gothenburg, I shall probably have an opportunity of learning other particulars.

There is also a house of correction at Christiania for trifling misdemeanours, where the women are confined to labour and imprisonment even for life. The state of the prisoners was represented to the Prince; in consequence of which, he visited the arsenal and house of correction. The slaves at the arsenal were loaded with irons of a great weight; he ordered them to be lightened as much as possible.

The people in the house of correction were commanded not to speak to him; but four women, condemned to remain there for life, got into the passage, and fell at his feet. He granted them a pardon; and inquiring respecting the treatment of the prisoners, he was informed that they were frequently whipped going in, and coming out; and for any fault, at the discretion of the inspectors. This custom he humanely abolished; though some of the principal inhabitants, whose situation in life had raised them above the temptation of stealing, were of opinion that these chastisements were necessary and wholesome.

In short, everything seems to announce that the Prince really cherishes the laudable ambition of fulfilling the duties of his station. This ambition is cherished and directed by the count Bernstof,* the prime minister of Denmark, who is universally celebrated for his abilities and virtue. The happiness of the people is a substantial eulogium; and, from all I gather, the inhabitants of Denmark and Norway are the least oppressed people of Europe. The press is free. They translate any of the French publications of the day, deliver their opinion on the subject, and discuss those it leads to with great freedom, and without fearing to displease the government.

On the subject of religion they are likewise becoming tolerant, at least, and perhaps have advanced a step further in freethinking. One writer has ventured to deny the divinity of Jesus Christ, and to question the necessity or utility of the Christian system, without being considered universally as a monster, which would have been the case a few years ago. They have translated many German works on education; and though they have not adopted any of their plans, it is become a subject of discussion. There are some grammar and free schools; but, from what I hear, not very good ones. All the children learn to read, write, and cast accounts, for the purposes of common life. They have no university; and nothing that deserves the name of science is taught; nor do individuals, by pursuing any branch of knowledge, excite a degree of curiosity which is the forerunner of improvement. Knowledge is not absolutely necessary to enable a considerable portion of the community to live; and, till it is, I fear, it never becomes general.

In this country, where minerals abound, there is not one

collection: and, in all probability, I venture a conjecture, the want of mechanical and chemical knowledge renders the silver mines unproductive; for the quantity of silver obtained every year is not sufficient to defray the expenses. It has been urged, that the employment of such a number of hands is very beneficial. But a positive loss is never to be done away; and the men, thus employed, would naturally find some other means of living, instead of being thus a dead weight on government, or rather on the community from whom its revenue is drawn.

About three English miles from Tonsberg there is a salt-work, belonging, like all their establishments, to government, in which they employ above an hundred and fifty men, and maintain nearly five hundred people, who earn their living. The clear profit, an increasing one, amounts to two thousand pounds sterling. And as the eldest son of the inspector, an ingenious young man, has been sent by the government to travel, and acquire some mathematical and chemical knowledge in Germany, it has a chance of being improved. He is the only person I have met with here who appears to have a scientific turn of mind. I do not mean to assert that I have not met with others, who have a spirit of inquiry.

The salt-works at St Ubes are basins in the sand, and the sun produces the evaporation: but here there is no beach. Besides, the heat of summer is so short-lived, that it would be idle to contrive machines for such an inconsiderable portion of the year. They therefore always use fires; and the whole establishment appears to be regulated with judgment.

The situation is well chosen and beautiful. I do not find, from the observation of a person who has resided here for forty years, that the sea advances or recedes on this coast.

I have already remarked, that little attention is paid to education, excepting reading, writing, and the rudiments of arithmetic; I ought to have added, that a catechism is carefully taught, and the children obliged to read in the churches, before the congregation, to prove that they are not neglected.

Degrees, to enable anyone to practise any profession, must be taken at Copenhagen; and the people of this country, having the good sense to perceive that men who are to live in a community should at least acquire the elements of their knowledge, and form their youthful attachments there, are seriously endeavouring to establish a university in Norway.* And Tonsberg, as a centrical place in the best part of the country, had the most suffrages; for, experiencing the bad effects of a metropolis, they have determined not to have it in or near Christiania. Should such an establishment take place, it will promote inquiry throughout the country, and give a new face to society. Premiums have been offered, and prize questions written, which I am told have merit. The building college-halls, and other appendages of the seat of science, might enable Tonsberg to recover its pristine consequence; for it is one of the most ancient towns of Norway, and once contained nine churches. At present there are only two. One is a very old structure, and has a Gothic respectability about it, which scarcely amounts to grandeur, because, to render a Gothic pile grand, it must have a huge unwieldiness of appearance. The chapel at Windsor may be an exception to this rule; I mean before it was in its present *nice*, *clean* state.* When I first saw it, the pillars within had acquired, by time, a sombre hue, which accorded with the architecture; and the gloom increased its dimensions to the eye by hiding its parts, but now it all bursts on the view at once; and the sublimity has vanished before the brush and broom; for it has been whitewashed and scraped till it is become as bright and neat as the pots and pans in a notable housewife's kitchen – yes; the very spurs on the recumbent knights were deprived of their venerable rust, to give a striking proof that a love of order in trifles, and taste for proportion and arrangement, are very distinct. The glare of light thus introduced, entirely destroys the sentiment these piles are calculated to inspire; so that, when I heard something like a jig from the organ-loft, I thought it an excellent hall for dancing or feasting. The measured pace of thought with which I had entered the cathedral, changed into a trip; and I bounded on the terrace, to see the royal family, with a number of ridiculous images in my head, that I shall not now recall.

The Norwegians are fond of music; and every little church has an organ. In the church I have mentioned, there is an inscription importing that a king,[1] James the sixth of Scotland,

---

[1] 'Anno 1589, St Martin's Day, which was the 11th day of November, on a Tuesday, came the high-born Prince and Lord Jacob Stuart, King in Scotland, to this Town, and the 25th Sunday after Trinity (Sunday) which was the 16th Day of November, stood his Grace in this Pew, and heard Scotch Preaching from the

and first of England,* who came with more than princely
gallantry, to escort his bride home, stood there, and heard divine
service.

There is a little recess full of coffins, which contains bodies
embalmed long since – so long, that there is not even a tradition
to lead to a guess at their names.

A desire of preserving the body seems to have prevailed in
most countries of the world, futile as it is to term it a preser-
vation, when the noblest parts are immediately sacrificed merely
to save the muscles, skin and bone from rottenness. When I was
shown these human petrifications, I shrunk back with disgust
and horror. 'Ashes to ashes!' thought I – 'Dust to dust!' – If this
be not dissolution, it is something worse than natural decay – It
is treason against humanity, thus to lift up the awful veil which
would fain hide its weakness. The grandeur of the active prin-
ciple is never more strongly felt than at such a sight; for nothing
is so ugly as the human form when deprived of life, and thus
dried into stone, merely to preserve the most disgusting image of
death. The contemplation of noble ruins produces a melancholy
that exalts the mind. – We take a retrospect of the exertions of
man, the fate of empires and their rulers; and marking the grand
destruction of ages, it seems the necessary change of time leading
to improvement. – Our very soul expands, and we forget our
littleness; how painfully brought to our recollection by such vain
attempts to snatch from decay what is destined so soon to perish.
Life, what art thou? Where goes this breath? this *I*, so much
alive? In what element will it mix, giving or receiving fresh
energy? – What will break the enchantment of animation? – For
worlds, I would not see a form I loved – embalmed in my heart
– thus sacrilegiously handled! – Pugh! my stomach turns. – Is
this all the distinction of the rich in the grave? – They had better
quietly allow the scythe of equality to mow them down with the

23rd Psalm, "The Lord is my Shepherd", etc. which M. David Lentz, Preacher
in Lith, then preached between 10 and 12.'

The above is an inscription which stands in St Mary's church, in Tonsberg.

It is known that King James the Sixth went to Norway, to marry Princess
Anna, the daughter of Frederick the Second, and sister to Christian the Fourth;
and that the wedding was performed at Oslo (now Christiania), where the
Princess, by contrary winds, was detained; but that the King, during this voyage,
was at Tonsberg, nobody would have known, if an inscription, in remembrance
of it, had not been placed in this church. [Author's note]

common mass, than struggle to become a monument of the instability of human greatness.

The teeth, nails and skin were whole, without appearing black like the Egyptian mummies; and some silk, in which they had been wrapped, still preserved its colour, pink, with tolerable freshness.

I could not learn how long the bodies had been in this state, in which they bid fair to remain till the day of judgment, if there is to be such a day; and before that time, it will require some trouble to make them fit to appear in company with angels, without disgracing humanity. – God bless you! I feel a conviction that we have some perfectible principle in our present vestment, which will not be destroyed just as we begin to be sensible of improvement; and I care not what habit it next puts on, sure that it will be wisely formed to suit a higher state of existence. Thinking of death makes us tenderly cling to our affections – with more than usual tenderness, I therefore assure you that I am your's, wishing that the temporary death of absence may not endure longer than is absolutely necessary.

1796

LETTER

Introductory to a Series of Letters on the Present Character of the French Nation

Paris, 15 February 1793

My dear friend,

It is necessary perhaps for an observer of mankind, to guard as carefully the first impression made by a nation, as by a countenance; because we imperceptibly lose sight of the national character, when we become more intimate with individuals. It is not then useless or presumptuous to note, that, when I first entered Paris, the striking contrast of riches and poverty, elegance and slovenliness, urbanity and deceit, every where caught my eye, and saddened my soul; and these impressions are still the foundation of my remarks on the manners, which flatter the senses, more than they interest the heart, and yet excite more interest than esteem.

The whole mode of life here tends indeed to render the people frivolous, and, to borrow their favourite epithet, amiable. Ever on the wing, they are always sipping the sparkling joy on the brim of the cup, leaving satiety in the bottom for those who venture to drink deep. On all sides they trip along, buoyed up by animal spirits, and seemingly so void of care, that often, when I am walking on the *Boulevards*, it occurs to me, that they alone understand the full import of the term leisure; and they trifle their time away with such an air of contentment, I know not how to wish them wiser at the expense of their gaiety. They play before me like motes in a sunbeam, enjoying the passing ray; whilst an English head, searching for more solid happiness, loses, in the analysis of pleasure, the volatile sweets of the moment. Their chief enjoyment, it is true, rises from vanity: but it is not the vanity that engenders vexation of spirit; on the contrary, it lightens the heavy burden of life, which reason too often weighs, merely to shift from one shoulder to the other.

Investigating the modification of the passion, as I would analyze the elements that give form to dead matter, I shall attempt to trace to their source the causes which have combined to render this nation the most polished, in a physical sense, and probably the most superficial in the world; and I mean to follow the windings of the various streams that disembogue into a terrific gulf, in which all the dignity of our nature is absorbed. For every thing has conspired to make the French the most sensual people in the world; and what can render the heart so hard, or so effectually stifle every moral emotion, as the refinements of sensuality?

The frequent repetition of the word French, appears invidious; let me then make a previous observation, which I beg you not to lose sight of, when I speak rather harshly of a land flowing with milk and honey. Remember that it is not the morals of a particular people that I would decry; for are we not all of the same stock? But I wish calmly to consider the stage of civilization in which I find the French, and, giving a sketch of their character, and unfolding the circumstances which have produced its identity, I shall endeavour to throw some light on the history of man, and on the present important subjects of discussion.

I wish I could first inform you that, out of the chaos of vices and follies, prejudices and virtues, rudely jumbled together, I saw the fair form of Liberty slowly rising, and Virtue expanding her wings to shelter all her children! I should then hear the account of the barbarities that have rent the bosom of France patiently, and bless the firm hand that lopt off the rotten limbs. But, if the aristocracy of birth is levelled with the ground, only to make room for that of riches, I am afraid that the morals of the people will not be much improved by the change, or the government rendered less venal. Still it is not just to dwell on the misery produced by the present struggle, without adverting to the standing evils of the old system. I am grieved – sorely grieved – when I think of the blood that has stained the cause of freedom at Paris; but I also hear the same live stream cry aloud from the highways, through which the retreating armies passed with famine and death in their rear, and I hide my face with awe before the inscrutable ways of providence, sweeping in such various directions the besom of destruction over the sons of men.

Before I came to France, I cherished, you know, an opinion, that strong virtues might exist with the polished manners produced by the progress of civilization; and I even anticipated the epoch, when, in the course of improvement, men would labour to become virtuous, without being goaded on by misery. But now, the perspective of the golden age, fading before the attentive eye of observation, almost eludes my sight; and, losing thus in part my theory of a more perfect state, start not, my friend, if I bring forward an opinion, which at first glance seems to be levelled against the existence of God! I am not become an Atheist, I assure you, by residing at Paris: yet I begin to fear that vice, or, if you will, evil, is the grand mobile of action, and that, when the passions are justly poised, we become harmless, and in the same proportions useless.

The wants of reason are very few, and, were we to consider dispassionately the real value of most things, we should probably rest satisfied with the simple gratification of our physical necessities, and be content with negative goodness: for it is frequently, only that wanton, the Imagination, with her artful coquetry, who lures us forward, and makes us run over a rough road, pushing aside every obstacle merely to catch a disappointment.

The desire also of being useful to others, is continually damped by experience; and, if the exertions of humanity were not in some measure their own reward, who would endure misery, or struggle with care, to make some people ungrateful, and others idle?

You will call these melancholy effusions, and guess that, fatigued by the vivacity, which has all the bustling folly of childhood, without the innocence which renders ignorance charming, I am too severe in my strictures. It may be so; and I am aware that the good effects of the revolution will be last felt at Paris where surely the soul of Epicurus has long been at work to root out the simple emotions of the heart, which being natural, are always moral. Rendered cold and artificial by the selfish enjoyments of the senses, which the government fostered, is it surprising that simplicity of manners, and singleness of heart, rarely appear, to recreate me with the wild odour of nature, so passing sweet?

Seeing how deep the fibres of mischief have shot, I sometimes ask, with a doubting accent, Whether a nation can go back to the purity of manners which has hitherto been maintained unsullied only by the keen air of poverty, when, emasculated by pleasure, the luxuries of prosperity are become the wants of nature? I cannot yet give up the hope, that a fairer day is dawning on Europe, though I must hesitatingly observe, that little is to be expected from the narrow principle of commerce which seems every where to be shoving aside the *point of honour* of the *noblesse*. I can look beyond the evils of the moment, and do not expect muddied water to become clear before it has had time to stand; yet, even for the moment, it is the most terrific of all sights, to see men vicious without warmth – to see the order that should be the superscription of virtue, cultivated to give security to crimes which only thoughtlessness could palliate. Disorder is, in fact, the very essence of vice, though with the wild wishes of a corrupt fancy humane emotions often kindly mix to soften their atrocity. Thus humanity, generosity, and even self-denial, sometimes render a character grand, and even useful, when hurried away by lawless passions; but what can equal the turpitude of a cold calculator who lives for himself alone, and considering his fellow-creatures merely as machines of pleasure, never forgets that honesty is the best policy? Keeping ever within the pale of the law, he crushes his thousands with impunity; but it is with that degree of management, which makes him, to borrow a significant vulgarism, a villain *in grain*. The very excess of his depravation preserves him, whilst the more respectable beast of prey, who prowls about like the lion, and roars to announce his approach, falls into a snare.

You may think it too soon to form an opinion of the future government, yet it is impossible to avoid hazarding some conjectures, when every thing whispers me, that names, not principles, are changed, and when I see that the turn of the tide has left the dregs of the old system to corrupt the new. For the same pride of office, the same desire of power are still visible; with this aggravation, that, fearing to return to obscurity after having but just acquired a relish for distinction, each hero, or philosopher, for all are dubbed with these new titles, endeavours to make hay while the sun shines; and every petty municipal officer, become the idol, or rather the tyrant of the day, stalks like a cock on a dunghill.

I shall now conclude this desultory letter which however will enable you to foresee that I shall treat more of morals than manners.

Yours ——

LETTERS TO GILBERT IMLAY

Letter 69

[*c*. 10 October 1795]

I write to you now on my knees; imploring you to send my child and the maid with ——, to Paris, to be consigned to the care of Madame ——, rue ——, section de ——. Should they be removed, —— can give their direction.

Let the maid have all my clothes, without distinction.

Pray pay the cook her wages, and do not mention the confession which I forced from her* – a little sooner or later is of no consequence. Nothing but my extreme stupidity could have rendered me blind so long. Yet, whilst you assured me that you had no attachment, I thought we might still have lived together.

I shall make no comments on your conduct; or any appeal to the world. Let my wrongs sleep with me! Soon, very soon shall

I be at peace. When you receive this, my burning head will be cold.

I would encounter a thousand deaths, rather than a night like the last. Your treatment has thrown my mind into a state of chaos; yet I am serene. I go to find comfort, and my only fear is, that my poor body will be insulted by an endeavour to recall my hated existence. But I shall plunge into the Thames where there is the least chance of my being snatched from the death I seek.

God bless you! May you never know by experience what you have made me endure. Should your sensibility ever awake, remorse will find its way to your heart; and, in the midst of business and sensual pleasure, I shall appear before you, the victim of your deviation from rectitude.

                                                              * * * *

Letter 70

                          Sunday Morning. [*c*. late October 1795]
I have only to lament, that, when the bitterness of death was past, I was inhumanly brought back to life and misery. But a fixed determination is not to be baffled by disappointment; nor will I allow that to be a frantic attempt, which was one of the calmest acts of reason. Did I care for what is termed reputation, it is by other circumstances that I should be dishonoured.

You say, 'that you know not how to extricate ourselves out of the wretchedness into which we have been plunged.' You are extricated long since. – But I forbear to comment. – If I am condemned to live longer, it is a living death.

It appears to me, that you lay much more stress on delicacy, than on principle; for I am unable to discover what sentiment of delicacy would have been violated, by your visiting a wretched friend – if indeed you have any friendship for me. – But since your new attachment is the only thing sacred in your eyes, I am silent – Be happy! My complaints shall never more damp your enjoyment – perhaps I am mistaken in supposing that even my death could, for more than a moment. – This is what you call magnanimity. – It is happy for yourself, that you possess this quality in the highest degree.

Your continually asserting, that you will do all in your power to contribute to my comfort (when you only allude to pecuniary assistance), appears to me a flagrant breach of delicacy. – I want

not such vulgar comfort, nor will I accept it.* I never wanted
but your heart – That gone, you have nothing more to give. Had
I only poverty to fear, I should not shrink from life. – Forgive
me then, if I say, that I shall consider any direct or indirect
attempt to supply my necessities, as an insult which I have not
merited – and as rather done out of tenderness for your own
reputation, than for me. Do not mistake me; I do not think that
you value money (therefore I will not accept what you do not
care for) though I do much less, because certain privations are
not painful to me. When I am dead, respect for yourself will
make you take care of the child.

I write with difficulty – probably I shall never write to you
again. – Adieu!

God bless you!

                                                    * * * *

Letter 71

[c. November 1795] Monday Morning.
I am compelled at last to say that you treat me ungenerously. I
agree with you that [Godwin omitted four lines here] But let the
obliquity now fall on me. – I fear neither poverty nor infamy. I
am unequal to the task of writing – and explanations are not
necessary. [Godwin omitted two lines here.] My child may have
to blush for her mother's want of prudence – and may lament
that the rectitude of my heart made me above vulgar precau-
tions; but she shall not despise me for meanness. – You are now
perfectly free.* – God bless you.

                                                    * * * *

Letter 73

I have been hurt by indirect enquiries, which appear to me not
to be dictated by any tenderness to me. – You ask 'If I am not
well or tranquil?' – They who think me so, must want a heart to
estimate my feelings by. – I choose then to be the organ of my
own sentiments.

I must tell you, that I am very much mortified by your
continually offering me pecuniary assistance – and, considering
your going to the new house, as an open avowal that you
abandon me, let me tell you that I will sooner perish than receive

any thing from you – and I say this at the moment when I am
disappointed in my first attempt to obtain a temporary supply.
But this even pleases me; an accumulation of disappointments
and misfortunes seems to suit the habit of my mind. –

Have but a little patience, and I will remove myself where it
will not be necessary for you to talk – of course, not to think of
me. But let me see, written by yourself – for I will not receive it
through any other medium – that the affair is finished. – It is an
insult to me to suppose, that I can be reconciled, or recover my
spirits; but, if you hear nothing of me, it will be the same thing
to you.

                                                    * * * *

Even your seeing me, has been to oblige other people, and not
to soothe my distracted mind.

Letter 74

[c. November 1795] Thursday Afternoon
Mr ——* having forgot to desire you to send the things of mine
which were left at the house, I have to request you to let ——*
bring them to ——.

I shall go this evening to the lodging; so you need not be
restrained from coming here to transact your business.* – And,
whatever I may think, and feel – you need not fear that I shall
publicly complain – No! If I have any criterion to judge of right
and wrong, I have been most ungenerously treated: but, wishing
now only to hide myself, I shall be as silent as the grave in which
I long to forget myself. I shall protect and provide for my child.
– I only mean by this to say, that you have nothing to fear from
my desperation.

                                                    Farewell.

                                                    * * * *

Letter 75

London, November 27 [1795]
The letter, without an address, which you put up with the letters
you returned,* did not meet my eyes till just now. – I had
thrown the letters aside – I did not wish to look over a register
of sorrow.

My not having seen it, will account for my having written to you with anger – under the impression your departure, without even a line left for me, made on me, even after your late conduct, which could not lead me to expect much attention to my sufferings.

In fact, 'the decided conduct, which appeared to me so unfeeling,' has almost overturned my reason; my mind is injured – I scarcely know where I am, or what I do. – The grief I cannot conquer (for some cruel recollections never quit me, banishing almost every other) I labour to conceal in total solitude. – My life therefore is but an exercise of fortitude, continually on the stretch – and hope never gleams in this tomb, where I am buried alive.

But I meant to reason with you, and not to complain. – You tell me, 'that I shall judge more coolly of your mode of acting, some time hence.' But is it not possible that *passion* clouds your reason, as much as it does mine? – and ought you not to doubt, whether those principles are so 'exalted', as you term them, which only lead to your own gratification? In other words, whether it be just to have no principle of action, but that of following your inclination, trampling on the affection you have fostered, and the expectations you have excited?

My affection for you is rooted in my heart. – I know you are not what you now seem – nor will you always act, or feel, as you do now, though I may never be comforted by the change. – Even at Paris,* my image will haunt you. – You will see my pale face – and sometimes the tears of anguish will drop on your heart, which you have forced from mine.

I cannot write. I thought I could quickly have refuted all your *ingenious* arguments; but my head is confused. – Right or wrong, I am miserable!

It seems to me, that my conduct has always been governed by the strictest principles of justice and truth. – Yet, how wretched have my social feelings, and delicacy of sentiment rendered me! – I have loved with my whole soul, only to discover that I had no chance of a return – and that existence is a burden without it.

I do not perfectly understand you. – If, by the offer of your friendship, you still only mean pecuniary support – I must again reject it. – Trifling are the ills of poverty in the scale of my misfortunes. – God bless you!

* * * *

I have been treated ungenerously – if I understand what is generosity. – You seem to me only to have been anxious to shake me off – regardless whether you dashed me to atoms by the fall. – In truth I have been rudely handled. *Do you judge coolly*, and I trust you will not continue to call those capricious feelings 'the most refined,' which would undermine not only the most sacred principles, but the affections which unite mankind. – You would render mothers unnatural – and there would be no such thing as a father! – If your theory of morals is the most 'exalted', it is certainly the most easy. – It does not require much magnanimity, to determine to please ourselves for the moment, let others suffer what they will!

Excuse me for again tormenting you, my heart thirsts for justice from you – and whilst I recollect that you approve Miss ——'s conduct – I am convinced you will not always justify your own.

Beware of the deceptions of passion! It will not always banish from your mind, that you have acted ignobly – and condescend to subterfuge to gloss over the conduct you could not excuse. – Do truth and principle require such sacrifices?

Letter 76

London, December 8 [1795]

Having just been informed that —— is to return immediately to Paris, I would not miss a sure opportunity of writing, because I am not certain that my last, by Dover has reached you.

Resentment, and even anger, are momentary emotions with me – and I wished to tell you, that if you ever think of me, it may not be in the light of an enemy.

That I have not been used *well* I must ever feel; perhaps, not always with the keen anguish I do at present – for I began even now to write calmly, and I cannot restrain my tears.

I am stunned! – Your late conduct still appears to me a frightful dream. —

Ah! ask yourself if you have not condescended to employ a little address, I could almost say cunning, unworthy of you? – Principles are sacred things – and we never play with truth, with impunity.

The expectation (I have too fondly nourished it) of regaining your affection, every day grows fainter and fainter. – Indeed, it seems to me, when I am not more sad than usual, that I shall never see you more. – Yet you will not always forget me. – You will feel something like remorse, for having lived only for yourself – and sacrificed my peace to inferior gratifications. In a comfortless old age, you will remember that you had one disinterested friend, whose heart you wounded to the quick. The hour of recollection will come – and you will not be satisfied to act the part of a boy, till you fall into that of a dotard. I know that your mind, your heart, and your principles of action, are all superior to your present conduct. You do, you must, respect me – and you will be sorry to forfeit my esteem.

You know best whether I am still preserving the remembrance of an imaginary being. – I once thought that I knew you thoroughly – but now I am obliged to leave some doubts that involuntarily press on me, to be cleared up by time.

You may render me unhappy; but cannot make me contempt-ible in my own eyes. – I shall still be able to support my child, though I am disappointed in some other plans of usefulness, which I once believed would have afforded you equal pleasure.

Whilst I was with you, I restrained my natural generosity, because I thought your property in jeopardy. – When I went to [Scandinavia], I requested you, *if you could conveniently*, not to forget my father, sisters, and some other people, whom I was interested about. – Money was lavished away,* yet not only my requests were neglected, but some trifling debts were not dis-charged, that now come on me. – Was this friendship – or generosity? Will you not grant you have forgotten yourself? Still I have an affection for you. – God bless you.

* * * *

Letter 77

[*c.* December 1795]

As the parting from you for ever is the most serious event of my life, I will once expostulate with you, and call not the language of truth and feeling ingenuity!

I know the soundness of your understanding – and know that it is impossible for you always to confound the caprices of every wayward inclination with the manly dictates of principle.

You tell me 'that I torment you.' – Why do I? Because you cannot estrange your heart entirely from me – and you feel that justice is on my side. You urge, 'that your conduct was unequivocal.' – It was not. – When your coolness has hurt me, with what tenderness have you endeavoured to remove the impression! – and even before I returned to England, you took great pains to convince me, that all my uneasiness was occasioned by the effect of a worn-out constitution – and you concluded your letter with these words, 'Business alone has kept me from you. – Come to any port, and I will fly down to my two dear girls with a heart all their own.'

With these assurances, is it extraordinary that I should believe what I wished? I might – and did think that you had a struggle with old propensities; but I still thought that I and virtue should at last prevail. I still thought that you had a magnanimity of character, which would enable you to conquer yourself.

——, believe me, it is not romance, you have acknowledged to me feelings of this kind. – You could restore me to life and hope, and the satisfaction you would feel, would amply repay you.

In tearing myself from you, it is my own heart I pierce – and the time will come, when you will lament that you have thrown away a heart, that, even in the moment of passion, you cannot despise. – I would owe every thing to your generosity – but, for God's sake, keep me no longer in suspense! – Let me see you once more! –

Letter 78

You must do as you please with respect to the child. – I could wish that it might be done soon, that my name may be no more mentioned to you. It is now finished. – Convinced that you have neither regard nor friendship, I disdain to utter a reproach, though I have had reason to think, that the 'forbearance' talked of, has not been very delicate. – It is however of no consequence. – I am glad you are satisfied with your own conduct.

I now solemnly assure you, that this is an eternal farewell. – Yet I flinch not from the duties which tie me to life.

That there is 'sophistry' on one side or other, is certain; but now it matters not on which. On my part it has not been a question of words. Yet your understanding or mine must be strangely warped – for what you term 'delicacy,' appears to me to be exactly the contrary. I have no criterion for morality, and have thought in vain, if the sensations which lead you to follow an ankle or step, be the sacred foundation of principle and affection. Mine has been of a very different nature, or it would not have stood the brunt of your sarcasms.

The sentiment in me is still sacred. If there be any part of me that will survive the sense of my misfortunes, it is the purity of my affections. The impetuosity of your senses, may have led you to term mere animal desire, the source of principle; and it may give zest to some years to come. – Whether you will always think so, I shall never know.

It is strange that, in spite of all you do, something like conviction forces me to believe, that you are not what you appear to be.

I part with you in peace.

ANNA SEWARD

ANNA SEWARD (1742–1809) developed an interest in poetry as an adolescent, but her literary career was initially impeded by her father, a clergyman, who forbade her to write poetry in case she thus became unattractive to men and therefore unmarriageable. Despite these precautions, Anna Seward, although she had inherited wealth, did not marry. Her sister died unexpectedly and Anna remained at home to look after her parents. Once she had declared her intention to remain single, she was no longer prevented from following her literary career. Her first success was *Elegy on Captain Cook* (1780) which was followed by *Monody on the Death of Major André* (1781). In 1784, she published a 'poetical novel', *Louisa*, and in 1799, her *Collection of Original Sonnets* appeared. Some of these had been published earlier in literary magazines. The texts of the letters are taken from *Letters of Anna Seward*, 1811, vol. 2, pp. 28–33, 247–50, and vol. 6, pp. 362–9. Biographical information comes from Sir Walter Scott's 'Introduction' to *The Poetical Works of Anna Seward with Extracts from her Literary Correspondence*, 3 vols, (1810), and Margaret Ashmun's *The Singing Swan: An Account of Anna Seward* (1931).

LETTER 5: TO JOSIAH WEDGWOOD*

18 February 1788

I am honoured and obliged by your endeavours to enlighten me on a subject so important to human virtue and human happiness. They have not been vain; and I blush for the coldness my late letter expressed, whose subject demanded the ardour of benevolent wishes, and of just indignation.

Let me, however, do myself the justice to observe, that my heart always recoiled with horror from the miseries which I heard were inflicted on the negro slaves; but I have had long acquaintance with a Mr Newton of this place, who made a large fortune in the East, where slavery pervades every opulent establishment. He constantly assured me, that the purchase, employment, and strict discipline of the negroes were absolutely necessary to maintain our empire, and our commerce, in the Indies. As constantly did he affirm, that they were of a nature so sordid and insensible, as to render necessary a considerable degree of severity, and to make much lenity alike injurious to the indulger and the indulged; that the accounts of the cruelties practised upon the slaves by their masters were false, or at least infinitely exaggerated. He observed, that the worst people will abstain from vice, when it is against their interest to practise it; that the high price and value of the subjugated, inevitably preserves them from the dire effects of this imputed barbarity.

When I sighed over the severe discipline, for the necessity of which he pleaded, I was desired to recollect the fate of the Ashwells – uncle and brother to young gentlewomen of this town. The former, a West India Planter, whose compassionate temper, which his nieces assert had been ever soft and indulgent, even to weakness, led him to give his slaves unusual relaxation from toil, and to take scrupulous care that they were constantly and plentifully supplied with wholesome food; yet was he murdered by them in the most cruel manner; and his nephew, then a youth of fourteen, *intentionally* murdered; they hamstringed, and cut off his left arm, and two of the fingers on his right hand, leaving him, as they thought, lifeless.

The last mentioned Mr Ashwell, who lives the hapless wreck of negro cruelty, uniformly confirmed to me, for I have often conversed with him, all Mr Newton had told me of the generally treacherous, ungrateful, and bloody temper of the negroes. Impressed with these ideas, I was led to consider the present efforts for their enfranchisement, as fruitless and dangerous, though just and humane; that the Scriptures, which often mention slavery, bear no testimony against it as impious; that, in some countries, the subjection of beings, that form the latest link in the chain descending from human to brute animality, was an evil inevitable, as war between nations has always been found in every climate.

Beneath the force of that melancholy conviction, I avoided reading any thing upon the subject; flattering myself, that if the abolition of a traffic so lamentable could be safely effected by our legislators, they, as Englishmen and Christians, would listen to merciful remonstrance, and feel themselves impelled to abolish it.

Your letter, and the tracts which accompanied it, have changed my ideas on the subject. They have given me indignant convictions, decided principles, and better hopes that the flood-gates of this overwhelming cruelty may be let down without ruin to our national interests.

But as to your exhortation that I would write a poem on the subject, I sicken at the idea of encountering the certain pains, and uncertain pleasures of publication, by committing this theme to my muse, fruitful as it is in the great nerves of poetry, pathos, and horror; and this, because I have no confidence that her voice would arrest the general attention. Better poetry than mine, though richly the product, is not the taste of this age. Mr Day's sublime poem, 'The Dying Negro',* passed away without its fame, though eminently calculated to impress the public with horror of the slave-trade.

You gratify me much by speaking so highly of my Elegies on Cook and André, and on Lady Millar. When the society for arts and sciences, of which my acquaintance, Sir Joseph Banks,* is President, struck a medal in honour of Captain Cook,* Mr Green of our museum had one, and indeed every person who had interested themselves at all publicly in the memory of that philanthropic hero.

> To me alone
> One of old Gideon's miracles was shown;
> For upon all the quicken'd ground

> The fruitful seed of Heaven did brooding lie,
> And nothing but the muses fleece was dry.[1]

Then the public hireling critics are not my friends; and I have personal enemies in some of them, rendered such by my sincerity, and because I could not stoop to flatter with praise the miserable rhymes they presented to me; and for that sin of omission to their vanity, they load my writings with imputed vulgarness, bombast, immorality, and obscenity itself, as the European Magazine and English Review testify. However contemptible such evidently groundless censure, it is not very pleasant to its object.

In losing Mr Bently,*[2] my muse lost a friend and protector. I had not the pleasure of being known to that gentleman, when he spoke to the public in such warm praise of my writings, either personally or by letter. He fanned her fires with the breath of ingenious, generous, classical, and discriminating praise. I knew not, at the time, to whom I was so much obliged.

That charming writer, Miss More, has given the world a poem on the Slave Trade; so has her ungrateful pupil Lactilla.* I have not yet seen either of those compositions; but I cannot prevail upon myself to give my scribbling foes new opportunity of venting their spleen, by speaking to the world of the inferiority of my attempt to that of the unlettered milk-woman's. So, I am sure, they would say, were I to write as well as Milton on the theme.

How should these reflections fail to extinguish the ardour of my exertion, when it feels inclined to struggle for an escape from common-life avocations to Aonian employments!* My only stimulus, from without, to an attempt on this occasion, is the consciousness that you, and a few other ingenious friends, are predisposed in its favour. I confess that to be a powerful one. During an whole hour after I received your letter, it maintained its ground ere it sunk beneath the snow-drifts of opposing recollections.

---

[1] From Cowley's* ode on being refused a place at court, with the hopes of which he had been flattered by Charles the Second, to whose interests he had devoted himself in that monarch's adversity. [Author's note]

[2] He was a reviewer in the poetic department of the *Monthly Review* for many years. [Author's note]

3 March 1789

Your charming poem on the Slave Trade is a most welcome present.* It would have given me great pleasure to have covered many pages in discriminating its various graces – but a recent inflammation in my eyes forbids the indulgence.

Self-partiality, which makes us fond of ideas and images that have arisen in our own minds, increases perhaps the solemn feelings, excited by the twelve first lines of your exordium. If your friend, Mr Hardinge, has thought it worth his while to preserve my letters, he could show you one, written last April, in answer to one of his, which requested me to employ my muse on this popular subject. That letter of mine to Mr Hardinge, described scenery, and expressed ideas exactly similar to those in the first twelve lines of your poem. I never committed them to measure, through utter want of time for compositions of any length. I could obtain it only by the sacrifice of more material things – my duties – my common-life business – and my friends.

Perhaps I wish this poem of yours had been written in the ten-feet couplet, of whose graces and powers you are so eminently mistress. I think that of eight feet requires the frequent intermixture of the line of seven syllables, in either very solemn, or very sprightly compositions, to give spirit and variety to the measure. Observe how often the seven feet line recurs in the Allegro, Il Penseroso,* and in Gray's Descent of Odin.*

Amongst many other happinesses in your last poem, it has great originality and beauty in its similes.

I am gratified that Mrs Siddons* chose one of my darling plays for her benefit. How charming must the Law of Lombardy* have been, arrayed in her graces, and in her powers! Its characters are drawn with the free hand of a master, who takes human nature rather than theatric precision for his model – and its language has Shakespearian ease and fire. Our public critics abuse it – but they are almost all composed of bad authors, whose enmity to good ones is inevitable, and, towards Mr Jephson,* national jealousy increases their venom.

Charming Mrs Piozzi* recommends Della Crusca's Diversity* to me, as an extremely fine poem – and Mr Hayley* tells me, that Mrs Smith's* Pegasus is of the true ethereal breed – of whose Sonnets, in my opinion, Colonel Barry, as justly as wittily, said, when he was last here, that the general run of them was two or three good lines, stolen from our most popular poets, dispersed here and there in each sonnet, with ten or a dozen others of very indifferent cement.

>   Alas! my gentle Helen, how must I,
>   Who will not flatter, and who dare not lie,

have wounded you with cold praise, had you sent me poems with as little original poetic matter as Mrs Smith's Sonnets; or strutting in such inflated defiance of every thing like common sense, as the compositions of Della Crusca! – not but there are considerable flashes of genius in the latter, but to me they serve only to make the general darkness more visible. Such odes as Diversity will confirm, instead of invalidating Mr Mason's objection to the irregular ode – yet, since Dryden* and Lord Lyttleton* have proved the possibility of making sublime and beautiful poems upon that model, I wonder at Mason's reprobating it. We may venture to pronounce, that a composition, which fails to interest us in irregular lyrics, would not please us better, if we were to see it reduced to the regular form – though fine odes are certainly the more perfect on that account. Adieu! my dear Miss Williams, – your's faithfully.

LETTER 66: TO SIR WALTER SCOTT*

24 August 1807

My temper is not suspicious, nor prone to busy itself with imaginary evils. Not therefore to friendship chilled by that personal intercourse which has increased its warmth on mine, did I impute your broken promise of an early letter on your return home, but solely to your expected press of electioneering business. Would to Heaven your silence had not been the consequence of more distressing circumstances!

I am gratified by your warm praise of my verses addressed to the young prodigy of the theatre.* He performed here during a fortnight, and absolutely enchanted us all, at once by his inspired representation on the stage, and by the unsoiled simplicity of his manners in private company, for he was much caressed and

invited. By the manager's contrivance of placing my indispens-
able arm-chair between the first and second scene, I was, without
the intervening glare of the lamps, enabled to see and hear him
in a nearness of situation highly favourable to the ever-varying
expression of his lovely features and impassioned countenance.
I saw him in five of his best characters.

Mr Mayne, a gentleman of genius and worth in this town,
attached himself to the youth with all a brother's kindness; took
long morning walks with him tête-à-tête. He assures me the
boy's heart is all truth and unaffected sensibility; that his
understanding is sound, and his imagination vivid.

With such excellent qualities of head and heart, cultivated by
an intimate knowledge of Shakespeare and our other best
dramatic writers, I think his professional talents will have no
great miss of what are called the classics. David Garrick,*
though born a gentleman, had not, I have understood, much
knowledge out of the theatric pale.

People who possess the learned languages set a higher value
upon them than perhaps they deserve. Recollecting how much
time and labour they had spent in acquiring them, they are
unwilling to believe them dispensable in any gentleman's edu-
cation. The writers of Great Britain equal, in every style of
composition, the proudest literary boasts of Greece and Rome,
or those of any living language. I cannot suppose that the being
able to read thoughts and sentiments, either of verse or prose, in
foreign tongues, which in equal force and beauty may be found
in our own, any great advantage to the understanding or
imagination, or to be essential in the education of any young
man not intended for divinity, physic, or law.

Old Betty* talks of placing his miraculous boy with a school-
master of eminence at Shrewsbury during three years, so soon
as the present summer closes. I foresee no great good in the
plan, – entertain no hope that, should it be realized, a mind
stored with poetic ideas, and enchanted by their influence, –
accustomed to universal attention, though unspoiled by the
homage, – used also to reign over the hearts of his audience, –
will be able to employ his thoughts on the conjugation of verbs,
and the toil of translation, to gather husks of learning, when the
seed-time and harvest-time of infancy has passed by. Kemble* is
a scholar and a fine actor, but his sister is a finer, and knows no
language but her own.

I was delighted to observe that Henry Betty's wonderful and unremitted exertions have not injured his constitution. His beautiful complexion has the deep glow of health, and his eyes its clearest lustre. His appetite is keen as Gil Blas';* he grows fast, and is plump and stout, and his voice is recovering fast from its 'mannish crack', as Shakespeare calls it. One of the players told me that it had greatly improved in the preceding six weeks. On its first break he should have been removed from the stage till it had acquired strength and fullness of tone. I believe it will be a very fine voice. The public have taken up the idea that it is spoiled, and perhaps the prejudice will be hard of removal. How often does excellence combat prejudice in vain!

If he lives and retains his health, tallness of figure will increase the power of that transcendent grace of motion already his; and I have no doubt but he will be a great and universal actor. His Loony Mactwolter has every excellence of Garrick's Abel Drugger;* the same simplicity of pure humour, nothing indebted to grimace and caricature. He set his audience in a roar of laughter, without one lurking, betraying smile on his own countenance, – precisely the dirty, ragged, lousy Irish tramper, with that mixture of odd, wild, yet grave wit and credulous folly, which mark the character of the Hibernian* peasantry, – and his brogue was native and incessant.

This astonishing transformation of half an hour from the graceful and impassioned Essex,* summoned to the block, and bending with agonized tenderness over his swooning wife, displayed to us all the versatility of his powers.

Surely Wordsworth* must be mad as was ever the poet Lee.* Those volumes of his,* which you were so good to give me, have excited, by turns, my tenderness and warm admiration, my contemptuous astonishment and disgust. The two latter rose to their utmost height while I read about his dancing daffodils, ten thousand, as he says, in high dance in the breeze beside the river, whose waves dance with them, and the poet's heart, we are told, danced too. Then he proceeds to say, that in the hours of pensive or of pained contemplation, these same capering flowers flash on his memory, and his heart, losing its cares, dances with them again.

Surely if his worst foe had chosen to caricature this egotistic manufacturer of metaphysic importance upon trivial themes, he could not have done it more effectually! Whenever Mr Wordsworth writes naturally he charms me, as in the Kitten and the Falling Leaves; Verses to the Spade of a Friend; Written on Brother's Water Bridge; The Sailor's Mother; three or four of the sonnets, and above all the Leech-Gatherer, which is a perfectly original and striking poem. If he had written nothing else, that composition might stamp him a poet of no common powers. The sonnet written on Westminster Bridge, is beautiful, unaffected, and grandly picturesque.

The ode, second volume, p. 147, is a mixture of his successful and unsuccessful attempts at sublimity. I delight in the five first stanzas; – then it goes rumbling down the dark profound of mysticism, whither my comprehension strives to follow him in vain. The lovely stanzas are a manifest imitation of an ode of Coleridge's,* of very superior beauty, beginning, 'Well, if the bard was weather-wise,' etc.

An anonymous present of three volumes came to me lately: Letters from England, by Don Manuel Espriella, translated from the Spanish. On many subjects they form a deeply-learned, and on all on which they treat, a very amusing work, abounding in the oddest possible sectarian anecdotes, and heretic history and information. Of our customs and manners, national virtues, prejudices, absurdities, and faults, it is a faithful picture; so faithful and comprehensive, as to make me doubt its being a translation. I think no foreigner either would or could take the trouble of tracing, with observation at once so extended and minute, the subtle maze of national characteristics.

These books appear to me likely to attract the attention of the higher class of readers, whom they are competent at once to interest and inform. They contain the best account I have seen of the Cumberland lakes. The author, whether foreigner or native, has drawn and discriminated their different features in the most distinct and vivid tints. He enables us to perceive the peculiar features of each picturesque mirror, its incumbent mountains and marginal woods; and conveys to his reader certain singularities of appearance, which no other tourist has noticed; which the eye of genius perhaps could only have remarked.

Two letters from the poetically-great Southey* have delighted me much. My avowed sense of Madoc's poetic excellence having reached his ear, it procured me the honour of its author's correspondence. He excites my concern and indignation by saying, that the profits on a year's sale of that glorious poem, amounted to L.3:17:1; a deep disgrace to the national sensibility and judgment.

Critics, who are either incapable of feeling poetic beauty, and mistake sublimity for bombast, or fraudulently withhold the praise they know to be due, are alike the foes of individual genius, and of the national credit, when thus they labour to rob a first-rate poet of fortune and of early celebrity. What caterpillars in the bright roses of poetry, what wasps and hornets on the feet of Colossal literature, are such impotent, or such dishonest deciders!

If I live I shall hope to see you again my guest, and for a longer period than that of your first, and recent and dearly welcome visit, with all that kindness of heart and hilarity of spirit which are so much your own, and which act upon our feelings like a May-day sun. Adieu!

CATHERINE MACAULAY

CATHERINE MACAULAY née Sawbridge, afterwards Graham (1731–91), was a republican historian and polemicist who advocated the extension of the suffrage, but not to women. But in her *Letters on Education* (1790) – written later in her life – she makes detailed references to the relationship between gender and possibilities of education. This collection of essays in the form of 'letters' includes discussion of the nurture of children generally and not merely of their formal education. Her 'theories' about how to bring up children from birth draw on her knowledge of other cultures as well as on her reading of other educational theorists of the day, such as Jean-Jacques Rousseau and Mme de Genlis. Macaulay is at her best when she writes on formal education; for example, her radical idea that boys and girls should be educated together is still a moot point today, whereas her notion that aristocratic women should not feel it incumbent on themselves to breastfeed seems somewhat illogical in the light of our current knowledge. Macaulay married twice, but had no children. It is primarily as an historian that Macaulay is most esteemed, publishing *The History of England from the Accession of James I* (1763–83), as well as pamphlets such as *Treatise on the Immutability of Moral Truth* (1783). Her publications have been neglected until comparatively recently, perhaps because her marriage to a man at least twenty years younger than herself made her infamous. The text comes from *Letters on Education* (1790), pp. 79–93 and 127–31. Biographical information comes from Bridget Hill, *The Republican Virago: The Life and Times of Catherine Macaulay, Historian* (1992).

Letter 14

Literary Education of Young Persons

'The most critical interval of human life,' says Rousseau, 'is that between the hour of birth, and twelve years of age. This is the time wherein vice and error take root, without our being possessed of any instrument to destroy them; and when the implement is found, they are so deeply grounded, that they are no longer to be eradicated. If children took a leap from their mother's breast, and at once arrived at the age of reason, the methods of education now usually taken with them would be very proper; but according to the progress of Nature, they require those which are very different. We should not tamper with the mind till it has acquired all its faculties: for it is impossible it should perceive the light we hold out, while it is blind, or that it should pursue over an immense plain of ideas, that route which reason hath so slightly traced, as to be perceptible only to the sharpest sight.'

This, and a great deal more to the same purpose, does Rousseau urge, for reducing the first parts of education to a system merely negative. The arguments of the author are very ingenious, and I so far agree with him as to think, that till the mind has attained sufficient strength to co-operate with its instructor, in rejecting by the dictates of judgment, improper associations of ideas, and in selecting such as are to be desired, it were better to leave it entirely to the simple impressions which it receives from example, and the experience of consequences. For opinions taken up on mere authority, must ever prevent original thinking, must stop the progress of improvement, and instead of producing rational agents, can only make man the mere ape of man.

It has been shrewdly observed by some writers, that we could be brought by education to adopt the greatest absurdities, as easily as the most reasonable propositions; and when we consider the opposite manners which have prevailed in different societies, the equal warmth with which they have been defended, and the implicit obedience which have been paid to them, we shall not find much reason to depend on authority for the truth of our opinions, or to value ourselves on a faculty which has had little to do in forming our principles of conduct.

To read virtue right, we must divest ourselves of all partialities and prejudices; and to divest oneself of all partialities and prejudices, is a task which perhaps has never been thoroughly accomplished by any man. However, to preserve as much as possible the independence of the mind, let us be very sparing of our precept to the credulous ears of infancy; and let us devote the first ten or twelve years of life to the strengthening of the corporal faculties, to the giving useful habits, and to those attainments which can be acquired, without burdening the mind with ideas which it cannot well comprehend. The Latin grammar; geography taught in the easiest and pleasantest manner; such parts of physics that lie open to the attention of children; writing, arithmetic, and the French language, which may be made easy to learn by having French domestics, are fully sufficient to fill up the time of childhood; and to exercise its growing faculties without the use of books, which I would seldom introduce, but with the view of amusement. These I would also confine to a very small number chosen for the simplicity of the subject, and for the purpose of entertainment; with an exception however in favour of such easy Latin authors as are used in the first classes of the public schools, in order to exemplify, by actual reading, those rules of grammer which are every day committed to memory. If any one of my pupils should show any marks of a more than ordinary vigor of intellect, or any great impatience to enlarge his ideas, I would at the age of ten years enter him into a course of reading, which should commence with the most celebrated fables in the English, Latin, and French languages. At the age of twelve, and not before, his studies may be extended to a proper selection of Plutarch's Lives in the English translation,* Addison's Spectators, Guthrie's Geographical Grammar, and Mentelle's Géographic Comparée, in the original: selected parts of these last books may be committed to memory; and Addison's Spectators ought to be written as exercises, and some passages parsed accurately in the manner in which a Latin or Greek lesson is usually analyzed. During this period, the English grammar ought to make part of the pupil's study, beginning with Ash's introduction to Lowth, and then with Lowth's introduction.*

At the age of fourteen, themes written in Latin and English should be exacted, with a proper attention to Dr Samuel Johnson's* practical precepts, by obliging the pupil to compose with celerity. Correctness of thought and composition will be acquired by time and labour; but a slowness in the collecting and arranging ideas, will ever attend the generality of persons, who have not from the beginning been necessitated by the force of authority to use dispatch.

At this period of life, I would recommend the commencing a course of history, beginning with Rollin's Ancient History, in French; then one of the best of the English histories in this language, and Livy's history in the original.*

The reading of Greek history may be postponed till the language is acquired; but the thread of the Roman history should be leisurely pursued through Livy, Dion, Cassius, Sallust, Tacitus, in Latin, and Ferguson and Gibbon in English.* The History of Modern Europe should succeed the study of the Greek history; and at the age of fifteen, the rudiments of this language should be taught, and the study pursued till a competent knowledge of it is acquired. At the age of sixteen, and not before, the pupil may commence a course of moral lectures, beginning with Cicero's Offices, and pursuing the thread of this study through Cicero, Plutarch, Epictetus, and Seneca.* At this age, if he is a pupil of taste, he will take great delight in Fenelon's Telemachus.* Rollin's Belles Lettres,* and the poets may now be introduced as a relief from the drier study of morals and history; but the English poetry I should confine to some selected plays of Shakespeare, to Addison's Cato,* to Steele's Conscious Lovers,* to Milton* and to Pope.* The French poetry I would limit to Boileau;* and some plays selected out of Corneille, Racine, Molière, and Voltaire's works;* and the Latin lectures to selected plays of Terence,* some select epigrams from Martial,* and to Virgil's Eneid and Georgics.* It may be unnecessary to say, that there are many pieces even of the moral Pope, very improper for the perusal of youth. His Abelard and Eloise is only fit for the autumnal season of life; and though it is painful to suppress the productions of genius and of labour, it would have been better if his imitations of Chaucer had been committed to the flames. As the tutor should always accompany his pupil in his lectures in poetry, he may take an opportunity to make observations on the potent power of numbers, and these he may illustrate by turning into plain prose some of the most striking parts of Pope's Essay on Man. The following brilliant passage will be found to be quite nonsense when stripped of the pomp of verse.

> From Nature's chain, whatever link you strike,
> Tenth, or ten thousandth breaks the chain alike;
> And, if each system in gradation roll
> Alike essential to the amazing whole,
> The least confusion but in one, not all
> That system only, but the whole must fall.
> Let earth unbalanced from her orbit fly,
> Planets and suns run lawless through the sky;
> Let ruling angels from their spheres be hurled,
> Being on being wrecked, and world on world:
> Heaven's whole foundations to their center nod,
> And Nature tremble to the throne of God.

If a man in plain prose was to say, that were one of the minutest tribes of the minuter being to be put out of existence, it would cause such confusion as to hurl ruling angels from their spheres, and make Nature tremble to the throne of God, we should either think him a bigot to the doctrine of a plenum, or regard him as a madman or a blockhead. Yet such are the charms of poetry, that most readers of this famous essay think they have gained a great many solid ideas from the most exceptionable passages; and even the philosopher gives way to the pleasures of sense, and suffers himself to be captivated by the power of harmony. The pupil, with proper stringency on this and on other passages of Pope's works, will be taught to admire without intoxication; and at the same time that he sets a just value on an art which can give to reason and to truth an irresistible strength, he will be ever on his guard against the delusive power of sound.

Some of the most elegant, forcible, and brilliant passages of the poets may form part of the exercises of the pupil, who should be made to repeat them aloud. If there are more than one pupil, one day in the week may be allotted for this purpose; but I would entirely prohibit the acting of plays, for these reasons; it requires more confidence than a young person ought to have, to acquit himself with spirit in the character of an actor; and such exercises induce a swelling bombast style of speaking, with an unnatural gesture and action. The stage actors are of all persons the worst models for oratory; they would meet with no admiration did they not outstep the modesty of nature; and our tastes are so vitiated by these representations, that a pupil would lose the applause he deserved did he condescend to excellence. During this period of education, when the pupil has made considerable advances in grammar and classical learning, he may improve his knowledge of ancient geography by the study of Cellarius.* The use of the globes may be now introduced, Ferguson's astronomy* taught, lectures on experimental philosophy attended, and the knowledge of natural history acquired by the perusal of those celebrated naturalists Pliny* and Buffon.*

Letter 15

Literary Education continued: Novels

[. . .]

But I must tell you, Hortensia, lest you should mistake my plan, that though I have been obliged (in order to avoid confusion) to speak commonly in the masculine character, that the same rules of education in all respects are to be observed to the female as well as to the male children, only to conform as much as rationally can be done to the customs of Europe; for we must make some difference in the sports of our pupils, after they have passed the period of mere childhood. The male pupils may be exercised with cricket, and such like games, and may be taught to ride and to fence; but this last, as a mere healthy exercise only, and not on the romantic notion of playing the knight errant, and acting criminally on a principle of honour. Our young ladies must also have their exercises; but we must confine these to walking, riding, dancing, and battledore.

But I beseech you, Hortensia, to give me your attention a little longer, or I shall have the formidable body of novel writers up in arms. What, not one novel allowed to amuse the private hour of leisure, after the fatigue of study? No closet recreation, where the mind may be at once delighted, and taught the refinement of modern sentiment? Where boys may learn the pleasures of la belle passion, and girls the endearments which attend a virtuous affection for a worthy object?

That a novel writer should behold his productions in a favourable light, does not surprize me; for to do these authors justice, they are in general ranged on the side of virtue, but they are apt to deceive. To draw a great variety of characters according to life, it is requisite to have a comprehensive knowledge of the human mind, or a peculiar dexterity in piercing through the veil which custom, and a regard for character, puts on. And it is the difficulty of copying Nature with exactness, and the circle of moral consequences, as they really exist, which occasion novel writers to draw situations unnaturally, and to give forced and exaggerated sentiments to their characters, and particularly to their hero and heroine. But the principal objection which lies against these compositions is, that they are all the history of lovers; and love tales are always improper for the ears of youth, whose mind should be ever open to the soft feelings of benevolence, but be kept as long as possible in ignorance of the melting sensations of what is called in pre-eminence, "the tender passion." A young reader soon finds out by the tenor of novel history, that love is an unconquerable passion; that every fine mind is subject to its infection; and that individuals are paired by some power of sympathy, to which they are so absolutely subjected, that the soft obdurate heart must yield when the destined object comes in view.

Many trips to Scotland* are undoubtedly projected and executed, and many unfortunate connections formed, from the influence which novels gain over the mind; and though criminal amours are in general censured in these works, yet an imprudent conduct through life is often the consequence of an improper association of ideas formed in youth.

Cervantes, Le Sage, and Fielding,* are undoubtedly strict copiers of Nature and as such, will ever give delight to the judicious reader. Don Quixote may be read at every period of life, without leaving any mischievous impression on the mind; but Le Sage's capital work, Gil Blas, is one of the last books which I should put into the hands of youth.

It is indeed an admirable picture of the deceit, roguery, folly, and vice, which is to be found in every rank of society, and as such, is capable of affording very instructive lessons to those who, having finished their education, are launching into the wide ocean of life, but the art of the writer is exerted to please the fancy, rather than to mend the heart.

The hero of his tale, though void of every principle of disinterested virtue, and soiled with a variety of moral blemishes, is raised from a low rank in life to the station of a Spanish nobleman; and the lively parts he possesses, his qualities of good humour, and his excellent address, plead so much in his favour, that the reader is not at all inclined to be angry at his success.

Fielding's works are in general liable to the same exceptions which lie against Le Sage. But his Joseph Andrews is so admirably conducted, and the hero is a character of such true virtue and simplicity, that this work may be read with safety, and even with improvement by youth. Cyrus's Travels,* a novel of the grave kind, may be added to this small list; but to Richardson, who is regarded as the most moral novel writer of the whole class, I should not pay the same compliment. It is true, that he is sublimely pathetic; and though prolix to a blameable degree, he will be always read, for the first time, with great satisfaction; but his history of Pamela,* which exhibits a pattern of chastity in low life, is conducted in such a manner as to render it totally unfit for the perusal of youth. His Clarissa Harlow* is not entirely free from the same exception; and though this novel is replete with religious and moral sentiments, and the obvious intent of the author is to dress virtue in an attractive garb, and to guard the inexperienced mind against the subtle attacks of vicious interested characters, yet he is not sufficiently correct in his ideas to set forth in his heroine an exact pattern of moral loveliness, nor to draw such a character of his rake, as should render him disgustful to the giddy part of the female sex.

Clarissa Harlow, though represented as a paragon of piety and moral excellence, is positive and conceited; and all her distresses are brought upon her by the adhering to some very whimsical notions which she has entertained of duty and propriety of conduct. She will not carry her submission far enough to render her father happy by marrying the man he has chosen for her husband; nor will she defend herself from his unjust resentment, by asserting her rights to an independent fortune left to her by an indulgent grandfather. She suffers herself to be tricked into the power of a known rake, and incurs the utmost injury from her situation, by neither taking the opportunities which offered to get clear of him, nor by insisting on his acting the honourable part. According to the rules of tragedy, the history closes with the death of the heroine; but this catastrophe is not so much the consequence of an oppressed mind, as a rigid adherence to the discipline of fasting, whilst under the alarming symptoms of a deep decline.

In the history of Sir Charles Grandison,* there is not so much sublime pathos; but the hero is a more unexceptionable character than that of Clarissa Harlow. Indeed, virtue in him, and in the heroine of this piece, appears sometimes in attitudes ridiculously stiff, and in a garb too pompous for exact imitation: it is also united to a visible portion of conceit; and on these reasons, I would postpone the perusal of this, as well as the histories of Pamela, and Clarissa Harlow, to an age when the judgment is sufficiently ripe to separate the wheat from the chaff.

You will perhaps wonder that I have not placed the Cecilia of Miss Burney,* in my select list: it is not that I am less an admirer than others of this lady's performance; her characters are just to a degree that surprises, when it is considered that they are drawn by a very young person. The conduct of her story is well conceived, her situations are in general natural, and virtue is every where inculcated by pleasing representations of it. But the conduct of the heroine in giving up a large fortune for the sake of marrying the heir of a family, whose absurd pride induce them to regard her with contempt; and the incident of her subsequent madness, may fill a young person's mind with too vast an idea of the power of love. I do not mean these observations as censures on her work; I am persuaded, that young persons will peruse it with pleasure, and advantage, when their education is complete, and their judgment sufficiently ripe to taste their beauties. Nor am I an enemy to these compositions in general. There are several which are not devoid of the power of pleasing and improving, though written by persons several degrees inferior to the capital authors just mentioned; and were they perused at a proper age, as a relaxation to severer studies, they would throw variety into domestic life, and serve as a good succedaneum to the unmeaning system of dissipation which at present prevails. But to confine literary occupation entirely to novels, and the lighter parts of the belle lettre, is a perversion of reason and common sense, which distinguishes the present age from every other which has succeeded the revival of letters, and cannot fail of having a powerful influence over the manners of society.

Letter 22

No *characteristic Difference in Sex*

The great difference that is observable in the characters of the sexes, Hortensia, as they display themselves in the scenes of social life, has given rise to much false speculation on the natural qualities of the female mind. – For though the doctrine of innate ideas, and innate affections, are in a great measure exploded by the learned, yet few persons reason so closely and so accurately on abstract subjects as through a long chain of deductions, to bring forth a conclusion which in no respect militates with their premises.

It is a long time before the crowd give up opinions they have been taught to look upon with respect; and I know many persons who will follow you willingly through the course of your argument, till they perceive it tends to the overthrow of some fond prejudice; and then they will either sound a retreat, or begin a contest in which the contender for truth, though he cannot be overcome, is effectually silenced, from the mere weariness of answering positive assertions, reiterated without end. It is from such causes that the notion of a sexual difference in the human character has, with a very few exceptions, universally prevailed from the earliest times, and the pride of one sex, and the ignorance and vanity of the other, have helped to support an opinion which a close observation of Nature, and a more accurate way of reasoning, would disprove.

It must be confessed, that the virtues of the males among the human species, though mixed and blended with a variety of vices and errors, have displayed a bolder and a more consistent picture of excellence than female species has hitherto done. It is on these reasons that, when we compliment the appearance of a more than ordinary energy in the female mind, we call it masculine, and hence it is, that Pope has elegantly said *a perfect woman's but a softer man.* And if we take in the consideration, that there can be but one rule of moral excellence for beings made of the same materials, organized after the same manner, and subjected to similar laws of Nature, we must either agree with Mr Pope, or we must reverse the proposition, and say, that *a perfect man is a woman formed after a coarser mold.* The difference that actually does subsist between the sexes, is too flattering for men to be willingly imputed to accident; for what accident occasions, wisdom might correct; and it is better, says Pride, to give up the advantages we might derive from the perfection of our fellow associates, than to own that Nature has been just in the equal distribution of her favours. These are the sentiments of the men; but mark how readily they are yielded to by the women; not from humility I assure you, but merely to preserve with character those fond vanities on which they set their hearts. No; suffer them to idolize their persons, to throw away their life in the pursuit of trifles, and to indulge in the gratification of the meaner passions, and they will heartily join in the sentence of their degradation.

Among the most strenuous asserters of a sexual difference in character, Rousseau is the most conspicuous, both on account of that warmth of sentiment which distinguishes all his writings, and the eloquence of his compositions: but never did enthusiasm and the love of paradox, those enemies to philosophical disquis- ition, appear in more strong opposition to plain sense than in Rousseau's definition of this difference. He sets out with a supposition, that Nature intended the subjection of the one sex to the other: that consequently there must be an inferiority of intellect in the subjected party: but as man is a very imperfect being, and apt to play the capricious tyrant, Nature, to bring things nearer to an equality, bestowed on the woman such attractive graces, and such an insinuating address, as to turn the balance on the other scale. Thus Nature, in a giddy mood, recedes from her purposes, and subjects prerogative to an influence which must produce confusion and disorder in the system of human affairs. Rousseau saw this objection; and in order to obviate it, he has made up a moral person of the union of the two sexes, which, for contradiction and absurdity, outdoes every metaphysical riddle that was ever formed in the schools. In short, it is not reason, it is not wit; it is pride and sensuality that speak in Rousseau, and, in this instance, has lowered the man of genius to the licentious pedant.

But whatever might be the wise purpose intended by Provi- dence in such a disposition of things, certain it is, that some degree of inferiority, in point of corporal strength, seems always to have existed between the two sexes; and this advantage, in the barbarous ages of mankind, was abused to such a degree, as to destroy all the natural rights of the female species, and reduce them to a state of abject slavery. What accidents have contributed in Europe to better their condition, would not be to my purpose to relate; for I do not intend to give you a history of women; I mean only to trace the sources of their peculiar foibles and vices; and these I firmly believe to originate in situation and education only: for so little did a wise and just Providence intend to make the condition of slavery an unalterable law of female nature, that in the same proportion as the male sex have consulted the interest of their own happiness, they have relaxed in their tyranny over women; and such is their use in the system of mundane creation, and such their natural influence over the male mind, that were these advantages properly exerted, they might carry every point of any importance to their honour and happiness. However, till that period arrives in which women will act wisely, we will amuse ourselves in talking of their follies.

The situation and education of women, Hortensia, is precisely that which must necessarily tend to corrupt and debilitate both the powers of mind and body. From a false notion of beauty and delicacy, their system of nerves is depraved before they come out of their nursery; and this kind of depravity has more influence over the mind, and consequently over morals, than is commonly apprehended. But it would be well if such causes only acted towards the debasement of the sex; their moral education is, if possible, more absurd than their physical. The principles and nature of virtue, which is never properly explained to boys, is kept quite a mystery to girls. They are told indeed, that they must abstain from those vices which are contrary to their personal happiness, or they will be regarded as criminals, both by God and man; but all the higher parts of rectitude, every thing that ennobles our being, and that renders us both innoxious and useful, is either not taught, or is taught in such a manner as to leave no proper impression on the mind. This is so obvious a truth, that the defects of female education have ever been a fruitful topic of declamation for the moralist; but not one of this class of writers have laid down any judicious rules for amendment. Whilst we still retain the absurd notion of a sexual excellence, it will militate against the perfecting a plan of education for either sex. The judicious Addison* animadverts on the absurdity of bringing a young lady up with no higher idea of the end of education than to make her agreeable to a husband, and confining the necessary excellence for this happy acquisition to the mere graces of person.

Every parent and tutor may not express himself in the same manner as is marked out by Addison: yet certain it is, that the admiration of the other sex is held out to women as the highest honour they can attain; and whilst this is considered as their *summum bonum*, and the beauty of their persons the chief *desideratum* of men, Vanity, and its companion Envy, must taint, in their characters, every native and every acquired excellence. Nor can you, Hortensia, deny, that these qualities, when united to ignorance, are fully equal to the engendering and rivetting all those vices and foibles which are peculiar to the female sex; vices and foibles which have caused them to be considered, in ancient times, as beneath cultivation, and in modern days have subjected them to the censure and ridicule of writers of all descriptions, from the deep thinking philosopher to the man of ton and gallantry, who, by the bye, sometimes distinguishes himself by qualities which are not greatly superior to those he despises in women. Nor can I better illustrate the truth of this observation than by the following picture, to be found in the polite and gallant Chesterfield.* 'Women,' says his Lordship, 'are only children of a larger growth. They have an entertaining tattle, sometimes wit; but for solid reasoning, and good sense, I never in my life knew one that had it, or who acted or reasoned in consequence of it for four and twenty hours together. A man of sense only trifles with them, plays with them, humours and flatters them, as he does an engaging child; but he neither consults them, nor trusts them in serious matters.'

1790

HELEN MARIA WILLIAMS

HELEN MARIA WILLIAMS (?1762–1827) wrote novels, poetry, letters and travel journals. In England in the 1780s, she became popular with her public, who praised her expression of sympathy for the underdog in some of her poems, such as *Peru* (1784) and *A Poem on the Bill Lately Passed for Regulating the Slave Trade* (1788). In 1787, William Wordsworth, who had met Williams, published his celebratory sonnet, 'On Seeing Miss Helen Maria Williams Weep at a Tale of Distress'. Prior to travelling to France in 1790, Williams published in her novel, *Julia*, a poem, 'The Bastille: A Vision', which showed her sympathy with the 1789 Revolution. She subsequently emigrated to France, and, apart from visits during 1790–1 and 1792, she did not return to England. Williams's most memorable writings are a series of letters which gave her first-hand accounts of the violent aftermath of the 1789 French Revolution: *Letters Written from France in the Summer of 1790* (1790) was followed by *Letters from France, 1792–6*. Her later volumes of prose included *Letters Containing a Sketch of the Politics of France* (1794) and *Sketches of the State of Manners and Opinions in the French Republic towards the Close of the Eighteenth Century* (1801). Williams's sympathies with the Girondists, subsequent to the September massacres, attracted condemnation in England. As well as this, Williams feared that her anti-Jacobinism, after the Girondists were defeated by the Jacobins in 1793, would get her into trouble with the French authorities. She was arrested in 1793, but subsequently released. She fled to Switzerland and did not return to Paris until after the fall of Robespierre. Williams's friendship, whether erotic or platonic, with a divorced man, John Hurford Stone, resulted in vituperation from British critics such as Horace Walpole. The text of her letter is taken from *Letters from France*, 2nd edn, vol. 2 (1792), pp. 22–32. Biographical

information comes from Janet Todd's Introduction to the Fac-
simile edition of *Letters from France: 1792–6* (1975) and *A
Dictionary of British and American Women Writers
1660–1800*, ed. Janet Todd (1987).

Letter 4

Before I suffered my friends at Paris to conduct me through the usual routine of convents, churches, and palaces, I requested to visit the Bastille; feeling a much stronger desire to contemplate the ruins of that building than the most perfect edifices of Paris. When we got into the carriage, our French servant called to the coachman, with an air of triumph, 'A la Bastille – mais nous n'y resterons pas.'* We drove under the porch which so many wretches have entered never to repass, and, alighting from the carriage, descended with difficulty into the dungeons, which were too low to admit of our standing upright, and so dark that we were obliged at noon-day to visit them with the light of a candle. We saw the hooks of those chains by which the prisoners were fastened round the neck to the walls of their cells; many of which, being below the level of the water, are in a constant state of humidity; and a noxious vapour issued from them, which more than once extinguished the candle, and was so insufferable that it required a strong spirit of curiosity to tempt one to enter. Good God! – and to these regions of horror were human creatures dragged at the caprice of despotic power. What a melancholy consideration, that

> Man! proud man,
> Drest in a little brief authority,
> Plays such fantastic tricks before high heaven,
> As make the angels weep.*

There appears to be a greater number of these dungeons than one could have imagined the hard heart of tyranny itself would contrive; for, since the destruction of the building, many subterraneous cells have been discovered underneath a piece of ground which was enclosed within the walls of the Bastille, but which formed a bank of solid earth before the horrid secrets of this prison-house were disclosed. Some skeletons were found in these recesses, with irons still fastened on their decaying bones.

After having visited the Bastille, we may indeed be surprised, that a nation so enlightened as the French, submitted so long to the oppressions of their government; but we must cease to wonder that their indignant spirits at length shook off the galling yoke.

Those who have contemplated the dungeons of the Bastille, without rejoicing in the French Revolution, may, for aught I know, be very respectable persons, and very agreeable companions in the hours of prosperity; but, if my heart were sinking with anguish, I should not fly to those persons for consolation. Sterne says, that a man is incapable of loving one woman as he ought, who has not a sort of affection for the whole sex; and as little should I look for particular sympathy from those who have no feelings of general philanthropy. If the splendour of a despotic throne can only shine like the radiance of lightning, while all around is involved in gloom and horror, in the name of heaven let its baleful lustre be extinguished forever. May no such strong contrast of light and shade again exist in the political system of France! but may the beams of liberty, like the beams of day, shed their benign influence on the cottage of the peasant, as well as on the place of the monarch! My Liberty, which for so many ages past has taken pleasure in softening the evils of the bleak and rugged climates of the North, in fertilizing a barren soil, in clearing the swamp, in lifting mounds against the inundations of the tempest, diffuse her blessings also on the genial land of France, and bid the husbandman rejoice under the shade of the olive and the vine!

The Bastille, which Henry the Fourth and his veteran troops assailed in vain,* the citizens of Paris had the glory of taking in a few hours. The avarice of Monsieur de Launay* had tempted him to guard this fortress with only half the complement of men ordered by the Government; and a letter which he received the morning of the 14th of July, commanding him to sustain the siege till the evening, when succour would arrive, joined to his own treachery towards the assailants, cost him his life.

The courage of the besiegers was inflamed by the horrors of the famine, there being at this time only twenty-four hours provision of bread in Paris. For some days the people had assembled in crowds round the shops of the bakers, who were obliged to have a guard of soldiers to protect them from the famished multitude; while the women, rendered furious by want, cried, in the resolute tone of despair, 'Il nous faut du pain pour nos enfants.'* Such was the scarcity of bread, that a French gentleman told me, that, the day preceding the taking of the Bastille, he was invited to dine with a *Négociant*;* and, when he went, was informed that a servant had been out five hours in search of bread, and had at last been able to purchase only one loaf.

It was at this crisis, it was to save themselves the shocking spectacle of their wives and infants perishing before their eyes, that the citizens of Paris flew to arms; and, impelled by such causes, fought with the daring intrepidity of men who had all that renders life of any value at stake, and who determined to die or conquer. The women too, far from indulging the fears incident to our feeble sex, in defiance of the cannon of the Bastille, ventured to bring victuals to their sons and husbands; and, with a spirit worthy of Roman matrons, encouraged them to go on. Women mounted guard in the streets, and, when any person passed, called out boldly, 'Qui va là?'*

A gentleman, who had the command of fifty men in this enterprise, told me, that one of his soldiers being killed by a cannonball, the people, with great marks of indignation, removed the corpse, and then, snatching up the dead man's hat, begged money for his interment, in a manner characteristic enough of that gaiety which never forsakes the French, even on occasions as would make any other people on earth serious. 'Madame, pour ce pauvre diable qui s'est fait tuer pour la Nation! – Monsieur, pour ce pauvre chien qui s'est fait tuer pour la Nation!'* This mode of supplication, though not very pathetic, obtained the end desired; no person being sufficiently obdurate to resist the powerful plea, 'qu'il s'est fait tuer pour la Nation!'

When the Bastille was taken, and the old man, of whom you have no doubt heard, and who had been confined in a dungeon thirty-five years, was brought into daylight, which had not for so long a space of time visited his eyes, he staggered, shook his white beard, and cried faintly, 'Messieurs, vous m'avez rendu un grand service, rendez-m'en un autre; tuez-moi! Je ne sais pas où aller.' – 'Allons, allons,' the crowd answered with one voice, 'la Nation te nourrira.'*

As the heroes of the Bastille passed along the streets after its surrender, the citizens stood at the doors of their houses, loaded with wine, brandy, and other refreshments, which they offered to these deliverers of their country; but they unanimously refused to taste any strong liquors, considering the great work they had undertaken as not yet accomplished, and being determined to watch the whole night, in case of any surprise.

All those who had assisted in taking the Bastille, were presented, by the Municipality of Paris, with a ribbon of the national colours; on which is stamped, enclosed in a circle of brass, an impression of the Bastille, and which is worn as a military order.

The Municipality of Paris also proposed a solemn funeral procession in memory of those who lost their lives in this enterprise; but, on making application to the National Assembly for a deputation of its members to assist at this solemnity, the Assembly were of opinion that these funeral honours should be postponed till a more favourable moment, as they might at present have a tendency to inflame the minds of the people.

I have heard several persons mention a young man, of a little insignificant figure, who, the day before the Bastille was taken, got up on a chair in the Palais Royal, and harangued the multitude, conjuring them to make a struggle for their liberty, and asserting, that now the moment was arrived. They listened to his eloquence with the most eager attention; and, when he had instructed as many as could hear him at one time, he requested them to depart, and repeated his harangue to a new set of auditors.

Among the dungeons of the Bastille are placed, upon a heap of stones, the figures of two men who contrived the plan of this fortress, where they were afterwards confined for life. These men are represented chained to the wall, and are beheld without any emotion of sympathy.

The person employed to remove the ruins of the Bastille, has framed of the stones eighty-three complete models of this building, which, with a true patriotic spirit, he has presented to the eighty-three departments of the kingdom, by way of hint to his countrymen to take care of their liberties in future.

1790

MARY HAYS

MARY HAYS (1760–1843) as a writer seemed to depend on the stimulus of other authors for her material, because often her works are responses to the works of others. She moved in dissenting circles and her first polemical pamphlet, *Cursory Remarks on an Enquiry into the Expediency and Propriety of Public or Social Worship* (1782), was in reaction to Gilbert Wakefield's attack on Dissenters who worshipped in public. Mary Wollstonecraft's *A Vindication of the Rights of Woman* (1792) made an impression on her, and her own *Letters and Essays, Moral and Miscellaneous* (1793) are partly in response to Wollstonecraft's themes. This is not surprising, given that she sought Wollstonecraft's advice before *Letters and Essays* was published. Her novels, *Memoirs of Emma Courtney* (1796) and *The Victim of Prejudice* (1799), drew partly on her own life for their material, just as Mary Wollstonecraft's *Mary: A Fiction* (1787) and *The Wrongs of Woman* (1798) drew on her life experiences. Hays's comprehensive *Female Biography: or Memoirs of Illustrious and Celebrated Women of All Ages and Countries* (1802) is an idiosyncratic history of women's achievements. After Hays met Hannah More and Maria Edgeworth, she wrote moralistic stories along the lines of More's didactic works for the poor. The text of Essay No. 3 is from *Letters and Essays, Moral and Miscellaneous*, pp. 19–30 (1793); and the essay, 'Improvements Suggested in Female Education', is from the *Monthly Magazine* (March 1797, pp. 193–5). Biographical information comes from *A Dictionary of British and American Women Writers 1660–1800* (1985), ed. Janet Todd, and from *The Love-Letters of Mary Hays (1779–1780)* (1925), ed. A. F. Wedd.

No. 3

Of all bondage, mental bondage is surely the most fatal; the absurd despotism which has hitherto, with more than gothic barbarity, enslaved the female mind, the enervating and degrading system of manners by which the understandings of women have been chained down to frivolity and trifles, have increased the general tide of effeminacy and corruption. To conform to the perpetual fluctuation of fashion (and few have the courage to dare the 'slow and moving finger of scorn', which is pointed at every external singularity) requires almost their whole time and attention, and leaves little leisure for intellectual improvement.

> Say dreamers of gay dreams!
> How will you weather an eternal night,
> Where such expedients fail!*

It has been alleged, that this constant variation of mode is serviceable to commerce, and promotes a brisk circulation of money; or with more propriety it might be said a quick succession of bankruptcies: but however this may be, it is I conceive making too expensive an offering at the golden shrine of Plutus* to sacrifice all the dignified and rational pursuits of life. A few distinguished individuals, feeling the powers of their own minds (for what can curb the celestial energy of genius?) are endeavouring to dispel the magical illusions of custom, and restore degraded woman to the glory of rationality, and to a fitness for immortality. The rights of woman, and the name of Wollstonecraft, will go down to posterity with reverence, when the pointless sarcasms of witlings are forgotten. I am aware that some men of real good sense and candour, have supposed that the idea of there being no sexual character, is carried in this most admirable work a little too far. Let them reflect for a moment on the extremes which the opposite opinion has produced; and say from whence arises the most formidable danger? Is there any cause to apprehend that we may subject our feelings too much to the guidance of reason? Or that we shall conduct

the business of our families with too much order and equity: to
the wise and good only, I now appeal! Would you not dare to
give up any of the allurements of the mistress (if indeed any
need be given up worth the preserving) to the refined pleasure
of living with a rational and equal companion? In such an
intercourse, when enlivened by love, if happiness resides on
earth, surely it is to be found! where the advantages are
reciprocal, for each reflects back with interest, the light they
receive. Similarity of mind and principle is the only true basis of
harmony. Great superiority of either side causes a narrow
jealousy, or a painful constraint; there is nothing so irksome as
to converse with people who cannot understand you.

Others (I mean the vulgar of every rank) terrified at the very
idea of our feeling and asserting our rights to rationality, raise
innumerable cavils and objections, all originating from the same
source, a pertinacious and jealous adherence to a narrow and
mistaken self-interest, and the petty word AUTHORITY. It is this
which makes the priest on certain occasions raise an alarm
about the safety of the church, the sovereign with paternal
solicitude endeavour to guard his people from light and knowl-
edge, by royal proclamations and prohibitions, and the Ephe-
sians* to exclaim that their 'craft is in danger'. Must I inform
these profound politicians, that every infringement of right
weakens duty, every stretch of prerogative gives a mortal wound
to monarchy, and every weak fence of proscription prepares the
way for their utter demolition, and for laying Hierarchy waste?
The love of arbitrary power, with morbid influence, corrupts
the human mind; and after the factitious strength of the delir-
ium, exhausted by the unnatural exertion, sinks into helpless
effeminacy and cowardly despondence, the usurper must sooner
or later be the victim of his usurpation.

Let those who love influence seek it by surer methods; bolts
and bars may confine for a time the feeble body, but can never
enchain the noble, the free-born mind; the only true grounds of
power are reason and affection, vows of obedience are lighter
than vanity, but the sensible heart rejoices to anticipate the
wishes of the object of its tenderness. Ye simple men! so tena-
cious of your prerogative, insinuate yourselves gently into our
affections and understandings, respect in us the majesty of
rationality, upon which ye so justly value yourselves, and ye will
have no cause to complain that like wayward children, spoilt by

equally misjudged caresses and correction, we in fact tyrannise over you by our caprices, while you are deluded with mock ensigns of power. And even where this is not the case, and the brute prevails over the weak infant, or the heart-broken slave, say! what are the mighty advantages ye reap from your dear-bought victory? Sullen acquiescence, gloomy resignation, fretful impatience, or degrading servility; all the virtues of the woman (for virtue is not the child of constraint) sunk in the poor spiritless contemptible slave; and when totally degraded by abject compliances to a tyrannical despot, every act of tame subjection to unreasonable requisitions, by weakening affection, clouding reason, and exciting disgust (for even the worm at times will turn upon the trampler) prepares the way for defection by undermining principle; and it is 'by good luck' only, if the effects are not such as a penetrating eye, going back to first causes, might without a prophetic spirit easily foresee, or if actuated by criminal and selfish motives as easily perhaps bring to pass.

> Let him ungenerous, who alone intent
> To bless himself – in eternal cares
> Well merited, consume his nights and days!
> Let barbarous nations whose inhuman love
> Is wild desire! let eastern tyrants
> From the light of heaven seclude their bosom
> Slaves! meanly possest of a mere lifeless
> Violated form!
> While those whom love cements in holy faith
> And equal transports, free as nature live,
> Disdaining fear.*

'Alas! (says the sensible writer of the Persian Letters)* I may find in Persia a seraglio composed of beautiful slaves, the mercenary or reluctant victims to gross and tyrannical desire. But what rational converse can I hope from these? What true affection? What solid peace? What heartfelt delight? But was Zelis my wife, in such a wife I should find the most endeared, most pleasing, most faithful friend! All the precautions of eastern jealousy would then be unnecessary; those wretched precautions! which if they bar the door against dishonour, shut out esteem, the life of friendship, and confidence, the soul of love.' Religion, reason, and affection, are stricter surer guards, than walls of adamant.

Lovers of truth! be not partial in your researches. Men of sense and science! remember, by degrading our understandings, you incapacitate us for knowing your value, and make cox-combs take place of you in our esteem. The ignorant and the vulgar prove their cunning by levelling principles; but you! how impolitic to throw a veil over our eyes, that we may not distinguish the radiance that surrounds you!

Objections are also made against the vindication of our rights, under the pretence, that by enlarging and ennobling our minds, we shall be undomesticated, and unfitted (I suppose is meant) for mere household drudges. With the excellent Dr Priestley,* I repeat 'this is a sordid and debasing prejudice,' of the fallacy of which I have been convinced both from experience and obser-vation. Numberless women have I known, whose studies (incapable of the 'epicurism of reason and religion') have been confined to Mrs Glasse's Art of Cookery,* and whose whole time has been spent in the kitchen, altercating with and changing of servants, provoking them to dishonesty by mean cautions, and narrow distrust; and immersed in unnecessary and dirty drudgery, have ruined their health, spoilt their tempers, neglected their persons, laid waste their minds, and sacrificed their friends, and after all these expensive forfeitures, have never attained the end; but have (to use a feminine phrase) muddled away their time and money in the disorderly management of hands without a head; been cheated by their dependents, because neither feeling respect nor attachment they have gloried in outwitting them; and their acquaintance, turning with disgust from their expensive and laboured treats, have sighed for the plain dish, the cordial and hospitable manners, 'the feast of reason and the flow of souls.' Contrast with this the following picture from Fitzosborne's charming Letters,* 'Her refined sense, and extensive knowledge have not raised her above the necessary acquisitions of female science; they have only taught her to fill that part of her character with higher grace and dignity. She enters into all the domestic duties of her station with the most consummate skill and prudence; her economical deportment is calm and steady; and she presides over her family like the intelligence of some planetary orb, conducting it in all its proper directions without violence, or disturbed effort.'

But the vindicator of female rights is thought by some sagacious married men to be incompetent to form any just opinion of the cares and duties of a conjugal state, from never having entered the matrimonial lists, because perhaps she has not met with the man who knows how properly to value her, or having met, may, alas! have lost. Wonderful free-masonry this! and ridiculous as wonderful. To be sure those who are eagerly engaged in play, with all their self-interest up in arms, are much better judges of the game than the cool impartial looker on; and a West-India Planter must understand the justice of the Slave-Trade far better than an English House of Commons, to say nothing of the very superior and extraordinary political wisdom necessarily belonging to the office of Prime Minister, of which the profane vulgar can form no idea! What nonsense this! Does it need a serious refutation? From such notions (most devoutly I repeat a part of the liturgy) good Lord deliver us.

'Every science (said the late Mr Robinson* in his political Catechism) beheld in the gross, resembles a loaded fruit tree in autumn; but as all the fruits and foliage and ramifications of the one, so all the departments of the other, may be reduced to a few first principles, and these comprehended, the whole is understood. Mystery,' he adds, 'is a fine material for manufacture.'

For once Rousseau does us justice, and writes, 'Notwithstanding the corrupt manners of the age, women are no more strangers than men to that rapturous enthusiasm with which the ideas of wisdom and virtue fire the soul.' Domestic concord is the lovely fruit of sympathy, congeniality, and kindred, sense and goodness. With equal sweetness and truth, sung the Poet in his admirable Indian Philosopher.

> Happy the youth that finds the bride,
> Whose birth is to his own allied,
>   The sweetest joy of life:
> But oh! the crowds of wretched souls,
> Fetter'd to minds of different moulds,
>   And chain'd to eternal strife.
>
> Some courteous angel tell me where,
> What distant lands this unknown fair,
>   Or distant seas detain?
> Swift as the wheel of nature rolls,
> I'd fly to meet and mingle souls,
>   And wear the joyful chain.*

1793

FROM THE *MONTHLY MAGAZINE*

Improvements Suggested in Female Education

To the Editor of the *Monthly Magazine*

Sir,

I am encouraged by your insertion of my defence of the talents of women, in reply to the strictures of A, B, and C,* to address you upon a subject, which, if not entirely depending upon the principle in question, is yet intimately connected with it. An eloquent advocate for the rights of her sex, and of humanity, waiving the controverted, though not unimportant, question, respecting sexual equality, contends, that our virtues and acquirements should be the same in nature, if differing in degree. In establishing this important truth, the deplorable consequences resulting from the distinctions hitherto adhered to in the education of the sexes, are painted with glowing colouring, and insisted upon in energetic language.

Female education, as at present conducted, is a complete system of artifice and despotism; all the little luxuriances and exuberances of character, which individualise the being, which give promise of, and lay the foundation for, future powers, are carefully lopped and pruned away; sincerity and candour are repressed with solicitude; the terrors of *opinion* are set in array, and suspended over the victim, till the enfeebled and broken spirit submits to the trammels, and, passive, tame, and docile, is stretched or shortened (as on the frame of the tyrant Procrustes)* to the *universal standard*. From woman, thus rendered systematically weak and powerless, to whom truth and morals have been confounded, inconsistent and contrary qualities are absurdly expected: for *principle*, it is attempted to substitute *rule* and dogma, while prejudice is combatted only by other prejudices, equally, if not still more pernicious. The majority of human beings have yet to learn, notwithstanding a daily and melancholy experience, the dangerous tendency of every species of imposition and falsehood: one erroneous idea, entangling itself with others, from the nature of association and mind, is sufficient to destroy the whole character, nay more, to poison a community. Not an action nor a thought can be entirely unconsequential; nothing is stationary; truth or error rapidly and incessantly propagates itself.

Sexual distinctions respecting chastity, an important branch
of temperance, have served but to increase the tide of profligacy,
and have been the fruitful source of the greater part of the
infelicity and corruption of society. 'Destroy love and friend-
ship,' says Hume,* 'what remains in the world worth accepting?'
To insist upon the tendency which libertinism and gross sensual-
ity must have to blunt the finer sensibilities, and vitiate the
delicacy of taste, which is favourable to the production of these
affections, would be unnecessary. One of the principal causes
which seems to have given rise to the present dissolute and venal
motives by which the intercourse of the sexes is influenced, is
perhaps the *dependence* for which women are uniformly edu-
cated. Upon the general enfeebling effects of this system I shall
not insist; its obvious consequences are sufficient for my present
purpose. The greater proportion of young women are trained
up by thoughtless parents, in ease and luxury, with no other
dependence for their future support than the precarious chance
of establishing themselves by marriage: for this purpose (the
men best know why) elaborate attention is paid to external
attractions and accomplishments, to the neglect of more useful
and solid acquirements. 'A young girl,' says Rousseau,* 'must
be trained up for a husband, like an Eastern beauty for a harem:'
and he was right; while they have but *one means* (every rule
admits of individual exceptions) not merely of gratifying the
heart (sensibility and nature will here always exert their honest
arts) but of satisfying their pride, their ambition, the laudable
desire of distinction, even of procuring a subsistence, or barely
the means of existing. If, thus situated, women marry from
mercenary and venal motives (the worst kind of prostitution)
with little delicacy or selection, is it reasonable to condemn
them? If misery, disgust, or infidelity result from such connec-
tions, ought it to be matter of surprise? Supposing they fail in
this *sole* method of procuring for themselves an establishment,
and such failures are frequent in this expensive and profligate
age, what is the consequence? Must we rigidly pursue and
censure these innocent and helpless victims to barbarous preju-
dice, should they prefer the flowery paths of pleasure, for which
their education has been in a great measure preparatory, to the
almost equally degrading alternative of servile occupation, or
the more specious, but not less galling situation of companion,
or humble martyr to the caprice of a fellow-being, not unfre-

quently rendered callous and despotic by prosperity and indulgence? One of the world's maxims, with a view to counteract other notions, equally false and pernicious, is that a woman having once deviated from chastity is to be considered as irreclaimable.

To demonstrate the truth of this philosophic and merciful adage, great care is taken to bar up every avenue against the return of this frail, unfortunate being, who, driven from the society and countenance of the virtuous and respectable, is reduced to associate with those whose habitual vices render them little calculated to assist her in regaining the path from which she has wandered. By these wise and humane methods, the tender, affectionate heart, betrayed, perhaps, by its own amiable susceptibility, and artless credulity, is precipitated by despair into real depravity. The numbers of women who are thus thrown into a state of abandoned profligacy are almost incalculable and incredible; while the universal contagion spreads through every rank, strikes at the root not only of the sweetest and most affecting felicities of life, but of the order and well-being of society. Men, satiated with beauty, marry merely for wealthy and convenience; while domestic happiness, and the tender confidence, and affecting endearments, of virtuous love, are almost as obsolete as the maxims of chivalry. In their stead, a heartless, mindless intercourse is substituted, the insidity of which is its least evil.

I am aware, that the absurd distinction alluded to, is deeply entangled with the system of property, and is one of those evils flowing from feudal institutions, the baneful effects of which can only cease with the renovation of civil society. Yet, in the meantime, its deplorable consequences might be ameliorated, by an alteration in the system of female education. Might not a part of the time wasted in the acquisition of useless and frivolous accomplishments, be devoted to the attainment of some ingenious art or useful trade, by which a young woman might hope to gain an honest and honourable independence, and be freed from the disgraceful necessity of bartering her person to procure a maintenance? Every parent having a family of daughters, for whom it is not in his power to make a suitable provision, is guilty of cruelty and vice, when he hazards their being exposed, helpless and unprotected, to the world. There are a variety of trades and professions, by their nature peculiarly appropriate to women, exercised, with very few exceptions, at present, entirely by men: to these many of the liberal arts might be added, also the knowledge and practice of arithmetic and book-keeping. A woman enabled to support herself, and to acquire property by her industry, would gain by regular occupation, and the health-ful exertion of her faculties, more firmness of mind and greater vigour of body. Marriages would be contracted from motives of affection, rather than of interest; and entered into with less apprehensions, when the whole burthen of providing for a family rested not upon the efforts of the man, but was cheerfully shared between the parties. It may be objected, that the weak-ness and cares of a mother, in bearing and nursing her offspring, must incapacitate her for farther exertion. This objection, with but few exceptions, might be proved futile, by the example of whole towns and communities; not to insist on the number of poor hard-labouring women, with large families (the support of which is thrown by a profligate husband wholly upon them) in this and in almost every other country. The constitution, strengthened by labour or wholesome exercise, would likewise acquire greater vigour, and many of those physical evils which afflict the female frame, in an enervated and artificial state of society, would be greatly alleviated, if not wholly removed. Those women whom disappointed affection, or personal disad-vantages, consigned to celebacy, in the exercise of body and mind, in occupations that promised competence or distinction, would be preserved from the numerous evils and follies, I might add, cruel insults, to which they are at present exposed.

The only happy life, it is justly observed, by Mr Hume, is that which is equally divided between action and rest (or relaxation). Duties will never be properly performed unless softened by pleasures: nor can pleasures deserve the title unless earned by business.

Inequality, in the present state of things, is not confined to property; while one part of the community, worn down by toil, sacrifice the *end* to the *means*, the remainder are sunk in a still more destructive incapacity or intolerable lassitude, from which there is no escape but by mischievous and dangerous exper-iments and exertions.

The prosperous or declining state of a nation might, perhaps, be more accurately deduced from the possession or want of private virtue and happiness, than from the condition of its revenue or its foreign connections. Government is valuable only as a *mean* of which individual *happiness* is the end: should this not be produced, the institution becomes vain or pernicious. Till one moral and mental standard is established for every rational agent, every member of a community, and a free scope afforded for the exertion of their faculties and talents, without distinction of rank or sex, *virtue* will be an empty name, and *happiness* elude our most anxious research.

1797

ANNA BARBAULD

ANNA LETITIA BARBAULD née Aikin (1743–1825) was a prolific writer of verse and essays. She had been educated at her father's school with her brother, John. With his assistance, she published her first volume, *Poems*, in 1773. In 1774, she married a dissenting clergyman, Rochemont Barbauld, and later set up a school for boys with him at Palgrave, Sussex, in order to make money. Anna Barbauld drew on her teaching at this school for her writing of *Devotional Pieces* (1775), *Lessons for Children* (1778), and *Hymns in Prose for Children* (1781). They closed this school in 1785 when Rochemont could no longer stand the strain of helping to run it, and, after travelling abroad, in 1787 Rochemont took charge of a dissenting chapel in the village of Hampstead, which, incidentally, Joanna Baillie attended. Anna Barbauld wrote political pamphlets at this period, including *An Address to the Opposers of the Repeal of the Corporation and Test Acts* (1791), *Civic Sermons to the People* (1792), and *Sins of the Government, Sins of the Nation* (1793). In 1802, Rochemont became minister at a chapel at Newington Green at Stoke Newington. When Rochemont's mental condition deteriorated, he had to be placed in a mental asylum. They had no children, but they adopted one of her brother's children, Charles Rochemont Aikin. After her husband's death in 1808, Anna Barbauld devoted her time to reviewing fiction for the *Monthly Magazine*, editing prose and poetry, and writing poetry. In 1820, she edited and introduced a reprinting of selected eighteenth-century novels, which included Samuel Richardson's *Clarissa Harlowe* (1747–8). Some of her letters to various friends and to her brother, John, have been published in *The Works of Anna Letitia Barbauld* (1825). She had earlier collaborated with her brother in the composition of moralistic essays (*Miscellaneous Pieces in Prose*, 1773). Although she was not a campaigner for women's rights, she supported the abolition of the slave trade, publishing her *Epistle to William Wilberforce* in 1791. Biog-

raphy comes from Lucy Aikin's Memoir in *The Works of Anna
Letitia Barbauld* (1825) and from Betsy Rodgers, *Georgian
Chronicle: Mrs Barbauld and Her Family* (1958). The text of
the letter comes from *The Works of Anna Letitia Barbauld*, vol.
2 (1825), pp. 116–18, and the extract from 'On the Origin and
Progress of Novel-Writing' from *The British Novelists* (1820),
pp. 44–56.

LETTER TO MRS CARR

We flattered ourselves with seeing some of the beauties of South Wales in coming hither, but we were completely disappointed by the state of the weather. This country is bleak and bare, with fine views of the sea, and a bold rocky coast, with a beach of fine hard sand. We have been much pleased with watching the coming in of the tide among the rocks, against which it dashes, forming columns of spray twenty and thirty foot high, accompanied with rainbows, and with a roar like distant cannon. There are fine caverns and recesses among the rocks; one particularly, which we took the opportunity of visiting yesterday, as it can only be entered at the ebb of the spring-tides. It is very spacious, beautifully arched, and composed of granite rocks finely veined with alabaster, which the imagination may easily form into a resemblance of a female figure, and is of course the Nereid of the grotto. We wished to have stayed longer; but our friend hurried us away, lest the tide should rush in, which it is supposed to do from subterraneous caverns, as it fills before the tide covers the sand of the adjacent beach. I was particularly affected with the fate of two lovers, (a young gentleman and lady from Clifton), whose friends were here for the sake of sea-bathing. They stole out early one morning by themselves, and strolled along the beach till they came to this grotto, which, being then empty, they entered. They admired the strata of rock leaning in different directions: they admired the incrustation which covers part of the side, exactly resembling honeycomb; various shells embedded in the rock; the sea-anemone spreading its purple fringe, – an animal flower clinging to the rocks. They admired the first efforts of vegetation in the purple and green tints occasioned by the lichens and other mosses creeping over the bare stone. They admired these together; they loved each other the more for having the same tastes; and they taught the echoes of the cavern to repeat the vows which they made of eternal constancy. In the mean time the tide was coming in: of this they were aware, as they now and then glanced their eye on the waves, which they saw advancing at a distance; but not knowing the peculiar nature of the cavern, they thought them-

selves safe; when on a sudden, as they were in the furthest part
of it, the waters rushed in from fissures in the rock with terrible
roaring. They climbed from ledge to ledge of the rocks, – but in
vain; the water rose impetuously, and at length filled the whole
grotto. Their bodies were found the next day, when the tide was
out, reclining on a shelf of rock; he in the tender attitude of
supporting her, in the very highest accessible part, and leaning
his own head in her lap, – so that he must have died first. Poor
lovers! If, however, you should be too much grieved for them,
you may impute the whole, if you please, to a waking *dream*
which I had in the grotto.

FROM 'ON THE ORIGIN AND PROGRESS OF NOVEL-WRITING'

For my own part, I scruple not to confess that, when I take up a
novel, my end and object is entertainment; and as I suspect that
to be the case with most readers, I hesitate not to say that
entertainment is their legitimate end and object. To read the
productions of wit and genius is a very high pleasure to all
persons of taste, and the avidity with which they are read by all
such shows sufficiently that they are calculated to answer this
end. Reading is the cheapest of pleasures: it is a domestic
pleasure. Dramatic exhibitions give a more poignant delight, but
they are seldom enjoyed in perfection, and never without
expense and trouble. Poetry requires in the reader a certain
elevation of mind and a practised ear. It is seldom relished unless
a taste be formed for it pretty early. But the humble novel is
always ready to enliven the gloom of solitude, to soothe the
languor of debility and disease, to win the attention from pain
or vexatious occurrences, to take man from himself, (at many
seasons the worst company he can be in,) and, while the moving
picture of life passes before him, to make him forget the subject
of his own complaints. It is pleasant to the mind to sport in the
boundless regions of possibility; to find relief from the sameness
of every-day occurrences by expatiating amidst brighter skies
and fairer fields; to exhibit love that is always happy, valour
that is always successful; to feed the appetite for wonder by a
quick succession of marvellous events; and to distribute, like a

ruling providence, rewards and punishments which fall just where they ought to fall.

It is sufficient therefore, as an end, that these writings add to the innocent pleasures of life; and if they do no harm, the entertainment they give is a sufficient good. We cut down the tree that bears no fruit, but we ask nothing of a flower beyond its scent and its colour. The unpardonable sin in a novel is dullness: however grave or wise it may be, if its author possesses no powers of amusing, he has no business to write novels; he should employ his pen in some more serious part of literature.

But it is not necessary to rest the credit of these works on amusement alone, since it is certain they have had a very strong effect in infusing principles and moral feelings. It is impossible to deny that the most glowing and impressive sentiments of virtue are to be found in many of these compositions, and have been deeply imbibed by their youthful readers. They awaken a sense of finer feelings than the commerce of ordinary life inspires. Many a young woman has caught from such works as *Clarissa** or *Cecilia*,* ideas of delicacy and refinement which were not, perhaps, to be gained in any society she could have access to. Many a maxim of prudence is laid up in the memory from these stores, ready to operate when occasion offers.

The passion of love, the most seductive of all the passions, they certainly paint too high, and represent its influence beyond what it will be found to be in real life; but if they soften the heart they also refine it. They mix with the common passions of our nature all that is tender in virtuous affection; all that is estimable in high principle and unshaken constancy; all that grace, delicacy, and sentiment can bestow of touching and attractive. Benevolence and sensibility to distress are almost always insisted on in modern works of this kind; and perhaps it is not exaggeration to say, that much of the softness of our present manners, much of that tincture of humanity so conspicuous amidst all our vices, is owing to the bias given by our dramatic writings and fictitious stories. A high regard to female honour, generosity, and a spirit of self-sacrifice, are strongly inculcated. It costs nothing, it is true, to an author to make his hero generous, and very often he is extravagantly so; still, sentiments of this kind serve in some measure to counteract the spirit of the world, where selfish considerations have always more than their due weight. In what discourse from the pulpit are religious feelings more strongly raised than in the prison sermon of *The Vicar of Wakefield*,* or some parts of *The Fool of Quality*?*

But not only those splendid sentiments with which, when properly presented, our feelings readily take part, and kindle as we read; the more severe and homely virtues of prudence and economy have been enforced in the writings of a Burney* and an Edgeworth.* Writers of their good sense have observed, that while these compositions cherished even a romantic degree of sensibility, the duties that have less brilliancy to recommend them were neglected. Where can be found a more striking lesson against unfeeling dissipation than the story of the *Harrels*?* Where have order, neatness, industry, sobriety, been recommended with more strength than in the agreeable tales of Miss Edgeworth? If a parent wishes his child to avoid caprice, irregularities of temper, procrastination, coquetry, affectation, – all those faults and blemishes which undermine family happiness, and destroy the every-day comforts of common life, – whence can he derive more impressive morality than from the same source? When works of fancy are thus made subservient to the improvement of the rising generation, they certainly stand on a higher ground than mere entertainment, and we revere while we admire.

Some knowledge of the world is also gained by these writings, imperfect indeed, but attained with more ease, and attended with less danger, than by mixing in real life. If the stage is a mirror of life, so is the novel, and perhaps a more accurate one, as less is sacrificed to effect and representation. There are many descriptions of characters in the busy world, which a young woman in the retired scenes of life hardly meets with at all, and many whom it is safer to read of than to meet; and to either sex it must be desirable that the first impressions of fraud, selfishness, profligacy and perfidy should be connected, as in good novels they always will be, with infamy and ruin. At any rate, it is safer to meet with a bad character in the pages of a fictitious story, than in the polluted walks of life; but an author solicitous for the morals of his readers will be sparing in the introduction of such characters. – It is an aphorism of Pope,

> Vice is a monster of such frightful mien
> As to be hated, needs but to be seen.

But he adds,

> But seen too oft, familiar with her face,
> We first endure, then pity, then embrace.*

Indeed the former assertion is not true without considerable modifications. If presented in its naked deformity, vice will indeed give disgust; but it may be so surrounded with splendid and engaging qualities, that the disgust is lost in admiration. Besides, though the selfish and mean propensities are radically unlovely, it is not the same with those passions which all have felt, and few are even desirous to resist. To present these to the young mind in the glowing colours of a Rousseau* or a Madame de Staël* is to awaken and increase sensibilities, which it is the office of wise restraint to calm and to moderate. Humour covers the disgust which the grosser vices would occasion; passion veils the danger of the more seducing ones.

After all, the effect of novel-reading must depend, as in every other kind of reading, on the choice which is made. If the looser compositions of this sort are excluded, and the senti-mental ones chiefly perused, perhaps the danger lies more in fixing the standard of virtue and delicacy too high for real use, than in debasing it. Generosity is carried to such excess as would soon dissipate even a princely fortune; a weak compas-sion often allows vice to escape with impunity; an overstrained delicacy, or regard to a rash vow, is allowed to mar all the prospects of a long life: dangers are despised, and self is annihilated, to a degree that prudence does not warrant, and virtue is far from requiring. The most generous man living, the most affectionate friend, the most dutiful child, would find his character fall far short of the perfections exhibited in a highly-wrought novel.

Love is a passion particularly exaggerated in novels. It forms the chief interest of, by far, the greater part of them. In order to increase this interest, a false idea is given of the importance of the passion. It occupies the serious hours of life; events all hinge upon it; every thing gives way to its influence, and no length of time wears it out. When a young lady, having imbibed these notions, comes into the world, she finds that this formidable passion acts a very subordinate part on the great theatre of the world; that its vivid sensations are mostly limited to a very early period; and that it is by no means, as the poet sings,

All the colour of remaining life.*

She will find but few minds susceptible of its more delicate
influences. Where it is really felt, she will see it continually
overcome by duty, by prudence, or merely by a regard for the
show and splendour of life; and that in fact it has a very small
share in the transactions of the busy world, and is often little
consulted even in choosing a partner for life. In civilized life
both men and women acquire so early a command over their
passions, that the strongest of them are taught to give way to
circumstances, and a moderate liking will appear apathy itself,
to one accustomed to see the passion painted in its most glowing
colours. Least of all will a course of novels prepare a young lady
for the neglect and tedium of life which she is perhaps doomed
to encounter. If the novels she reads are virtuous, she has learned
how to arm herself with proper reserve against the ardour of her
lover; she has been instructed how to behave with the utmost
propriety when run away with, like *Miss Byron*,* or locked up
by a cruel parent, like *Clarissa*; but she is not prepared for
indifference and neglect. Though young and beautiful, she may
see her youth and beauty pass away without conquests, and the
monotony of her life will be apt to appear more insipid when
contrasted with scenes of perpetual courtship and passion.

It may be added with regard to the knowledge of the world,
which, it is allowed, these writings are calculated in some degree
to give, that, let them be as well written and with as much
attention to real life and manners as they can possibly be, they
will in some respects give false ideas, from the very nature of
fictitious writing. Every such work is a *whole*, in which the fates
and fortunes of the personages are brought to a conclusion,
agreeably to the author's own preconceived idea. Every incident
in a well written composition is introduced for a certain purpose,
and made to forward a certain plan. A sagacious reader is never
disappointed in his forebodings. If a prominent circumstance is
presented to him, he lays hold on it, and may be very sure it will
introduce some striking event; and if a character has strongly
engaged his affections, he need not fear being obliged to
withdraw them; the personages never turn out differently from
what their first appearance gave him a right to expect; they
gradually open, indeed; they may surprise, but they never
disappoint him. Even from the elegance of a name he may give

a guess at the amenity of the character. But real life is a kind of chance-medley, consisting of many unconnected scenes. The great author of the drama of life has not finished his piece; but the author must finish his; and vice must be punished and virtue rewarded in the compass of a few volumes; and it is a fault in *his* composition if every circumstance does not answer the reasonable expectations of the reader. But in real life our reasonable expectations are often disappointed; many incidents occur which are like 'passages that lead to nothing', and characters occasionally turn out quite different from what our fond expectations have led us to expect.

In short, the reader of a novel forms his expectations from what he supposes passes in the mind of the author, and guesses rightly at his intentions, but would often guess wrong if he were considering the real course of nature. It was very probable, at some periods of his history, that *Gil Blas*,* if a real character, would come to be hanged; but the practised novel-reader knows well that no such event can await the hero of the tale. Let us suppose a person speculating on the character of *Tom Jones** as the production of an author, whose business it is pleasingly to interest his readers. He has no doubt but that, in spite of his irregularities and distresses, his history will come to an agreeable termination. He has no doubt but that his parents will be discovered in due time; he has no doubt but that his love for *Sophia** will be rewarded sooner or later with her hand; he has no doubt of the constancy of that young lady, or of their entire happiness after marriage. And why does he foresee all this? Not from the real tendencies of things, but from what he has discovered of the author's intentions. But what would have been the probability in real life? Why, that the parents would either never have been found, or have proved to be persons of no consequence – that *Jones* would pass from one vicious indulgence to another, till his natural good disposition was quite smothered under his irregularities – that *Sophia* would either have married her lover clandestinely, and have been poor and unhappy, or she would have conquered her passion and married some country gentleman with whom she would have lived in moderate happiness, according to the usual routine of married life. But the author would have done very ill so to have constructed his story. If *Booth* had been a real character, it is probable his *Amelia** and her family would not only have been

brought to poverty, but left in it; but to the reader it is much
more probable that by some means or other they will be rescued
from it, and left in possession of all the comforts of life. It is
probable in *Zeluco** that the detestable husband will some way
or other be got rid of; but woe to the young lady, who, when
married, should be led, by contemplating the possibility of such
an event, to cherish a passion which ought to be entirely
relinquished!

Though a great deal of trash is every season poured out upon
the public from the English presses, yet in general our novels are
not vicious; the food has neither flavour nor nourishment, but
at least it is not poisoned. Our national taste and habits are still
turned towards domestic life and matrimonial happiness, and
the chief harm done by a circulating library is occasioned by the
frivolity of its furniture, and the loss of time incurred. Now and
then a girl perhaps may be led by them to elope with a coxcomb;
or, if she is handsome, to expect the homage of a *Sir Harry* or
My lord, instead of the plain tradesman suitable to her situation
in life; but she will not have her mind contaminated with such
scenes and ideas as Crebillon,* Louvet,* and others of that class
have published in France.

And indeed, notwithstanding the many paltry books of this
kind published in the course of every year, it may safely be
affirmed that we have more good writers in this walk living at
the present time, than at any period since the days of Richardson
and Fielding. A very great proportion of these are ladies: and
surely it will not be said that either taste or morals have been
losers by their taking the pen in hand. The names of D'Arblay,*
Edgeworth, Inchbald,* Radcliffe,* and a number more will
vindicate this assertion. [. . .]

1820

JOANNA BAILLIE

JOANNA BAILLIE (1762–1851), a poet and dramatist, was born in Bothwell, Lanarkshire, where she lived until the age of seven. The family then moved with their clergyman father to Hamilton. At the age of ten, Joanna was sent to a boarding-school in Glasgow. When her father died in 1778, the sixteen-year-old Joanna lived with her mother and sister at Long Calderwood, her mother's family home near Glasgow. Here she spent her time walking and reading, indirectly gathering the material which she later used to good effect in her poems. In 1783, she moved to London with her mother and sister in order to live for a time in Windmill Street with her brother until the three women settled in the village of Hampstead, near London. Her first volume, *Poems: Wherein it is Attempted to Describe Certain Views of Nature and Rustic Manners* (1790), which she published anonymously, received only one review, albeit favourable, in the November 1791 issue of the *Monthly Review*. The book did not sell. Baillie, who had become a regular guest at her aunt's, Anne Hunter's, *conversazione*, in London, then turned to drama as a means of gaining a readership. She published, at first anonymously, *A Series of Plays, in which it is Attempted to Delineate the Stronger Passions of the Mind* (3 vols, 1798–1812). Her first volume, known as *Plays on the Passions* (1798), included her 'Introductory Discourse', which is concerned with her ideas about writing 'works which most strongly characterize human nature in the middling and lower classes of society'. During her lifetime these 'closet dramas' were much read but seldom performed in theatres. Only seven of her twenty-eight dramas have been staged. In 1823, she published a volume of her own 'literary ballads', *Metrical Legends of Exalted Characters*. In 1840, she revised her 1790 *Poems* and added some uncollected later poems, entitling this volume *Fugitive Verses*. My biographical information comes from Margaret S. Carhart's *The Life and Work of Joanna Baillie* (1923), and the text from *A Series of Plays, in which it is Attempted to Delineate the Stronger Passions of the Mind*, vol. 1 (1798), pp. 18–26.

From 'Introductory Discourse'

Our desire to know what men are in the closet as well as the field, by the blazing hearth, and at the social board, as well as in the council and the throne, is very imperfectly gratified by real history; romance writers, therefore, stepped boldly forth to supply the deficiency; and tale writers, and novel writers, of many descriptions, followed after. If they have not been very skilful in their delineations of nature; if they have represented men and women speaking and acting as men and women never did speak or act; if they have caricatured both our virtues and our vices; if they have given us such pure and unmixed, or such heterogeneous combinations of character as real life never presented, and yet have pleased and interested us, let it not be imputed to the dulness of man in discerning what is genuinely natural in himself. There are many inclinations belonging to us, besides this great master-propensity of which I am treating. Our love of the grand, the beautiful, the novel, and above all of the marvellous, is very strong; and if we are richly fed with what we have a good relish for, we may be weaned to forget our native and favourite aliment. Yet we can never so far forget it, but that we will cling to, and acknowledge it again, whenever it is presented before us. In a work abounding with the marvellous and unnatural, if the author has any how stumbled upon an unsophisticated genuine stroke of nature, we will immediately perceive and be delighted with it, though we are foolish enough to admire at the same time, all the nonsense with which it is surrounded. After all the wonderful incidents, dark mysteries, and secrets revealed, which eventful novel so liberally presents to us; after the beautiful fairy ground, and even the grand and sublime scenes of nature with which descriptive novel so often enchants us; those works which most strongly characterize human nature in the middling and lower classes of society, where it is to be discovered by stronger and more unequivocal marks, will ever be the most popular. For though great pains have been taken in our higher sentimental novels to interest us in the delicacies, embarrassments, and artificial distresses of the more refined part of society, they have never been able to cope in the public opinion with these. The one is a dressed and beautiful pleasure-ground, in which we are enchanted for a while, amongst the delicate and unknown plants of artful cultivation; the other is a rough forest of our native land; the oak, the elm, the hazel, and the bramble are there; and amidst the endless varieties of its paths we can wander for ever. Into whatever scenes the novelist may conduct us, what objects soever he may present to our view, still is our attention most sensibly awake to every touch faithful to nature; still are we upon the watch for every thing that speaks to us of ourselves.

The fair field of what is properly called poetry, is enriched with so many beauties, that in it we are often tempted to forget what we really are, and what kind of beings we belong to. Who in the enchanted regions of simile, metaphor, allegory and description, can remember the plain order of things in this every-day world? From heroes whose majestic forms rise like a lofty tower, whose eyes are lightning, whose arms are irresistible, whose course is like the storms of heaven, bold and exalted sentiments we will readily receive; and will not examine them very accurately by that rule of nature which our own breast prescribes to us. A shepherd whose sheep, with fleeces of the purest snow, browse the flowery herbage of the most beautiful vallies; whose flute is ever melodious, and whose shepherdess is ever crowned with roses; whose every care is love, will not be called very strictly to account for the loftiness and refinement of his thoughts. The fair Nymph, who sighs out her sorrows to the conscious and compassionate wilds; whose eyes gleam like the bright drops of heaven; whose loose tresses stream to the breeze, may say what she pleases with impunity. I will venture, however, to say, that amidst all this decoration and ornament, all this loftiness and refinement, let one simple trait of the human heart, one expression of passion genuine and true to nature, be introduced, and it will stand forth alone in the boldness of reality, whilst the false and unnatural around it, fades away upon every side, like the rising exhalations of the morning. With admiration, and often with enthusiasm we proceed on our way through the grand and the beautiful images, raised to our imagination by the lofty Epic muse; but what even here are those things that strike upon the heart; that we feel and remember? Neither the descriptions of war, the sound of the trumpet, the clanging of arms, the combat of heroes, nor the death of the mighty, will interest our minds like the fall of the feeble stranger, who simply expresses the anguish of his soul, at the thoughts of that far-distant home which he must never return to again, and closes his eyes amongst the ignoble and forgotten; like the timid stripling goaded by the shame of reproach, who urges his trembling steps to the fight, and falls like a tender flower before the first blast of winter. How often will some simple picture of this kind be all that remains upon our minds of the terrific and magnificent battle, whose description we have read with admiration! How comes it that we relish so much the episodes of an heroic poem? It cannot merely be that we are pleased with a resting-place, where we enjoy the variety of contrast; for were the poem of the simple and familiar kind, and an episode after the heroic style introduced into it, ninety readers out of an hundred would pass over it altogether. Is it not that we meet such a story, so situated, with a kind of sympathetic good will, as in passing through a country of castles and of palaces, we should pop unawares upon some humble cottage, resembling the dwellings of our own native land, and gaze upon it with affection. The highest pleasures we receive from poetry, as well as from the real objects which surround us in the world, are derived from the sympathetic interest we all take in beings like ourselves; and I will even venture to say, that were the grandest scenes which can enter into the imagination of man, presented to our view and all reference to man completely shut out from our thoughts, the objects that composed it would convey to our minds little better than dry ideas of magnitude, colour, and form; and the remembrance of them would rest upon our minds like the measurement and distances of the planets.

If the study of human nature then, is so useful to the poet, the novelist, the historian, and the philosopher, of how much greater importance must it be to the dramatic writer? To them it is a powerful auxiliary, to him it is the centre and strength of the battle. If characteristic views of human nature enliven not their pages, there are many excellencies with which they can, in some degree, make up for the deficiency; it is what we receive from them with pleasure rather than demand. But in his works no richness of invention, harmony of language, nor grandeur of sentiment will supply the place of faithfully delineated nature.

The poet and the novelist may represent to you their great characters from the cradle to the tomb. They may represent them in any mood or temper, and under the influence of any passion which they see proper, without being obliged to put words into their mouths, those great betrayers of the feigned and adopted. They may relate every circumstance however trifling and minute, that serves to develop their tempers and dispositions. They tell us what kind of people they intend their men and women to be, and as such we receive them. If they are to move us with any scene of distress, every circumstance regarding the parties concerned in it, how they looked, how they moved, how they sighed, how the tears gushed from their eyes, how the very light and shadow fell upon them, is carefully described, and the few things that are given them to say along with all this assistance, must be very unnatural indeed if we refuse to sympathise with them. But the characters of the drama must speak directly for themselves. Under the influence of every passion, humour, and impression; in the artificial veilings of hypocrisy and ceremony, in the openness of freedom and confidence, and in the lonely hour of meditation they speak. He who made us hath placed within our breast a judge that judges instantaneously of every thing they say. We expect to find them creatures like ourselves; and if they are untrue to nature, we feel that we are imposed upon; as though the poet had introduced to us for brethren, creatures of a different race, beings of another world.

As in other works deficiency in characteristic truth may be compensated by excellencies of a different kind, in the drama characteristic truth will compensate every other defect. Nay, it will do what appears a contradiction; one strong genuine stroke of nature will cover a multitude of sins even against nature herself. When we meet in some scene of a good play a very fine stroke of this kind, we are apt to become so intoxicated with it, and so perfectly convinced of the author's great knowledge of the human heart, that we are unwilling to suppose that the whole of it has not been suggested by the same penetrating spirit. Many well-meaning enthusiastic critics have given themselves a great deal of trouble in this way; and have shut their eyes most ingeniously against the fair light of nature for the very love of it. They have converted, in their great zeal, sentiments palpably false, both in regard to the character and situation of the persons who utter them, sentiments which a child or a clown would detect, into the most skilful depictments of the heart. I can think of no stronger instance to show how powerfully this love of nature dwells within us.

1798

HANNAH MORE

HANNAH MORE (1745–1833) was an essayist, poet and play-wright who gradually became more oriented towards religious didacticism, renouncing art except when used in the service of her moral aims. She had four sisters who continued to make their own living by running a girls' boarding-school after Hannah left this work in 1790 in order to marry. Her fiancé, Edward Turner, who was twenty years her senior, could not be brought to marry her, so he settled an annuity of £200 on her as recompense for the waste of her time. She was thus able to live independently on this income which she augmented by writing poetry and plays, and later, moralistic essays and religious stories and ballads. Much of her early writing belongs to the eighteenth century in theme and style as well as date, but by the late 1780s, through the aegis of her close friend William Wilberforce, she began to concern herself with the plight of the worst-off – African slaves at first, and later, the poorer working-classes and the unemployed – and to direct her writing towards their improvement. The text of the extract from *Strictures on the Modern System of Female Education* comes from *The Works of Hannah More*, new edn, vol. 5 (1830), pp. 126–40, and 'Unprofitable Reading' comes from *Moral Sketches of Prevailing Opinions and Manners, Foreign and Domestic: with Reflections on Prayer* (1819), pp. 236–49. Biographical information comes from Mary Alden Hopkins, *Hannah More and Her Circle* (1947), *The Letters of Hannah More*, ed. and introd. R. Brimley Johnson (1925), and William Roberts, *Memoirs of the Life and Correspondence of Mrs Hannah More*, 3 vols (1835).

Chapter 8

On Female Study, and Initiation into Knowledge. – Error of Cultivating the Imagination to the Neglect of the Judgment. – Books of Reasoning Recommended

As this little work by no means assumes the character of a general scheme of education, the author has purposely avoided expatiating largely on any kind of instruction, but as it happens to be connected, either immediately or remotely, with objects of a moral or religious nature. Of course, she has been so far from thinking it necessary to enter into the enumeration of those popular books which are used in general instruction, that she has purposely forborne to mention any. With such books the rising generation is far more copiously and ably furnished than any that has preceded it; and, out of an excellent variety, the judicious instructor can hardly fail to make such a selection as shall be beneficial to the pupil.

But while due praise ought not to be withheld from the improved methods of communicating the elements of general knowledge, yet is there not some danger that our very advantages may lead us into error, by causing us to repose so confidently on the multiplied helps which facilitate the entrance into learning, as to render our pupils superficial through the very facility of acquirement? Where so much is done for them, may they not be led to do too little for themselves? and besides that exertion may slacken for want of a spur, may there not be a moral disadvantage in possessing young persons with the notion that learning may be acquired without diligence, and knowledge be attained without labour? Sound education never *can* be made a 'primrose-path of dalliance'. Do what we will we cannot *cheat* children into learning, or *play* them into knowledge, according to the conciliating smoothness of the modern creed, and the selfish indolence of modern habits. There is no idle way to any acquisitions which really deserve the name. And as Euclid,* in order to repress the impetuous vanity of greatness, told his sovereign that there was no royal way to geometry, so the fond mother may be assured that there is no short cut to any other kind of learning; no privileged bye-path cleared from the thorns and briars of repulse and difficulty, for the accommodation of opulent inactivity or feminine weakness. The tree of knowledge, as a punishment, perhaps, for its having been at first unfairly tasted, cannot now be climbed without difficulty; and this very circumstance serves afterwards to furnish not only literary pleasures, but moral advantages. For the knowledge which is acquired by unwearied assiduity is lasting in the possession, and sweet to the possessor; both, perhaps, in proportion to the cost and labour of the acquisition. And though an abler teacher ought to endeavour, by improving the communicating faculty in himself (for many know what they cannot teach), to soften every difficulty; yet, in spite of the kindness and ability with which he will smooth every obstruction, it is probably among the wise institutions of Providence that great difficulties should still remain. For education is but an initiation into that life of trial to which we are introduced on our entrance into this world. It is the first breaking-in to that state of toil and labour to which we are born, and to which sin has made us liable; and in this view of the subject the pains taken in the acquisition of learning may be converted to higher uses than such as are purely literary.

Will it not be ascribed to a captious singularity, if I venture to remark that real knowledge and real piety, though they may have gained in many instances, have suffered in others from that profusion of little, amusing, sentimental books with which the youthful library overflows? Abundance has its dangers as well as scarcity. In the first place, may not the multiplicity of these alluring little works increase the natural reluctance to those more dry and uninteresting studies, of which, after all, the rudiments of every part of learning *must* consist? And, secondly, is there not some danger (though there are many honourable exceptions) that some of those engaging narratives may serve to infuse into the youthful heart a sort of spurious goodness, a confidence of virtue, a parade of charity? And that the benevolent actions with the recital of which they abound, when they are not made to flow from any source but *feeling*, may tend to inspire a self-complacency, a self-gratulation, a 'stand by, for I am holier than thou'? May not the success with which the good deeds of the little heroes are uniformly crowned; the invariable reward which is made the instant concomitant of well-doing, furnish the young reader with false views of the condition of life, and the nature of the divine dealings with men? May they not help to suggest a false standard of morals, to infuse a love of popularity and an anxiety for praise, in the place of that simple and unostentatious rule of doing whatever good we do, *because it is the will of God*? The universal substitution of this principle would tend to purify the worldly morality of many a popular little story. And there are few dangers which good parents will more carefully guard against than that of giving their children a mere political piety; that sort of religion which just goes to make people more respectable, and to stand well with the world; a religion which is to save appearances without inculcating realities; a religion which affects to 'preach peace and good will to men', but which forgets to give 'glory to God in the highest'.

There is a certain precocity of mind which is much helped on by these superficial modes of instruction; for frivolous reading will produce its correspondent effect, in much less time than books of solid instruction; the imagination being liable to be worked upon, and the feelings to be set a going, much faster than the understanding can be opened and the judgment enlightened. A talent for conversation should be the result of instruction, not its precursor: it is a golden fruit when suffered to ripen gradually on the tree of knowledge; but if forced in the hot-bed of a circulating library, it will turn out worthless and vapid in proportion as it was artificial and premature. Girls who have been accustomed to devour a multitude of frivolous books, will converse and write with a far greater appearance of skill, as to style and sentiment, at twelve or fourteen years old, than those of a more advanced age, who are under the discipline of severer studies; but the former having early attained to that low standard which had been held out to them, become stationary; while the latter, quietly progressive, are passing through just gradations to a higher strain of mind; and those who early begin with talking and writing like women, commonly end with thinking and acting like children.

I would not, however, prohibit such works of imagination as suit this early period. When moderately used, they serve to stretch the faculties and expand the mind; but I should prefer works of vigorous genius and pure unmixed fable to many of those tame and more affected moral stories, which are not grounded on Christian principle. I should suggest the use, on the one hand, of original and acknowledged fictions; and, on the other, of accurate and simple facts; so that truth and fable may ever be kept separate and distinct in the mind. There is something that kindles fancy, awakens genius, and excites new ideas in many of the bold fictions of the East. And there is one peculiar merit in the Arabian and some other Oriental tales, which is, that they exhibit striking, and, in many respects, faithful views of the manners, habits, customs, and religion of their respective countries; so that some tincture of real local information is acquired by the perusal of the wildest fable, which will not be without its uses in aiding the future associations of the mind in all that relates to Eastern history and literature.

The irregular fancy of women is not sufficiently subdued by early application, nor tamed by labour, and the kind of knowledge they commonly do acquire is easily attained; and being chiefly some slight acquisition of the memory, something which is given them to get off by themselves, and not grounded in their minds by comment and conversation, it is easily lost. The superficial *question*-and-*answer* way, for instance, in which they often learn history, furnishes the mind with little to lean on: the events being detached and separated, the actions having no links to unite them with each other; the characters not being interwoven by mutual relation; the chronology being reduced to disconnected dates, instead of presenting an unbroken series; of course, neither events, actions, characters, nor chronology, fasten themselves on the understanding, but rather float in the memory as so many detached episodes, than contribute to form the mind and to enrich the judgment of the reader, in the important science of men and manners.

The swarms of *Abridgments, Beauties*, and *Compendiums*, which form too considerable a part of a young lady's library, may be considered, in many instances, as an infallible receipt for making a superficial mind. The *names* of the renowned characters in history thus become familiar in the mouths of those who can neither attach to the ideas of the person the series of his actions, nor the peculiarities of his character. A few fine passages from the poets (passages, perhaps, which derived their chief beauty from their position and connection) are huddled together by some extract-maker, whose brief and disconnected patches of broken and discordant materials, while they inflame young readers with the vanity of reciting, neither fill the mind nor form the taste; and it is not difficult to trace back to their shallow sources the hackneyed quotations of certain *accomplished* young ladies, who will be frequently found not to have come legitimately by any thing they know. I mean, not to have drawn it from its true spring, the original works of the author from which some *beauty-monger* has severed it. Human inconsistency in this, as in other cases, wants to combine two irreconcilable things: it strives to unite the reputation of knowledge with the pleasures of idleness, forgetting that nothing that is valuable can be obtained without sacrifices, and that, if we would purchase knowledge, we must pay for it the fair and lawful price of time and industry. For this *extract-reading*, while it accommodates itself to the convenience, illustrates the character, of the age in which we live. The appetite for pleasure, and that love of ease and indolence which is generated by it, leave little time or taste for sound improvement; while the vanity, which is equally a characteristic of the existing period, puts in its claim also for indulgence, and contrives to figure away by these little snatches of ornamental reading, caught in the short intervals of successive amusements.

Besides, the taste, thus pampered with delicious morsels, is early vitiated. The young reader of these *clustered beauties* conceives a disrelish for every thing which is plain, and grows impatient, if obliged to get through those equally necessary though less showy parts of a work, in which, perhaps, the author gives the best proof of his judgment by keeping under that occasional brilliancy and incidental ornament, of which these superficial students are in constant pursuit. In all well-written books, there is much that is good which is not dazzling; and these shallow critics should be taught, that it is for the embellishment of the more tame and uninteresting parts of his work, that the judicious poet commonly reserves those flowers, whose beauty is defaced when they are plucked from the garland into which he had so skilfully woven them.

The remark, however, as far as it relates to abridgments, is by no means of general application: there are many valuable works, which, from their bulk, would be almost inaccessible to a great number of readers, and a considerable part of which may not be generally useful. Even in the best written books there is often superfluous matter; authors are apt to get enamoured of their subject, and to dwell too long on it: every person cannot find time to read a longer work on any subject, and yet it may be well for them to know something on almost every subject; those, therefore, who abridge voluminous works judiciously, render service to the community. But there seems, if I may venture the remark, to be a mistake in the *use* of abridgments. They are put systematically into the hands of *youth*, who have, or ought to have, leisure for the works at large; while abridgments seem more immediately calculated for persons in more advanced life, who wish to recall something they had forgotten; who want to restore old ideas rather than acquire new ones; or they are useful for persons immersed in the business of the world, who have little leisure for voluminous reading: they are excellent to refresh the mind, but not competent to form it: they serve to bring back what had been formerly known, but do not supply a fund of knowledge.

Perhaps there is some analogy between the mental and bodily conformation of women. The instructor, therefore, should imitate the physician. If the latter prescribe bracing medicines for a body of which delicacy is the disease, the former would do well to prohibit relaxing reading for a mind which is already of too soft a texture, and should strengthen its feeble tone by invigorating reading.

By softness, I cannot be supposed to mean imbecility of understanding, but natural softness of heart, and pliancy of temper, together with that indolence of spirit which is fostered by indulging in seducing books, and in the general habits of fashionable life.

I mean not *here* to recommend books which are immediately religious, but such as exercise the reasoning faculties, teach the mind to get acquainted with its own nature, and to stir up its own powers. Let not a timid young lady start if I should venture to recommend to her, after a proper course of preparatory reading, to swallow and digest such strong meat as Watts's* or Duncan's little book of Logic,* some parts of Mr Locke's Essay on the Human Understanding,* and Bishop Butler's Analogy.* Where there is leisure, and capacity, and an able friend to comment and to counsel, works of this nature might be profitably substituted in the place of so much English Sentiment,

French Philosophy, Italian Love-Songs, and fantastic German imagery and magic wonders. While such enervating or absurd books sadly disqualify the reader for solid pursuit or vigorous thinking, the studies here recommended would act upon the constitution of the mind as a kind of alterative, and, if I may be allowed the expression, would help to brace the intellectual stamina.

This suggestion is, however, by no means intended to exclude works of taste and imagination, which must always make the ornamental part, and of course a very considerable part of female studies. It is only intimated, that they should not form them entirely and exclusively. For what is called dry tough reading, independent of the knowledge it conveys, is useful as a habit, and wholesome as an exercise. Serious study serves to harden the mind for more trying conflicts; it lifts the reader from sensation to intellect; it abstracts her from the world and its vanities; it fixes a wandering spirit and fortifies a weak one; it divorces her from matter; it corrects that spirit of trifling which she naturally contracts from the frivolous turn of female conversation and the petty nature of female employments; it concentrates her attention, assists her in a habit of excluding trivial thoughts, and thus even helps to qualify her for religious pursuits. Yes, I repeat it, there is to woman a Christian use to be made of sober studies; while books of an opposite cast, however unexceptionable they may be sometimes found in point of expression, however free from evil in its more gross and palpable shapes, yet from their very nature and constitution they excite a spirit of relaxation, by exhibiting scenes and suggesting ideas which soften the mind and set the fancy at work: they take off wholesome restraints, diminish sober-mindedness, impair the general powers of resistance, and at best feed habits of improper indulgence, and nourish a vain and visionary indolence, which lays the mind open to error and the heart to seduction.

Women are little accustomed to close reasoning on any subject; still less do they inure their minds to consider particular parts of a subject: they are not habituated to turn a truth round, and view it in all its varied aspects and positions; and this, perhaps, is one cause of the too great confidence they are disposed to place in their own opinions. Though their imagination is already too lively, and their judgment naturally incorrect; in educating them we go on to stimulate the imagination, while we neglect the regulation of the judgment. They already want ballast, and we make their education consist in continually crowding more sail than they can carry. Their intellectual powers being so little strengthened by exercise, makes every petty business appear a hardship to them; whereas serious study would be useful, were it only that it leads the mind to the habit of conquering difficulties. But it is peculiarly hard to turn at once from the indolent repose of light reading, from the concerns of mere animal life, the objects of sense, or the frivolousness of female chit-chat; it is peculiarly hard, I say, to a mind so softened, to rescue itself from the dominion of self-indulgence, to resume its powers, to call home its scattered strength, to shut out every foreign intrusion, to force back a spring so unnaturally bent, and to devote itself to religious reading, to active business, to sober reflection, to self-examination. Whereas to an intellect accustomed to think at all, the difficulty of thinking seriously is obviously lessened.

Far be it from me to desire to make scholastic ladies or female dialecticians; but there is little fear that the kind of books here recommended, if thoroughly studied, and not superficially skimmed, will make them pedants, or induce conceit; for by showing them the possible powers of the human mind, you will bring them to see the littleness of their own: and surely to get acquainted with the mind, to regulate, to inform it; to show it its own ignorance and its own weakness, does not seem the way to puff it up. But let her who is disposed to be elated with her literary acquisitions check the rising vanity by calling to mind the just remark of Swift, 'that after all her boasted acquirements, a woman will, generally speaking, be found to possess less of what is called learning than a common school-boy'.

Neither is there any fear that this sort of reading will convert ladies into authors. The direct contrary effect will be likely to be produced by the perusal of writers who throw the generality of readers at such an unapproachable distance as to check presumption, instead of exciting it. Who are those ever-multiplying authors, that with unparalleled fecundity are overstocking the world with their quick-succeeding progeny? They are NOVEL-WRITERS: the easiness of whose productions is at once the cause of their own fruitfulness, and of the almost infinitely numerous race of imitators to whom they give birth. Such is the frightful facility of this species of composition, that every raw girl, while she reads, is tempted to fancy that she can also write. And as Alexander,* on perusing the Iliad, found by congenial sympathy the image of Achilles stamped on his own ardent soul, and felt himself the hero he was studying; and as Corregio,* on first beholding a picture which exhibited the perfection of the graphic art, prophetically felt all his own future greatness, and cried out in rapture, 'And I, too, am a painter!' so a thorough-paced novel-reading Miss, at the close of every tissue of hackneyed adventures, feels within herself the stirring impulse of corresponding genius, and triumphantly exclaims, 'And I, too, am an author!' The glutted imagination soon overflows with the redundance of cheap sentiment and plentiful incident, and by a sort of arithmetical proportion, is enabled by the perusal of any three novels, to produce a fourth; till every fresh production, like the prolific progeny of Banquo, is followed by

Another, and another, and another!*

Is a lady, however destitute of talents, education, or knowledge of the world, whose studies have been completed by a circulating library, in any distress of mind? the writing a novel suggests itself as the best soother of her sorrows! Does she labour under any depression of circumstances? writing a novel occurs as the readiest receipt for mending them! and she solaces her imagination with the conviction that the subscription which has been extorted by her importunity, or given to her necessities, has been offered as a homage to her genius; and this confidence instantly levies a fresh contribution for a succeeding work. Capacity and cultivation are so little taken into the account, that writing a book seems to be now considered as the only sure resource which the idle and the illiterate have always in their power.

May the Author be indulged in a short digression, while she remarks, though rather out of its place, that the corruption occasioned by these books has spread so wide, and descended so low, as to have become one of the most universal, as well as most pernicious, sources of corruption among us. Not only among milliners, mantua-makers, and other trades where numbers work together, the labour of one girl is frequently sacrificed that she may be spared to read those mischievous books to the others; but she has been assured by clergymen who have witnessed the fact, that they are procured and greedily read in the wards of our hospitals! an awful hint, that those who teach the poor to read, should not only take care to furnish them with principles which will lead them to abhor corrupt books, but that they should also furnish them with such books as shall strengthen and confirm their principles.

1799

FROM *MORAL SKETCHES OF PREVAILING OPINIONS AND MANNERS*

Unprofitable Reading

We have already ventured to allude to the disproportionate quantity of human life which is squandered in the ever multiplying haunts of public dissipation: but as this is an evil too notorious to require any fresh animadversion, we shall not stop to insist on the excess to which it is carried, but shall advert to another, which, if less ostensible, is scarcely less mischievous – we allude to the increased and increasing prevalence of idle reading.

For whether a large proportion of our probationary being – time, that precious talent assigned us for providing for the treasures of eternity, – be consumed in unprofitable reading at home, or in frivolous diversions abroad, the effect on the state of the mind is not very dissimilar. The difference between private excess and public intoxication, is not very material as to its effects on the individual: the chief difference lies in the example and the expenses; for the mind is nearly as much unfitted for sober duties by the one, as by the other.

It is the same principle which influences the inveterate novel reader, and the never-wearied pursuer of public dissipation; only its operation is different in different tempers. The active and lively trifler seeks to lose reflection in the bustling crowd; while the more indolent alienates her mind from what is right, without any exertion of the body. In one it is the imagination which is acted upon; in the other, the senses. In one sense, indeed, the domestic idleness is the worst; because it wraps itself up in its own comparative merit, and complacently reposes on its superior sobriety; for, if the spirits are more agitated in the one case, in the other they sink into a more perilous indolence. The scenes acted over by the imagination in private, have also a superiority in mischief over those of actual, busy gaiety in others, as being more likely to be retained and repeated. Instances, however, are not rare, in which a thorough manager contrives to make both meet. In this union the injury is doubled.

But it will be urged by the too ready advocates, that *all* these books are not wicked. It is readily granted. Many works of fiction may be read with safety, some even with profit; but the constant familiarity even with such as are not exceptionable in themselves, relaxes the mind that wants hardening, dissolves the heart which wants fortifying, stirs the imagination which wants quieting, irritates the passions which want calming, and, above all, disinclines and disqualifies for active virtues, and for spiritual exercises. The habitual indulgence in such reading is a silent, mining mischief. Though there is no act, and no moment, in which any open assault on the mind is made, as in the instances previously noticed, yet the constant habit performs the work of a mental atrophy; it produces all the symptoms of decay, and the danger is not less for being more gradual, and, therefore, less suspected.

The general manners are becoming more and more relaxed. Even the old restraints, which had a regard to appearances, were not without their use. The writer remembers to have heard Dr Johnson* reprove a young lady in severe terms, for quoting a sentiment from Tom Jones* – a book, he said, which, if a modest lady had done so improper a thing as to read, she should not do so immodest a thing as to avow.

Many instances might be adduced to prove, that the age is gradually grown less scrupulous. We will give only one. Another young lady, independent and rich, about the same time was tempted to send for Rousseau's Heloise.* A very little progress in the work convinced her, that it was neither safe for her to read, nor, having read it, could she either modestly confess it, or conscientiously deny the perusal, if questioned. Her virtue conquered her curiosity; she sent away, unread, a book which may now be seen lying openly on the tables of many who would be shocked at the slightest imputation on the delicacy of their minds, or the scrupulousness of their morals.

But to limit the evil of idle reading to the single article of *time*: – It is, perhaps, not too much to assert, that if the hours spent by the higher and middle classes in this profitless perusal could be counted, they would, probably, far exceed in number those spent by the gay in more ostensible and public dissipation. Nay; we are almost tempted to say, that if, to the account of time dissipated by the latter, were added the hours spent by both classes in acts of devotion and serious reading, perhaps the total aggregate would be exceeded in number by the hours thrown away in the retirement of idle readers.

We are the more earnest on this subject, from being in possession of some facts which evince beyond any persuasions, which confirm beyond any arguments, the perils which we may be thought too warm in deprecating. Among the overflowing number of fictitious writings, not a few are there in the English, and still more and worse in the French and German schools, in which the intrigue between the already married hero and heroine is opened by means so apparently innocent, and conducted so gradually, and with so much plausibility, as, for a time, to escape detection. Vicious scenes are artfully kept out of sight, while virtuous principles are silently, but systematically, undermined, till the imagination, that notorious corrupter of the heart, has had time to prepare the work of destruction. Such fascinating qualities are lavished on the seducer, and such attractive graces on the seduced, that the images indulged with delight by the fancy, carry on the reader imperceptibly to a point which is not so far from their indulgence in the act as some imagine. Such soothing apologies for an amiable weakness, that is, in plain English, for the breach of the seventh Commandment, are made by the writer, that the reader begins to think her judgment is convinced, as well as her inclination gratified; and the polluted mind, brought into the state, of all others, the least willing, and the least able, to resist practical crime, is ready to exclaim, with the satirist of political vices,

That *not* to be corrupted is the shame.[*]

Thus the violation of as awful a prohibition as any in the decalogue, is softened down into a pardonable weakness. The stabbing the peace and honour of the husband, and the barbarous desertion of the innocent babes, or the still deeper wound given to the grown up daughters, is reduced to a venial fault, for which the irresistibleness of the temptation is shamelessly, but too successfully pleaded.

In tracing the effect, almost exclusively, of the unrestrained indulgence in these soothing pictures of varnished corruption, we could, were it prudent, produce actual instances of this breach of solemn vows, this total abandonment of all the proprieties, and all the duties of life: and it is too probable, that, besides the known instances to which allusion is here made, many more might be adduced as having imbibed from the same sources the rudiments of moral misery, which has alarmingly swelled the recent list of divorces, and thus render it more than probable, that the circulating library is no unfrequent road to Doctors' Commons.*

There are distinctions and gradations maintained by the squanderers of time in their several ways, of which the well-employed do not perceive the difference. Many who would turn with contempt from the card-table, think little of giving days and nights to these pernicious, or, at best, unimproving fictions – an exchange without being an improvement; for the volumes do not, like the cards, confine the mischief to the time they are in the hands, but, as we have observed, often leave impressions behind them when the others are forgotten.

How gladly should we limit these observations to persons whose time is turned to little account, and spent with little scruple, in *any* amusement which is not obviously corrupt! But it is with real reluctance we take the liberty to animadvert on the same error, though not carried to the same excess, in persons of a higher strain of character, persons of correct manners and considerable attainments. Do not many such tolerate in their families abundance of reading which, to say the least, is not improving, and of which, frequently, this would be too gentle a censure? Even where the books contain little that is coarse or corrupt, still it must be repeated, the prodigious quantity of life they consume must exceedingly deduct from that which would otherwise be allotted to more wholesome studies.

And this is not all. – We hear passages, not the most pure in point of delicacy, and quite unequivocal in point of impiety, repeated with enthusiasm by young ladies, from the works of a noble, but profligate and infidel poet:* a poet rich in abused genius, and abounding in talents, ungratefully employed to dishonour Him who gave them. – But from the same fair lips, we hear little of Milton and of Spenser, of Cowper and of Young, of Thompson and of Goldsmith, of Gray and of Beattie,* names once dear to every lover of enchanting song.

Nor need we look back exclusively to departed genius, for the innocent and refreshing delights of poetry. The muses have living votaries, who pour forth strains at once original, mellifluous, and chaste.

What shall we presume to say to sober-minded parents, even to grave clergymen, who not only do not prohibit the authors of the school in question; who not only do not restrain their daughters from being students in it, but who not unfrequently introduce, as part of the family reading, poetry, which if it contain not the gross expressions, and vulgar wickedness of the wits of Charles's days,* is little less profane in principle, or corrupt in sentiment? There is some knowledge which it is a praise not to know; and the vice in this case being somewhat 'refined through certain strainers', furnishes at once a temptation and an apology.

It may be urged, in vindication of this remissness, that as soon as young persons get out of their parents' hands, they will naturally choose their books for themselves. This is granted. – But is not every year which prolongs their precious innocence, a year gained? May not, within that period, the nascent libertinism be checked, with ardent imagination fixed to other pursuits, the sentiment of virtue kindled, the taste for purity confirmed, and the habit and love of prayer established? And, above all, is it not a pity that they should be able hereafter to plead as an apology for their intimacy with such books, that they were introduced to them by a fond and careful parent?

May we not take the liberty to ask of worthy, but, in this instance, injudicious parents, is this practice quite consistent with the command given to fathers, even under a darker dispensation, that they should not limit the improvement of their children to any set hours, but that they should 'teach them diligently, sitting in the house, and walking by the way, rising up, and lying down?'*

1819

MARY ROBINSON

MARY ROBINSON née Darby (1758–1800), novelist, playwright and poet, attended for a time the school run by Hannah More's sisters in Bristol. After her marriage at the age of sixteen, she took up acting when her profligate husband, Thomas Robinson, landed them in a debtors' prison. She became the mistress of the Prince of Wales for a year, and received an annuity of £500 when he broke off their relationship. She had an affair with Colonel Banastre Tarleton but became ill, and this affair finally ended when he married an heiress. Despite ill-health, Robinson took to writing to help support herself, her daughter and her mother. Her literary and social notoriety during her lifetime had its origins in her role as mistress, especially to the Prince of Wales. Her works include *Poems* (1775), *Captivity, A Poem; and Celadon and Lydia, A Tale* (1777), *The Beauties of Mrs Robinson, Selected and Arranged from her Poetical Works* (1791), *Poems* (1791–3), *Sight, The Cavern of Woe and Solitude* (1793), *Sappho and Phaon* (1796), *Lyrical Tales* (1800), and *The Mistletoe, A Christmas Tale in Verse* (1800). She began her *Memoirs* in 1800, but this work remained unfinished at her death, and was published posthumously in 1801, with additional material by her daughter, Maria E. Robinson. *Letter to the Women of England on the Injustice of Subordination* (1799) was initially published under the pseudonym of 'Anne Frances Randall', but the second edition of this work (1799) was conclusively attributed to Mary Robinson in the *Monthly Review*, 1800, vol. 31, p. 331. The text of the opening passage of *Letter to the Women of England* ... comes from the first edition of 1799, pp. 1–17. The excerpt from her *Memoirs* and also biographical information come from the *Memoirs of Mary Robinson ('Perdita')*, ed. and introd. J. Fitzgerald Molloy (1895), pp. 1–3, 6–11, and 20–24. Additional biographical information is from DNB.

FROM *LETTER TO THE WOMEN OF ENGLAND ON THE INJUSTICE OF SUBORDINATION*

Custom, from the earliest periods of antiquity, has endeavoured to place the female mind in the subordinate ranks of intellectual sociability. WOMAN has ever been considered as a lovely and fascinating part of the creation, but her claims to mental equality have not only been questioned, by envious and interested sceptics; but, by a barbarous policy in the other sex, considerably depressed, for want of liberal and classical cultivation. I will not expatiate largely on the doctrines of certain philosophical sensualists, who have aided in this destructive oppression, because an illustrious British female, (whose death has not been sufficiently lamented, but to whose genius posterity will render justice) has already written volumes in vindication of 'The Rights of Woman'.*[1] But I shall endeavour to prove that, under the present state of mental subordination, universal knowledge is not only benumbed and blighted, but true happiness, originating in enlightened manners, retarded in its progress. Let WOMAN once assert her proper sphere, unshackled by prejudice, and unsophisticated by vanity; and pride, (the noblest species of pride,) will establish her claims to the participation of power, both mentally and corporeally.

In order that this letter may be clearly understood, I shall proceed to prove my assertion in the strongest, but most undecorated language. I shall remind my enlightened countrywomen that they are not the mere appendages of domestic life, but the partners, the equal associates of man: and, where they excel in intellectual powers, they are no less capable of all that prejudice and custom have united in attributing, exclusively, to the thinking faculties of man. I argue thus, and my assertions are incontrovertible.

[1] The writer of this letter, though avowedly of the same school, disdains the drudgery of servile imitation. The same subject may be argued in a variety of ways; and though this letter may not display the philosophical reasoning with which *The Rights of Woman* abounded, it is no less suited to the purpose. For it requires a *legion of Wollstonecrafts* to undermine the poisons of prejudice and malevolence.

Supposing that destiny, or interest, or chance, or what you will, has united a man, confessedly of a weak understanding, and corporeal debility, to a woman strong in all the powers of intellect, and capable of bearing the fatigues of busy life: is it not degrading to humanity that such a woman should be the passive, the obedient slave, of such an husband? Is it not repugnant to all the laws of nature, that her feelings, actions, and opinions, should be controlled, perverted, and debased, by such an help-mate? Can she look for protection to a being, whom she was formed by the all wise CREATOR, to protect? Impossible, yet, if from prudence, or from pity, if for the security of worldly interest, or worldly happiness, she presumes to take a lead in domestic arrangements, or to screen her wedded shadow from obloquy or ruin, what is she considered by the imperious sex? but an usurper of her husband's rights; a domestic tyrant; a vindictive shrew; a petticoat philosopher; and a disgrace to that race of mortals, known by the degrading appellation of the *defenceless sex*.

The barbarity of custom's law in this *enlightened* country, has long been exercised to the prejudice of woman:[1] and even the laws of honour have been perverted to oppress her. If a man receive an insult, he is justified in seeking retribution. He may chastise, challenge, and even destroy his adversary. Such a proceeding in MAN is termed honorable; his character is exonerated from the stigma which calumny attached to it; and his courage rises in estimation, in proportion as it exemplifies his revenge. But were a WOMAN to attempt such an expedient, however strong her sense of injury, however invincible her fortitude, or important the preservation of character, she would be deemed a murderess. Thus, custom says, you must be free from error; you must possess an unsullied fame: yet, if a slanderer, or a libertine, even by the most unpardonable falsehoods, deprive you of either reputation or repose, you have no remedy. He is received in the most fastidious societies, in the cabinets of nobles, at the toilettes of coquets and prudes, while

---

[1] The Mahometans are said to be of opinion that women have no souls! Some British husbands would wish to evince that they have no senses, or at least not the privilege of using them: for a modern wife, I mean to say that which is denominated a *good one*, should neither hear, see, speak, nor feel, if she would wish to enjoy any tolerable portion of tranquillity.

you must bear your load of obloquy, and sink beneath the uniting efforts of calumny, ridicule, and malevolence. Indeed we have scarcely seen a single instance where a professed libertine has been either shunned by women, or reprobated by men, for having acted either unfeelingly or dishonorably towards what is denominated the *defenceless sex*. Females, by this mis-judging lenity, while they give proofs of a degrading triumph, cherish for themselves that anguish, which, in their turn, they will, unpitied, experience.

Man is able to bear the temptations of human existence better than woman, because he is more liberally educated, and more universally acquainted with society. Yet, if he has the temerity to annihilate the bonds of moral and domestic life, he is acquitted; and his enormities are placed to the account of *human frailty*. But if WOMAN advance beyond the boundaries of decorum,

> Ruin ensues, reproach, and endless shame,
> And one false step, entirely damns her fame.*

Such partial discriminations seem to violate all laws, divine and human! If WOMAN be the weaker creature, her frailty should be the more readily forgiven. She is exposed by her personal attractions, to more perils, and yet she is not permitted to bear that shield, which man assumes; she is not allowed the exercise of *courage* to repulse the enemies of her fame and happiness; though, if she is wounded, – she is *lost for ever*!

Supposing that a WOMAN has experienced every insult, every injury, that her vain-boasting, high-bearing associate, man, can inflict: imagine her, driven from society; deserted by her kindred; scoffed at by the world; exposed to poverty; assailed by malice; and consigned to scorn: with no companion but sorrow, no prospect but disgrace; she has no remedy. She appeals to the feeling and reflecting part of mankind; they pity, but they do not seek to redress her: she flies to her own sex; they not only condemn, but they avoid her. She talks of punishing the villain who has destroyed her: he smiles at the menace, and tells her, *she is*, a WOMAN.

Let me ask this plain and rational question, – is not woman a human being, gifted with all the feelings that inhabit the bosom of man? Has not woman affections, susceptibility, fortitude, and an acute sense of injuries received? Does she not shrink at the touch of persecution? Does not her bosom melt with sympathy, throb with pity, glow with resentment, ache with sensibility, and burn with indignation? Why then is she denied the exercise of the nobler feelings, an high consciousness of honour, a lively sense of what is due to dignity of character? Why may not woman resent and punish? Because the long established laws of custom, have decreed her *passive*! Because she is by nature organized to feel every wrong more acutely, and yet, by a barbarous policy, denied the power to assert the first of Nature's rights, self-preservation.

How many vices are there that men perpetually indulge in, to which women are rarely addicted. Drinking, in man, is reckoned a proof of good fellowship; and the *bon vivant* is considered as the best and most desirable of companions. Wine, as far as it is pleasant to the sense of tasting, is as agreeable to woman as to man: but its use to excess will render either brutal. Yet man *yields* to its influence, because he is the *stronger-minded* creature; and woman *resists* its power over the senses, because she is the *weaker*. How will the *superiorly* organized sex defend this contradiction? Man will say his passions are stronger than those of women; yet we see women rush not only to ruin, but to death, for objects they love; while men exult in an unmeaning display of caprice, intrigue, and seduction; frequently, without even a zest for the vices they exhibit. The fact is simply this: the passions of men originate in sensuality; those of women, in sentiment: man loves corporeally, woman mentally: which is the nobler creature?

Gaming is termed, in the modern vocabulary, a masculine vice. Has vice then a *sex*? Till the passions of the mind in man and woman are separate and distinct, till the sex of vital animation, denominated soul, be ascertained, on what pretext is woman deprived of those amusements which man is permitted to enjoy? If gaming be a vice (though every species of commerce is nearly allied to it), why not condemn it wholly? why suffer man to persevere in the practice of it; and yet in woman execrate its propensity? Man may enjoy the convivial board, indulge the caprices of his nature; he may desert his home, violate his marriage vows, scoff at the moral laws that unite society, and set even religion at defiance, by oppressing the defenceless; while woman is condemned to bear the drudgery of domestic life, to vegetate in obscurity, to *love* where she abhors, to *honour* where she despises, and to *obey*, while she shudders at subordination. Why? Let the most cunning sophist, answer me, WHY?

If women sometimes, indeed too frequently, exhibit a frivolous species of character, we should examine the evil in which it orginates, and endeavour to find a cure. If the younger branches of some of our nobility are superficially polished, and wholly excluded from essential knowledge, while they are regularly initiated in the mysteries of a gaming table, and the mazes of intrigue, can we feel surprized at their soon discovering an aptitude to evince their hereditary follies? We know that women, like princes, are strangers to the admonitions of truth; and yet we are astonished when we behold them emulous of displaying every thing puerile and unessential; and aiming perpetually at arbitrary power, without one mental qualification to authorize dominion. From such women, the majority of mankind draw their opinions of sexual imbecility; and, in order that their convenient plea may be sanctioned by example, they continue to debilitate the female mind, for the sole purpose of enforcing subordination.

Yet, the present era has given indisputable proofs, that WOMAN is a thinking and an enlightened being! We have seen a Wollstonecraft, a Macaulay, a Sévigné;* and many others, now living, who embellish the sphere of literary splendour, with genius of the first order. The aristocracy of kingdoms will say, that it is absolutely necessary to extort obedience: if all were masters, who then would stoop to serve? By the same rule, man exclaims, If we allow the softer sex to participate in the intellectual rights and privileges we enjoy, who will arrange our domestic drudgery? who will reign (as Stephano* says, while we are vice-roys over them) in our household establishments? who will rear our progeny; obey our commands; be our affianced vassals; the creatures of our pleasures? I answer, women, but they will not be your slaves; they will be your associates, your equals in the extensive scale of civilized society; and in the indisputable rights of nature.[1]

In the common occurrences and occupations of life, what in

[1] The ancient Romans were more liberal, even during the reigns of their most atrocious tyrants: and it is to be presumed that the intellectual powers of British women, were they properly expanded, are, at least, equal to those of Roman ladies.

man is denominated high-spirit, is in WOMAN termed vindictive.
If a man be insulted and inflicts a blow upon his assailant, he is
called a brave and noble-minded creature! If WOMAN acts upon
the same principle of resistance, she is branded as a Zantippe;
though in such a situation she would scarcely meet with a
Socrates,* even if, in the scale of comparison, she possessed
stronger corporeal, as well as mental, powers, than the object of
her resentment.

How comes it, that in this age of reason we do not see
statesmen and orators selecting women of superior mental
acquirements as their associates? Men allow that women are
absolutely necessary to their happiness, and that they 'had been
brutes' without them. But the poet did not insinuate that none
but silly or ignorant women were to be allowed the *supreme
honour* of unbrutifying man, of rendering his life desirable, and
of 'smoothing the rugged path of care' with their endearments.
The ancients were emulous of patronizing, and even of cultivat-
ing the friendship of enlightened women. But a British Demos-
thenes, a Pythagoras, a Leontius, a Eustathius, or a Brutus,*
would rather pass his hours in dalliance with an unlettered
courtezan, than in the conversation of a Theano, a Themiste, a
Cornelia, a Sosipatra, or a Portia.* What is this display of
mental aristocracy? what but the most inveterate jealousy; the
most pernicious and refined species of envy and malevolence?

Let me ask the rational and thinking mortal, why the graces
of feminine beauty are to be constituted emblems of a debilitated
mind? Does the finest symmetry of form, or the most delicate
tint of circulation, exemplify a tame submission to insult or
oppression? Is strength of intellect, in woman, bestowed in vain?
Has the SUPREME DISPOSER OF EVENTS given to the female soul
a distinguished portion of energy and feeling, that the one may
remain inactive, and the other be the source of her destruction?
Let the moralist think otherwise. Let the contemplative philo-
sopher examine the proportions of human intellect; and let us
hope that the immortality of the soul springs from causes that
are not merely *sexual*.

Cicero* says, 'There was, from the beginning such a thing as
Reason; a direct emanation from nature itself, which prompted
to good, and averted from evil.' Reason may be considered as
a part of soul; for, by its powers, we are taught intuitively to
hope for a future state. Cicero did not confine the attribute of

Reason to sex; such doctrine would have been completely
Mahometan!

The most celebrated painters have uniformly represented
angels as of no sex. Whether this idea originates in theology, or
imagination, I will not pretend to determine; but I will boldly
assert that there is something peculiarly unjust in condemning
woman to suffer every earthly insult, while she is allowed a sex;
and only permitting her to be happy, when she is divested of it.
There is also something profane in the opinion, because it
implies that an all-wise Creator sends a creature into the world,
with a sexual distinction, which shall authorise the very extent
of mortal persecution. If men would be completely happy by
obtaining the confidence of women, let them unite in confessing
that mental equality, which evinces itself by indubitable proofs
that the soul has no sex. If, then, the cause of action be the
same, the effects cannot be dissimilar. [. . .]

1799

FROM *MEMOIRS OF MARY ROBINSON*

At the period when the ancient city of Bristol was besieged by
Fairfax's army, the troops being stationed on a rising ground in
the vicinity of the suburbs, a great part of the venerable minster
was destroyed by the cannonading before Prince Rupert surren-
dered to the enemy; and the beautiful Gothic structure, which at
this moment fills the contemplative mind with melancholy awe,
was reduced to but little more than one-half of the original
fabric.* Adjoining to the consecrated hill, whose antique tower
resists the ravages of time, once stood a monastery of monks of
the order of St Augustine. This building formed a part of the
spacious boundaries which fell before the attacks of the enemy,
and became a part of the ruin, which never was repaired or re-
raised to its former Gothic splendours.

On this spot was built a private house, partly of simple, and
partly of modern architecture. The front faced a small garden,
the gates of which opened to the Minster Green (now called the
College Green); the west side was bounded by the cathedral,
and the back was supported by the ancient cloisters of St
Augustine's monastery. A spot more calculated to inspire the

soul with mournful meditation can scarcely be found amidst the monuments of antiquity.

In this venerable mansion there was one chamber whose dismal and singular constructure left no doubt of its having been a part of the original monastery. It was supported by the mouldering arches of the cloisters, dark, Gothic, and opening on the minster sanctuary, not only by casement windows that shed a dim mid-day gloom, but by a narrow winding staircase, at the foot of which an iron-spiked door led to the long gloomy path of cloistered solitude. This place remained in the situation in which I describe it in the year 1776, and probably may, in a more ruined state, continue so to this hour.

In this awe-inspiring habitation, which I shall henceforth denominate the Minster House, during a tempestuous night, on the 27th of November, 1758, I first opened my eyes to this world of duplicity and sorrow. I have often heard my mother say that a more stormy hour she never remembered. The wind whistled round the dark pinnacles of the minster tower and the rain beat in torrents against the casements of her chamber. Through life the tempest has followed my footsteps, and I have in vain looked for a short interval of repose from the perseverance of sorrow.

In the male line I am descended from a respectable family in Ireland, the original name of which was MacDermott. From an Irish estate, my great-grandfather changed it to that of Darby. My father, who was born in America, was a man of strong mind, high spirit, and great personal intrepidity. Many anecdotes, well authenticated, and which, being irrefragable, are recorded as just tributes to his fame and memory, shall, in the course of these memoirs, confirm this assertion. [. . .]

My mother was born at Bridgwater, in Somersetshire, in the house near the bridge, which is now occupied by Jonathan Chub, Esq., a relation of my beloved and lamented parent, and a gentleman who, to acknowledged worth and a powerful understanding, adds a superior claim to attention by all the acquirements of a scholar and a philosopher.

My mother, who never was what may be called a handsome woman, had nevertheless, in her youth, a peculiarly neat figure, and a vivacity of manner which obtained her many suitors. Among others, a young gentleman of good family, of the name of Storr, paid his addresses. My father was the object of my

mother's choice, though her relations rather wished her to form
a matrimonial alliance with Mr S. The conflict between affection
and duty was at length decided in favour of my father, and the
rejected lover set out in despair for Bristol. From thence, in a
few days after his arrival, he took his passage in a merchantman
for a distant part of the globe; and from that hour no intelligence
ever arrived of his fate or fortune. I have often heard my mother
speak of this gentleman with regret and sorrow.

My mother was between twenty and thirty years of age at the
period of her marriage. The ceremony was performed at Dun-
yatt, in the county of Somerset. My father was shortly after
settled at Bristol, and during the second year after their union a
son was born to bless and honour them.

Three years after my mother gave birth to a daughter, named
Elizabeth, who died of the small-pox at the age of two years and
ten months. In the second winter following this event, which
deeply afflicted the most affectionate of parents, I was born. She
had afterwards two sons: William, who died at the age of six
years; and George, who is now a respectable merchant at
Leghorn, in Tuscany.

All the offspring of my parents were, in their infancy, uncom-
monly handsome, excepting myself. The boys were fair and
lusty, with auburn hair, light blue eyes, and countenances
peculiarly animated and lovely. I was swarthy; my eyes were
singularly large in proportion to my face, which was small and
round, exhibiting features peculiarly marked with the most
pensive and melancholy cast.

The great difference betwixt my brothers and myself, in point
of personal beauty, tended much to endear me to my parents,
particularly to my father, whom I strongly resembled. The early
propensities of my life were tinctured with romantic and singular
characteristics; some of which I shall here mention, as proofs
that the mind is never to be diverted from its original bent, and
that every event of my life has more or less been marked by the
progressive evils of a too acute sensibility.

The nursery in which I passed my hours of infancy was so
near the great aisle of the minster, that the organ, which re-
echoed its deep tones, accompanied by the chaunting of the
choristers, was distinctly heard both at morning and evening
service. I remember with what pleasure I used to listen, and how
much I was delighted whenever I was permitted to sit on the

winding steps which led from the aisle to the cloisters. I can at this moment recall to memory the sensations I then experienced – the tones that seemed to thrill through my heart, the longing which I felt to unite my feeble voice to the full anthem, and the awful though sublime impression which the church service never failed to make upon my feelings. While my brothers were playing on the green before the minster, the servant who attended us has often, by my earnest entreaties, suffered me to remain beneath the great eagle which stood in the centre of the aisle, to support the book from which the clergyman read the lessons of the day; and nothing could keep me away, even in the coldest seasons, but the stern looks of an old man, whom I named Black John from the colour of his beard and complexion, and whose occupations within the sacred precincts were those of a bell-ringer and sexton.

As soon as I had learned to read my great delight was that of learning epitaphs and monumental inscriptions. A story of melancholy import never failed to excite my attention; and before I was seven years old I could correctly repeat Pope's Lines to the Memory of an Unfortunate Lady;* Mason's Elegy on the Death of the beautiful Countess of Coventry,* and many smaller poems on similar subjects. I had then been attended two years by various masters. Mr Edmund Broadrip taught me music, my father having presented me with one of Kirkman's finest harpsichords, as an encitement to emulation. Even there my natural bent of mind evinced itself. The only melody which pleased me was that of the mournful and touching kind. Two of my earliest favourites were the celebrated ballad by Gay,* beginning, ''Twas when the sea was roaring,' and the simple pathetic stanzas of 'The Heavy Hours,' by the poet Lord Lyttelton.* These, though nature had given me but little voice, I could at seven years of age sing so pathetically that my mother, to the latest hour of her life, never could bear to hear the latter of them repeated. They reminded her of sorrows in which I have since painfully learned to sympathize.

The early hours of boarding-school study I passed under the tuition of the Misses More, sisters to the lady of that name whose talents have been so often celebrated.* The education of their young pupils was undertaken by the five sisters. 'In my mind's eye' I see them now before me; while every circumstance of those early days is minutely and indelibly impressed upon my memory.

I remember the first time I ever was present at a dramatic representation: it was the benefit of that great actor* who was proceeding rapidly towards the highest paths of fame, when death dropped the oblivious curtain, and closed the scene for ever. The part which he performed was King Lear; his wife, afterwards Mrs Fisher, played Cordelia, but not with sufficient *éclat* to render the profession an object for her future exertions. The whole school attended; Mr Powel's two daughters being then pupils of the Misses More. Mrs John Kemble, then Miss P. Hopkins, was also one of my school-fellows, as was the daughter of Mrs Palmer, formerly Miss Pritchard, and afterwards Mrs Lloyd. I mention these circumstances merely to prove that memory does not deceive me. [. . .]

I was not then quite ten years old, though so tall and formed in my person that I might have passed for twelve or thirteen. My brother George was a few years younger. On our arrival in London we repaired to my father's lodgings in Spring Gardens. He received us, after three years' absence, with a mixture of pain and pleasure; he embraced us with tears, and his voice was scarcely articulate. My mother's agitation was indescribable; she received a cold embrace at their meeting – it was the last she ever received from her alienated husband.

As soon as the first conflicts seemed to subside, my father informed my mother that he was determined to place my brother and myself at a school in the vicinity of London; that he purposed very shortly returning to America, and that he would readily pay for my mother's board in any private and respectable family. This information seemed like a death-blow to their domestic hopes. A freezing, formal, premeditated separation from a wife who was guiltless of any crime, who was as innocent as an angel, seemed the very extent of decided misery.

It was in vain that my mother essayed to change his resolution, and influence his heart in pronouncing a milder judgment; my father was held by a fatal fascination; he was the slave of a young and artful woman, who had availed herself of his American solitude, to undermine his affections for his wife and the felicity of his family.

This deviation from domestic faith was the only dark shade that marked my father's character. He possessed a soul brave, liberal, enlightened and ingenuous. He felt the impropriety of his conduct. Yet, though his mind was strongly organized, though his understanding was capacious, and his sense of honour delicate even to fastidiousness, he was still the dupe of his passions, the victim of an unfortunate attachment.

Within a few days of our arrival in London we were placed for education in a school at Chelsea. The mistress of this seminary was perhaps one of the most extraordinary women that ever graced, or disgraced, society; her name was Meribah Lorrington. She was the most extensively accomplished female that I ever remember to have met with; her mental powers were no less capable of cultivation than superiorly cultivated. Her father, whose name was Hull, had from her infancy been the master of an academy at Earl's Court, near Fulham; and early after his marriage losing his wife, he resolved on giving this daughter a masculine education. Meribah was early instructed in all the modern accomplishments, as well as in classical knowledge. She was mistress of the Latin, French, and Italian languages; she was said to be a perfect arithmetician and astronomer, and possessed the art of painting on silk to a degree of exquisite perfection. But, alas! with all these advantages she was addicted to one vice, which at times so completely absorbed her faculties as to deprive her of every power, either mental or corporeal. Thus, daily and hourly, her superior acquirements, her enlightened understanding, yielded to the intemperance of her ruling infatuation, and every power of reflection seemed lost in the unfeminine propensity.

All that I ever learned I acquired from this extraordinary woman. In those hours when her senses were not intoxicated, she would delight in the task of instructing me. She had only five or six pupils, and it was my lot to be her particular favourite. She always, out of school, called me her little friend, and made no scruple of conversing with me (sometimes half the night, for I slept in her chamber), on domestic and confidential affairs. I felt for her a very sincere affection, and I listened with peculiar attention to all the lessons she inculcated. Once I recollect her mentioning the particular failing which disgraced so intelligent a being. She pleaded, in excuse of it, the immitigable regret of a widowed heart, and with compunction declared that she flew to intoxication as the only refuge from the pang of prevailing sorrow. I continued more than twelve months under the care of Mrs Lorrington, during which period my mother boarded in a clergyman's family at Chelsea. I applied rigidly to study, and acquired a taste for books, which has never, from that time, deserted me. Mrs Lorrington frequently read to me after school hours, and I to her. I sometimes indulged my fancy in writing verses, or composing rebuses, and my governess never failed to applaud the juvenile compositions I presented to her. Some of them, which I preserved and printed in a small volume shortly after my marriage, were written when I was between twelve and thirteen years of age; but as love was the theme of my poetical phantasies, I never showed them to my mother till I was about to publish them.

It was my custom, every Sunday evening, to drink tea with my mother. During one of those visits a captain in the British navy, a friend of my father's, became so partial to my person and manners that a proposal of marriage shortly after followed. My mother was astonished when she heard it, and, as soon as she recovered from her surprise, inquired of my suitor how old he thought me; his reply was, 'About sixteen.' My mother smiled, and informed him that I was then not quite thirteen. He appeared to be sceptical on the subject, till he was again assured of the fact, when he took his leave with evident chagrin, but not without expressing his hopes that, on his return to England – for he was going on a two years' expedition – I should be still disengaged. His ship foundered at sea a few months after, and this amiable gallant officer perished.

I had remained a year and two months with Mrs Lorrington, when pecuniary derangements obliged her to give up her school. Her father's manners were singularly disgusting, as was his appearance; for he wore a silvery beard which reached to his breast; and a kind of Persian robe which gave him the external appearance of a necromancer. He was of the Anabaptist persuasion, and so stern in his conversation that the young pupils were exposed to perpetual terror. Added to these circumstances, the failing of his daughter became so evident, that even during school hours she was frequently in a state of confirmed intoxication. These events conspired to break up the establishment, and I was shortly after removed to a boarding-school at Battersea.

The mistress of this seminary, Mrs Leigh, was a lively, sensible, and accomplished woman; her daughter was only a few years older than myself, and extremely amiable as well as lovely. Here I might have been happy, but my father's remissness in sending pecuniary supplies, and my mother's dread of pecuniary inconvenience, induced her to remove me; my brother, nevertheless, still remained under the care of the Reverend Mr Gore, at Chelsea. [. . .]

1801

FANNY BURNEY

FANNY [FRANCES] BURNEY (afterwards Mme d'Arblay) (1752–1840) published her first novel, *Evelina* (1777), when she was twenty-five. Her father, Dr Charles Burney, a musician, teacher, and historian of music, introduced her to his literary circle which included Dr Johnson and Hester Thrale. Fanny Burney then turned her talents, which she honed throughout her life by writing letters and a diary, to satiric comedy, but her satire, *The Witlings*, was virtually suppressed by her father and Fanny's friend, Samuel Crisp, who were afraid that the subjects of her satire would recognize themselves in her play. Fanny Burney wrote another novel, *Cecilia* (1782), which was well received. But her father then induced Fanny to take up the position of Second Keeper of the Robes for the Queen, which Fanny kept up for five years. She also wrote three blank verse dramas, only one of which was produced. But this employment, although secure, thwarted her literary inclinations, and she became ill. She sought her release from this permanent post, and, when she left, was awarded a pension of £100 per annum. In 1793, at the age of 42, she married General Alexandre d'Arblay, a French emigré, and with him and their son, Alexander, lived in France from 1802 to 1812. She wrote two more novels, *Camilla* (1796) and *The Wanderer* (1814) and three further unpublished comedies. Her *Memoirs of Dr Burney* (1832) were not well received, but her voluminous diaries give lively detailed accounts of her experiences, such as her observation of the aftermath of the Battle of Waterloo (1815). The texts come from *Diary and Letters of Mme d'Arblay* (1842–6), vol. 3, pp. 173–8, and vol. 6, pp. 276–86. Biographical information comes from Maggie Lane's *Literary Daughters* (1989), pp. 25–50.

FROM *DIARY AND LETTERS*

1802

Paris, 15 April 1802

'The book-keeper came to me eagerly, crying *"vite, vite, Madame, prenez votre place dans la diligence, car voici un Monsieur Anglais, qui surement va prendre la meilleure!" – en effet*,'* ce Monsieur Anglais did not disappoint his expectations, or much raise mine; for he not only took the best place, but contrived to ameliorate it by the little scruple with which he made every other worse, from the unbridled expansion in which he indulged his dear person, by putting out his elbows against his next, and his knees and feet against his opposite neighbour. He seemed prepared to look upon all around him with a sort of sulky haughtiness, pompously announcing himself as a commander of distinction who had long served at Gibraltar and various places, who had travelled thence through France, and from France to Italy, who was a native of Scotland, and of proud, though unnamed genealogy; and was now going to Paris purposely to behold the First Consul, to whom he meant to claim an introduction through Mr Jackson. His burnt complexion, Scotch accent, large bony face and figure, and high and distant demeanour, made me easily conceive and believe him a highland chief. I never heard his name, but I think him a gentleman born, though not gently bred.

The next to mention is a Madame *Raymond* or *Grammont*, for I heard not distinctly which, who seemed very much a gentlewoman, and who was returning to France, too uncertain of the state of her affairs to know whether she might rest there or not. She had only one defect to prevent my taking much interest in her; this was, not merely an avoidance, but a horror of being touched by either of my children; who, poor little souls, restless and fatigued by the confinement they endured, both tried to fling themselves upon every passenger in turn; and though by every one they were sent back to their sole prop, they were by no one repulsed with such hasty displeasure as by this old lady, who seemed as fearful of having the petticoat of her gown, which was stiff, round, and bulging, as if lined with parchment, deranged, as if she had been attired in a hoop for Court.

The third person was a Madame Blaizeau, who seemed an exceeding good sort of a woman, gay, voluble, good humoured, and merry. All we had of amusement sprung from her sallies, which were uttered less from a desire of pleasing others, her very natural character having none of the high polish bestowed by the Graces, than from a jovial spirit of enjoyment which made them produce pleasure to herself. She soon and frankly acquainted us she had left France to be a governess to some young ladies before the Revolution, and under the patronage, as I think, of the Duke of Dorset; she had *been courted*, she told us, by an English gentleman farmer, but he would not change his religion for her, nor she for him, and so, when every thing was bought for her wedding, they broke off the connexion; and she afterwards married a Frenchman. She had seen a portrait, set richly in diamonds, of the King, prepared for a present to the First Consul; and described its superb ornaments and magnificence, in a way to leave no doubt of the fact. She meant to stop at *St Denys*, to enquire if her mother yet lived, having received no intelligence from or of her, these last ten eventful years!

At Canterbury, while the horses were changed, my little ones and I went to the cathedral; but dared merely seize sufficient time to view the outside and enter the principal aisle. I was glad even of that much, as its antique grandeur gave me a pleasure which I always love to cherish in the view of fine old cathedrals, those most permanent monuments of what our ancestors thought reverence to God, as manifested in munificence to the place dedicated to his worship.

At Dover we had a kind of dinner-supper in one, and my little boy and girl and I retired immediately after it, took some tea in our chamber, and went to rest.

Friday, 16 April
As we were not to sail till twelve, I had hoped to have seen the Castle and Shakspeare's Cliff,* but most unfortunately it rained all the morning, and we were confined to the inn, except for the interlude of the custom-house, where, however, the examination was so slight, and made with such civility, that we had no other trouble with it than a wet walk and a few shillings.

Our passports were examined; and we then went to the port,

and, the sea being perfectly smooth, were lifted from the quay
to the deck of our vessel with as little difficulty as we could have
descended from a common chair to the ground.

The calm which caused our slow passage and our sickness,
was now favourable, for it took us into the port of Calais so
close and even with the quay, that we scarcely accepted even a
hand to aid us from the vessel to the shore.

The quay was lined with crowds of people, men, women, and
children, and certain amphibious females, who might have
passed for either sex, or anything else in the world, except what
they really were, European women! Their men's hats, men's
jackets, and men's shoes; their burnt skins, and most savage-
looking petticoats, hardly reaching, nay, not reaching their
knees, would have made me instantly believe any account I
could have heard of their being just imported from the wilds of
America.

The vessel was presently filled with men, who, though dirty
and mean, were so civil and gentle, that they could not displease,
and who entered it so softly and quietly, that, neither hearing
nor seeing their approach, it seemed as if they had availed
themselves of some secret trap-doors through which they had
mounted to fill the ship, without sound or bustle, in a single
moment. When we were quitting it, however, this tranquillity as
abruptly finished, for in an instant a part of them rushed round
me, one demanding to carry Alex., another Adrienne, another
seizing my écritoire, another my arm, and some one, I fear, my
parasol, as I have never been able to find it since.

We were informed we must not leave the ship till Monsieur le
Commissaire arrived to carry us, I think, to the municipality of
Calais to show our passports. Monsieur le Commissaire, in
white with some red trappings, soon arrived, civilly hastening
himself quite out of breath to save us from waiting. We then
mounted the quay, and I followed the rest of the passengers,
who all followed the commissary, accompanied by two men
carrying the two children, and two more carrying, one my
écritoire, and the other insisting on conducting its owner. The
quantity of people that surrounded and walked with us, sur-
prised me; and their decency, their silence, their quietness
astonished me. To fear them was impossible, even in entering
France with all the formed fears hanging upon its recent though
past horrors.

But on coming to the municipality, I was, I own, extremely ill at ease, when upon our gouvernante's desiring me to give the commissary my passport, as the rest of the passengers had done, and my answering it was in my écritoire, she exclaimed, '*Vite! vite! cherchez-le, ou vous serez arrêtée!*'* You may be sure I was quick enough! – or at least tried to be so, for my fingers presently trembled, and I could hardly put in the key.

In the hall to which we now repaired, our passports were taken and deposited, and we had new ones drawn up and given us in their stead. On quitting this place we were accosted by a new crowd, all however as gentle, though not as silent, as our first friends, who recommended various hotels to us, one begging we would go to Grandsire, another to Duroc, another to Meurice – and this last prevailed with the gouvernante, whom I regularly followed, not from preference, but from the singular horror my otherwise worthy and well-bred old lady manifested, when, by being approached by the children, her full round coats risked the danger of being modernized into the flimsy, falling drapery of the present day.

At Meurice's our goods were entered, and we heard that they would be examined at the custom-house in the afternoon. We breakfasted, and the crowd of fees which were claimed by the captain, steward, sailors, carriers, and heaven knows who besides, are inconceivable. I gave whatever they asked, from ignorance of what was due, and from fear of offending those of whose extent still less of whose use of power I could form no judgment. I was the only one in this predicament; the rest refusing or disputing every demand. They all, but us, went out to walk; but I stayed to write to my dearest father, to Mrs Lock, and my expecting mate.

We were all three too much awake by the new scene to try for any repose, and the hotel windows sufficed for our amusement till dinner; and imagine, my dearest sir, how my repast was seasoned, when I tell you that, as soon as it began, a band of music came to the window and struck up '*God save the King*'. I can never tell you what a pleased emotion was excited in my breast by this sound on a shore so lately hostile, and on which I have so many, so heartfelt motives for wishing peace and amity perpetual!

This over, we ventured out of the hotel to look at the street. The day was fine, the street was clean, two or three people who passed us, made way for the children as they skipped out of my hands, and I saw such an unexpected appearance of quiet, order, and civility, that, almost without knowing it, we strolled from the gate, and presently found ourselves in the market-place, which was completely full of sellers, and buyers, and booths, looking like a large English fair.

The queer, gaudy jackets, always of a different colour from the petticoats of the women, and their immense wing-caps, which seemed made to double over their noses, but which all flew back so as to discover their ears, in which I regularly saw large and generally drop gold ear-rings, were quite as diverting to myself as to Alex. and Adrienne. Many of them, also, had gold necklaces, chains, and crosses; but ear-rings all: even the maids who were scrubbing or sweeping, ragged wretches carrying burdens on their heads or shoulders, old women selling fruit or other eatables, gypsey-looking creatures with children tied to their backs – all wore these long, broad, large, shining ear-rings.

Beggars we saw not – no, not one, all the time we stayed or sauntered; and for civility and gentleness, the poorest and most ordinary persons we met or passed might be compared with the best dressed and best looking walkers in the streets of our metropolis, and still to the disadvantage of the latter. I cannot say how much this surprised me, as I had conceived an horrific idea of the populace of this country, imagining them all transformed into bloody monsters.

Another astonishment I experienced equally pleasing, though not equally important to my ease; I saw innumerable pretty women and lovely children, almost all of them extremely fair. I had been taught to expect nothing but mahogany complexions and hideous features instantly on crossing the strait of Dover. When this, however, was mentioned in our party afterwards, the Highlander exclaimed, 'But Calais was in the hands of the English so many years, that the English race there is not yet extinct.'

The perfect security in which I now saw we might wander about, induced us to walk over the whole town, and even extend our excursions to the ramparts surrounding it. It is now a very clean and pretty town, and so orderly that there was no more tumult or even noise in the market-place, where the people were so close together as to form a continual crowd, than in the bye-streets leading to the country, where scarcely a passenger was to

be seen. This is certainly a remark which, I believe, could never
be made in England.

When we returned to the hotel, I found all my fellow-travellers
had been to the custom-house! I had quite forgotten, or rather
neglected to enquire the hour for this formality, and was
beginning to alarm myself lest I was out of rule, when a young
man, a commissary, I heard, of the hotel, came to me and asked
if I had anything contraband to the laws of the Republic. I
answered as I had done before. 'Mais, Madame, avez-vous
quelque chose de neuf?' 'Oui, Monsieur.' – 'Quelques jupons?'
'Beaucoup, Monsieur.' – 'Quelques bas de coton?' 'Plusieurs,
Monsieur.' – 'Eh bien! Madame, tout cela sera saisi.' – 'Mais,
Monsieur! quand ce n'est pas du tout pour vendre, seulement
pour porter?' 'C'est égal, Madame, tout ça sera saisi.' – 'Eh!
mais que faut-il donc faire?' 'Il faut, Madame, payer généreuse-
ment; et si vous êtes bien sûre qu'il n'y a rien à vendre, alors
peut-être – '*

I entreated him to take charge himself as to what was *right*
and *generous*, and he readily undertook to go through the
ceremony for me without my appearing. I was so much fright-
ened, and so happy not to be called upon personally, that I
thought myself very cheaply off in his after-demand of a guinea
and a half. I had two and a half to pay afterwards for additional
luggage.

We found reigning through Calais a general joy and satisfac-
tion at the restoration of *Dimanche* and abolition of *Décade*.* I
had a good deal of conversation with the maid of the inn, a tall,
fair, extremely pretty woman, and she talked much upon this
subject, and the delight it occasioned, and the obligation all
France was under to the Premier Consul for restoring religion
and worship.

Sunday, 18 April
We set off for Paris at five o'clock in the morning. The country
broad, flat, or barrenly steep – without trees, without buildings,
and scarcely inhabited – exhibited a change from the fertile
fields, and beautiful woods and gardens, and civilization of
Kent, so sudden and unpleasant that I only lamented the fatigue
of my position, which regularly impeded my making use of this
chasm of pleasure and observation for repose. This part of
France must certainly be the least frequented, for we rarely met

a single carriage, and the villages, few and distant, seemed to
have no intercourse with each other. *Dimanche*, indeed, might
occasion this stiffness, for we saw, at almost all the villages, neat
and clean peasants going to or coming from mass, and seeming
indescribably elated and happy by the public permission of
divine worship on its originally appointed day.

I was struck with the change in Madame Raymond, who
joined us in the morning from another hotel. Her hoop was no
more visible; her petticoats were as lank, or more so, than her
neighbours'; and her distancing the children was not only at an
end but she prevented me from renewing any of my cautions to
them, of not incommoding her; and when we were together a
few moments, before we were joined by the rest, she told me,
with a significant smile, not to tutor the children about her any
more, as she only avoided them from having something of
consequence to take care of, which was removed. I then saw she
meant some English lace or muslin, which she had carried in a
petticoat, and, since the Custom-house examination was over,
had now packed in her trunk.

Poor lady! I fear this little merchandise was all her hope of
succour on her arrival! She is amongst the emigrants who have
twice or thrice returned, but not yet been able to rest in their
own country.

What most in the course of this journey struck me, was the
satisfaction of all the country people, with whom I could
converse, at the restoration of the *Dimanche*; and the boasts
they now ventured to make of having never kept the *Décade*,
except during the dreadful reign of Robespierre,* when not to
oppose any of his severest decrees was insufficient for safety, it
was essential even to existence to observe them with every
parade of the warmest approval.

The horrible stories from every one of that period of wanton
as well as political cruelty, I must have judged exaggerated,
either through the mist of fear or the heats of resentment, but
that, though the details had innumerable modifications, there
was but one voice for the excess of barbarity.

At a little hamlet near Clermont, where we rested some time,
two good old women told us that this was the happiest day
('twas Sunday) of their lives; that they had lost *le bon Dieu* for
these last ten years, but that Bonaparte had now found him! In
another cottage we were told the villagers had kept their own

Curé all this time concealed, and though privately and with fright, they had thereby saved their souls through the whole of the bad times! And in another, some poor creatures said they were now content with their destiny, be it what it might, since they should be happy, at least, in the world to come; but that while denied going to mass, they had all their sufferings aggravated by knowing that they must lose their souls hereafter, besides all that they had to endure here!

O my dearest father! that there can have existed wretches of such diabolical wickedness as to have snatched, torn, from the toiling indigent every ray even of future hope! Various of these little conversations extremely touched me; nor was I unmoved, though not with such painful emotion, on the sight of the Sunday night dance, in a little village through which we passed, where there seemed two or three hundred peasants engaged in that pastime; all clean and very gaily dressed, yet all so decent and well behaved, that, but for the poor old fiddlers, we might have driven on, and not have perceived the rustic ball.

Here ends the account of my journey, and if it has amused my dearest father, it will be a true delight to me to have scribbled it. My next letter brings me to the capital, and to the only person who can console me for my always lamented absence from himself.

Witness, F. D'ARBLAY

1815

It is not near the scene of battle that war, even with victory, wears an aspect of felicity – no, not even in the midst of its highest resplendence of glory. A more terrific or afflicting sojourn than that of Brussels at this period can hardly be imagined.* The universal voice declared that so sanguinary a battle as that which was fought almost in its neighbourhood, and quite within its hearing, never yet had spread the plains with slaughter; and though exultation cannot ever have been prouder, nor satisfaction more complete, in the brilliancy of success, all my senses were shocked in viewing the effects of its attainment. For more than a week from this time I never approached my window but to witness sights of wretchedness. Maimed, wounded, bleeding, mutilated, tortured victims of this exterminating contest passed by every minute: the fainting, the sick, the dying, and the dead, on brancards, in carts, in waggons, succeeded one another without intermission. There seemed to be a whole and a large army of disabled or lifeless soldiers! All that was intermingled with them bore an aspect of still more poignant horror; for the Bonapartian prisoners, who were now poured into the city by hundreds, had a mien of such ferocious desperation, where they were marched on, uninjured, from having been taken by surprise or overpowered by numbers; or faces of such anguish, where they were drawn on in open vehicles, the helpless victims of gushing wounds or horrible dislocations, that to see them without commiseration for their sufferings, or admiration for the heroic, however misled enthusiasm, to which they were martyrs, must have demanded an apathy dead to all feeling but what is personal, or a rancour too ungenerous to yield even to the view of defeat. Both the one set and the other of these unhappy warriors endured their calamities with haughty forbearance of complaint. The maimed and lacerated, while their ghastly visages spoke torture and death, bit their own clothes, perhaps their flesh! to save the loud utterance of their groans; while those of their comrades who had escaped these corporeal inflictions seemed to be smitten with something between remorse and madness that they had not forced themselves on to destruction ere thus they were exhibited in dreadful parade through the streets of that city they had been sent forth to conquer. Others of these wretched prisoners had, to me, as I first saw them, the air of the lowest and most disgusting of Jacobins,* in dirty tattered vestments of all sorts and colours, or soiled carters' frocks; but disgust was soon turned to pity, when I afterwards learnt that these shabby accoutrements had been cast over them by their conquerors after despoiling them of their own.

Everybody was wandering from home; all Brussels seemed living in the streets. The danger to the city, which had imprisoned all its inhabitants except the rabble or the military, once completely passed, the pride of feeling and showing their freedom seemed to stimulate their curiosity in seeking details on what had passed and was passing. But neither the pride nor the joy of victory was anywhere of an exulting nature. London and Paris render all other places that I, at least, have dwelt in, tame and insipid. Bulletins in a few shop-windows alone announced to the general public that the Allies had vanquished and that Bonaparte was a fugitive.

I met at the Embassade an old English officer who gave me most interesting and curious information, assuring me that in the carriage of Bonaparte, which had been seized, there were proclamations ready printed, and even dated from the palace of Lachen, announcing the downfall of the Allies and the triumph of Bonaparte!

But no satisfaction could make me hear without deadly dismay and shuddering his description of the field of battle. Piles of dead! – Heaps, masses, hills of dead bestrewed the plains!

I met also Colonel Jones; so exulting in success! so eager to remind me of his assurances that all was safe!

And I was much interested in a narration made to me by a wounded soldier, who was seated in the courtyard of the Embassade. He had been taken prisoner after he was severely wounded, on the morning of the 18th, and forced into a wood with many others, where he had been very roughly used, and stripped of his coat, waistcoat, and even his shoes; but as the fortune of the day began to turn, there was no one left to watch him, and he crawled on all-fours till he got out of the wood, and was found by some of his roving comrades.

The most common adventure of this sort, when heard at the moment of action, and from the principal in what is narrated, has an interest.

Thousands, I believe I may say without exaggeration, were employed voluntarily at this time in Brussels in dressing wounds and attending the sick beds of the wounded. Humanity could be carried no further; for not alone the Belgians and English were thus nursed and assisted, nor yet the Allies, but the prisoners also; and this, notwithstanding the greatest apprehensions being prevalent that the sufferers, from their multitude, would bring pestilence into the heart of the city.

The immense quantity of English, Belgians, and Allies, who were first, of course, conveyed to the hospitals and prepared houses of Brussels, required so much time for carriage and placing, that although the carts, waggons, and every attainable or seizeable vehicle were unremittingly in motion – now coming, now returning to the field of battle for more, – it was nearly a week, or at least five or six days, ere the unhappy wounded prisoners, who were necessarily last served, could be accommodated. And though I was assured that medical and surgical aid was administered to them wherever it was possible, the blood

that dried upon their skins and their garments, joined to the
dreadful sores occasioned by this neglect, produced an effect so
pestiferous, that, at every new entry, eau de Cologne, or vinegar,
was resorted to by every inhabitant, even amongst the shop-
keepers, even amongst the commonest persons, for averting the
menaced contagion.

Even the churches were turned into hospitals, and every house
in Brussels was ordered to receive or find an asylum for some of
the sick.

The Boyds were eminently good in nursing, dressing wounds,
making slops, and administering comfort amongst the maimed,
whether friend or foe. Madame d'Henin sent her servants, and
money, and cordials to all the French that came within her
reach; Madame de la Tour du Pin was munificent in the same
attentions; and Madame de Maurville never passed by an
opportunity of doing good. M. de Beaufort, being far the richest
of my friends at this place, was not spared; he had officers and
others quartered upon him without mercy.

We were all at work more or less in making lint. For me, I
was about amongst the wounded half the day, the *British,
s'entend*! The rising in France for the honour of the nation now,
and for its safety in independence hereafter, was brilliant and
delightful, spreading in some directions from La Manche to La
Méditerranée: the focus of loyalty was Bordeaux. Le Roi left
Gand the 22nd. [. . .] The noble Blücher* entered France at
Mortes le Château. '*Suivez les vite,*' he cried, '*mes enfants! ou
demain nous les aurons encore sur les bras!*'* *On dit* that the
Duke of Wellington* avowed he more than once thought the
battle lost! The efforts made by Bonaparte were stupendous,
and his Imperial Guards fought with a *dévouement*, an enthusi-
asm, that showed they thought victory and their leader must be
one. It was not till six o'clock that the Duke felt his real
advantage. He was everywhere in the field, and ran the most
terrible risks, for which he is equally blamed and admired: but
the stake was so prodigious! the victory or defeat so big with
enormous consequences!

Meanwhile, to put a stop as much as possible to the alarming
putrid exhalations, three thousand peasants were employed all
at once in burying the heaps of dead on the plains!

This, at least, was the current account at Brussels. [. . .]

JANE TAYLOR

JANE TAYLOR (1783-1824) was an engraver and writer who wrote essays, a novel, *Display* (1815), and poetry mainly for young people and children. She often collaborated with her sister, Ann (later Mrs Gilbert) in the writing of poems for children. Some of Jane and Ann Taylor's poems, such as 'Twinkle, twinkle, little star', became popular nursery rhymes. Jane Taylor's satires for young adults – *Essays in Rhyme on Morals and Manners* (1816) – are sometimes overly didactic, but, as in 'Recreation', are occasionally humorous. This poem might be read in conjunction with Jane Taylor's 'The Troublesome Friend' and its parallel letter of response, which she published under the pseudonym of 'Q.Q.' in *Youth's Magazine*. She contributed a variety of essays and letters to this weekly between 1816 and 1822, using at times a comic style with a Christian didactic aim. Jane and Ann Taylor's joint publications for children include *Original Poems for Infant Minds* (1804–5), *Rhymes for the Nursery* (1806), *Limed Twigs to Catch Young Birds* (1808), *Signor Topsy-Turvy's Wonderful Magic Lantern* (1808), *Hymns for Infant Minds* (1810), *Original Hymns for Sunday School* (1812), and *The Linnet's Life* (1822). Prose extracts are taken from *The Contributions of QQ to a Periodical Work*, ed. Isaac Taylor (1823), pp. 156–63, 263–70; and *Memoirs and Poetical Remains of the Late Jane Taylor: with Extracts from her Correspondence*, ed. Isaac Taylor, 2nd edn, vol. 2, pp. 141–5. Biographical information comes from D. M. Armitage, *The Taylors of Ongar* (1939) and Jane Taylor's *Prose and Poetry*, introd. F. V. Barry (1925).

FROM *LETTER TO MISS S.L.C.*

Colchester, 20 December 1805

Mr dear L,

If four or five years ago you had suffered so long a chasm to be made in our correspondence, I should doubtless have indulged in some such painful soliloquy as you have prepared for me: or perhaps in a yet more touching and plaintive strain. But now, enjoying all the sober nationality of mature age – now, having happily past that wild and fanciful season, by some denominated the '*silly age*' – or, at least, being a degree or two more rational than I was then, I feel far more disposed to attribute the long intervals to which every correspondence is liable, to some of those thousand nameless hindrances which every day presents, and to that inconvenient spirit of procrastination of which most of us more or less partake, than to declining affection, to fickleness, or to affront. Perhaps it may have occurred to you in the course of this long period, which I fear has nearly put you out of breath, that I have been speaking one word for you, and two for myself: – it would be very unfair for you to suppose so; but even should your supposition be just, you will allow that to afford another person one third of a good thing, that might have been all one's own, is no mean proportion. But now it will be making a poor return for all this generosity if you should become more than ever remiss in your communications; and then make yourself easy by thinking that Jane will only impute it to 'some nameless hindrance, or an inconvenient spirit of procrastination.'

But now for your grave and appropriate question, namely – 'What do you think of this famous victory?'* — To which, after due consideration, I reply – Why pray what do *you* think of it? for I make little doubt that we have thought much alike on the subject. Should you however question this, and suppose that my humbler ideas have not stretched to the same height as yours, I will convince you of the contrary, by endeavouring to recall some of the reflections that were inspired by this 'famous victory'. And first, I thought that – it was a very 'famous victory'; did not you? – and besides this, and much more, I thought a great many things that the newspapers had very

obligingly thought, ready for me. Well but to speak in a graver
strain; and if you are disposed to hear what I have really thought
about our late glorious victories; – why read on: –

Now, impressed with the idea that my private opinion could
in no way affect the public weal, I have allowed myself to form
one, without restraint; well knowing that I might vainly endeav-
our to pluck one leaf from the hero's laurel, even if I were
disposed to do so, which I assure you I am not. For every one
who performs his part with zeal and success, claims respect: –
and who can deny that Nelson has nobly performed his? But tell
me is the character of the warrior in itself to be admired? or
rather, can it be loved? From what motives does a man at first
devote himself to the trade of war? Do you not think it is more
often from a desire of glory, than from patriotism? And now,
though I have often endeavoured to discover what there is either
amiable or generous in the love of *glory*, I have never yet been
able to discern it. I cannot tell how or why it is a less selfish
principle than the love of riches. Is not he in reality the truest
patriot who fills up his station in private life well – he who loves
and promotes peace, both public and private, who knowing that
his country's prosperity depends much more on its *virtue*, than
its arms, resolves that his individual endeavours shall not be
wanting to promote this desirable end? And is not he the
greatest hero who is able to despise public honours for the sake
of private usefulness – he who has learned to subdue his own
inclinations, to deny himself every gratification inconsistent with
virtue and piety, who has conquered his passions, and subdued
his own spirit? surely he is 'greater than he that taketh a city' –
or a squadron. If the great men of the earth did but act on these
principles, our heroes would be sadly at a loss for want to
employment; I fear they would be obliged to turn to making
plough-shares and pruning hooks.

Now perhaps you will call me an ungrateful creature; but
really I think I am not so. Though, certainly, I have not joined
without some secret misgivings of heart in the unqualified
plaudits that have sounded from all quarters. If so many brave
men *must* be sacrificed, I heartily rejoice that the dear bought
victory was ours. But how is it possible, while we regard them
not merely as the machines of war, but as immortal beings, to
rejoice without sorrow and dismay in the result of the
rencontre? . . .

THE TROUBLESOME FRIEND *

Editor,
Youth's Magazine

Sir,

In the hope that some of your correspondents may offer a few remarks on the subject on which I am about to address you, I have been induced to lay before you certain grievances under which I have long privately groaned: and as it is possible that others besides myself may have similar things to complain of, you may, by the insertion of my letter, be rendering a public service while conferring a private obligation.

You must know that the house adjoining my Father's is occupied by a family with whom we are on terms of intimacy. The eldest daughter especially, being a girl of my own age, I have always considered as a particular friend; and notwithstanding the complaints I am about to lay before you, I really feel a sincere regard for her; although I will not deny that the warm affection which I at first entertained is greatly damped by the continual vexations to which her conduct exposes me. In short, Sir, she is one of those good sort of people whose misfortune it is to be *very* soon affronted.

Now it is needless to state how many occasions will perpetually occur, between such near neighbours, of taking offence where there is a disposition to do so; – and that, notwithstanding the most sincere and diligent efforts on one part to avoid them. Being myself one of a large family, my time is very much occupied by domestic affairs; besides by attention to those pursuits which are necessary to the completion of my education. Now it unfortunately happens that our neighbour, although in circumstances apparently similar to my own, has, or makes a much larger portion of leisure than I can command; and hence arises one of the principal sources of uneasiness between us. She is so much *hurt*, as her phrase is, that I am not ready and willing at all times of the day *to step in*, or to have a gossip over the garden wall. Now, although no one can enjoy the pleasures of society more than I do at proper seasons, yet I must say it is no enjoyment to me to have the regular and agreeable routine of my daily avocations liable to perpetual interruption. It is however on this account that my troublesome friend is perpetu-

reproaching me with being – 'a bad neighbour' – 'unsociable' – 'proud'; and with being indifferent to her society.

I do assure you that I cannot pace up and down our garden walk with a book in my hand, but at the hazard of giving offence; for if she should happen to be within sight, and if I should not happen to raise my head to nod to her, and say Good morning, it will take her a week to pardon the neglect. Then, it would surprise you to hear the plausible manner she has of representing her grievances; so that when her complaints have been repeated to me by some *mutual friend*, I have really begun to fancy myself quite in the wrong; and yet upon the coolest reflection I cannot accuse myself of misconduct in this matter.

My friend is wont, with a very resigned, pathetic, and reasonable sort of look and manner to make such complaints as the following. – 'I do feel a little hurt, I must confess; – so much attention as I have shown to her, and so much regard as, I can truly say, I feel for her. Why, I have known her pass our parlour window twenty times in a day, when she knows I have been sitting there, without once giving herself the trouble to turn her head to nod to me; – is not this a little strange, so intimate as we are?'

'Certainly, it is,' says our mutual friend.

'Well, and then she makes an excuse of being so vastly busy: for my part I've no notion of being too busy to speak to a friend; have you?'

'Certainly not.'

'Well, one can never step in there but one seems to be interrupting them: and it is quite a favour to get her to bring her work, and sit an hour with one in the morning: in short, I have done asking her. I don't deny that she is willing to come in and do one a kindness, when it is needed; but I like a friend to be a friend at all times; and in my opinion there's nothing so charming as a sociable disposition; for my own part this is so much *my* temper, that, as I often say, I feel these slights the more: and certainly at times, I cannot help feeling a little hurt.'

In this style, as I have been repeatedly informed, she makes out a case against me. But as I never take any other notice of such charges than by doing all in my power to show her real friendship, we might go on tolerably, if it were not that sometimes, owing to some unforeseen occurrence, or mistake, which it is impossible always to guard against, my friend takes more serious offence: – so much so, at times, that during many weeks she has refused to speak to me. I should be ashamed to call the attention of your readers to the detail of affairs so trifling, if it were not for the sake of illustrating my meaning; with this view I will mention an instance or two of the kind.

The last time that she appeared so much offended, it was in consequence of my having omitted to send her a formal invitation to spend the evening with me. Wishing to see several of my young friends, I had previously consulted with her about the day, and, having fully agreed together when it should be, I sat down to write the notes to my other friends, without its even occurring to me that she would expect any further notice. However, to my great surprise, she did not join our party; and when I sent in to inquire the reason, she returned me only a cold and formal excuse. It was in vain that I endeavoured to recollect any thing I had done or left undone that could have vexed her; and it was not till weeks afterwards that she condescended to explain the cause of her displeasure. Now really, if I had thought of writing her a note of invitation, I should have been in equal danger of giving offence; for then, it is probable she would have accused me of being too ceremonious with her.

I should be more ready to suspect that the blame was on my part, if it were not that others of her acquaintance make the same complaints. We are both of us teachers in our Sunday School; and there is no situation, as you may be aware, in which a quarrelsome or peevish disposition is more likely to show itself. You will not be surprised, therefore, when I say that my poor neighbour is continually taking umbrage with one of her fellow teachers: when any fresh arrangement takes place in the classes, she seldom fails to complain that all the most stupid children are selected for her. Her attendance at the school is not the most regular; yet no one can offer her the kindest remonstrance on this subject, or suggest the smallest improvement in her method of teaching, without the certainty of her being highly offended. If any new plans are projected without consulting her, that is sure to be considered as a personal affront; and if, on the other hand, she is consulted, we are equally sure of her objecting to what is proposed. She is always complaining that she has so little to do with the management of the school: and indeed she is so constantly dissatisfied, that her services are much less acceptable than they would otherwise be: for there is, you know, trouble and difficulty and fatigue enough in a Sunday School, without having our embarrassments increased by disagreements among the teachers.

Having been so long used to the peculiarity of my friend's temper, I was really scarcely aware of the degree of bondage and restraint which is imposed upon me, until lately when she was absent from home on a visit of some months. I cannot adequately describe to you how much I felt at liberty as soon as she was gone. I could now walk in the garden without looking fifty ways to see if she was within sight. I could go out, or come in, read, or write, or take a walk with any other friend, and all with a degree of freedom and comfort unknown heretofore. And the glow of sincere pleasure with which I should otherwise have welcomed her return, was (I do not deny it) damped exceedingly by the recollection of the trouble it would inevitably bring upon me.

Now surely that must be a serious fault in a person's character, which, in spite of many good qualities, renders her company burdensome, and her absence a deliverance: and if any thing could be suggested that might successfully represent the weakness and unreasonableness of such a disposition, it would at once do a real service to all such troublesome friends, and inspire with the warmest gratitude all their troubled acquaintance.

I am, Sir, your obedient servant,
PENELOPE

A LETTER TO WHOMSOEVER IT MAY CONCERN*

Dear Reader,

Happening to glance my eye upon the title of a paper in the last number of the Youth's Magazine, I was induced to put on my spectacles, and give it a reading: and although many of those who contribute to its pages are doubtless better prepared, in most respects, than myself, to reply to it, yet on one account I feel peculiarly qualified to accept the challenge there given: – it is that I myself, for a considerable portion of my life, was one of the society of *troublesome friends*.

I can assign more reasons than one for my having long withdrawn from that society; but must frankly acknowledge that the primary cause was my having few friends left to be troublesome to. This circumstance at once afforded me leisure for reflection and roused me to it: for observing that my society was shunned, first by one, and then by another of my associates, I began to employ many solitary hours in endeavouring to discover the cause; and after various unsuccessful attempts to trace it to the misconduct of others, I was at last compelled to suspect that, after all, the fault might be in myself.

Without troubling you with the long course of experiment and observation by which I was led to this unpleasant conclusion, I shall content myself with stating it to be my settled conviction that, an excessive sensibility to injury – a readiness to take offence on small occasions – a disposition to jealousy, proceed from nothing so much as a tendency to overrate our own worth and consequence. Hence it is that we entertain unreasonable expectations of the attentions due to us from others; and the inevitable disappointment which ensues, mortifies our vanity and self-love, and produces that fretful, complaining, or resentful temper which gives so much trouble to our neighbours, and ten-fold more uneasiness to ourselves.

Persons whose misfortune it is to magnify their own consequence, instead of making a liberal allowance for similar infirmities in their neighbours, expect that every body should regard them in the same disproportionate view, and are first astonished, and then hurt, when they discover how far this is from being the case. She who is always thinking of herself, imagines that others must be always thinking of her; at least she thinks it ought to be so; though of all persons, such a one is the least likely to excite a lively interest in those around her.

Another cause of the disposition in question I discovered to be, in my own case, the want of a sufficient interest in the useful employments of life; which left me at leisure to indulge that idle and gossipping turn of mind from whence mischief of one sort or another is sure to arise. When, as a resource from the painfulness of my reflections, I began to engage more heartily in my pursuits, it was astonishing how much less inclination I felt to watch the motions and arraign the conduct of my neighbours. Being fully occupied myself, I often quite forgot to notice whether they paid me proper attentions or not; and a thousand little things passed unnoticed, at which I should most certainly have taken offence, had I been on the look out for it. I also acquired by this means, a little more charity in judging of the conduct of my neighbours; for it could not but occur to my mind that whereas, while I was busily engaged in my own occupations I had little leisure to think of *them*; so they, for a reason equally good, might sometimes lose a lively recollection *even of me*. That very common admonition – to *mind one's own business*, is really an excellent one; for while an energetic attention to one's own affairs effectually checks an impertinent and mischievous curiosity about the conduct of other people, it by no means prevents a benevolent concern for their welfare, or activity in their service, when they may happen to require it. Thus I found that while I became less and less inclined to break off an interesting employment in order to watch whether one neighbour went by without calling, or whether another paid me some expected attention, I was yet much more willing than heretofore to give up some portion of my time to them when I could do them any good by that means.

There was another consideration which had great efficacy in curing me, if I am cured, of my troublesome propensities; and that was the utter *unavailingness* of my resentments. When I was affronted, and determined to show it, I soon discovered that nobody cared much whether I was pleased or angry. People in general seemed perfectly contented to wait till my anger was over. A few more good tempered ones, who endeavoured to explain and to conciliate, I could see smiled secretly at my infirmity; while the more ill-natured laughed at it without disguise. So that I found I was always the chief sufferer, and the chief loser, by my ill humour. When, from motives of pique, I absented myself from any company, the circumstance, as I have had opportunities enough of discovering, excited no regret; but very often the reverse: so that I began to be thoroughly tired of indulging resentments which punished no one but myself.

As it is common to pass from one extreme to another, so I am suspected by some of having now become too insensible to this sort of injury. Whether that be the case I will not determine; but this I know, that if I err on this side, it is the most peaceful and comfortable fault I ever fell into. In fact it is so difficult a thing to offend me now, that those – if there are any such – who would wish to do so, must I am sure give up the attempt in despair. I am far from being ignorant that I occasionally experience, like other people, little slights and neglects from the carelessness, selfishness, or ill-nature of my neighbours; but as this rarely happens from those whom I love and esteem, I must confess that it gives the smallest possible disturbance to my tranquillity. If any one treats me with rudeness or neglect, I perceive that that person knows not how to behave; and I feel the same sort of compassion and indulgence towards the party that one does on remarking any other species of awkwardness in ill-bred people.

As to my happiness, that is so greatly independent of others – so much regulated by my own conduct and internal tranquillity – that it cannot be moved by such things. It is, indeed, since I have learned the happy art of looking within for entertainment and satisfaction, and depended on my own resources, that I have become so much less troublesome to others than formerly. And it is well for me that this change has taken place; for as I am now growing old, and have nothing to recommend me to the notice of any one, being neither rich, nor witty, nor entertaining; think, I beseech you, what an unhappy and forlorn creature I should be if my happiness still depended upon the flattering attentions of my neighbours. I assure you if that were the case, I should have little enough. And while I am upon this subject I will take the liberty to say, that it does appear to me that much of the dissatisfaction, fretfulness, and uneasiness, visible in persons in the decline of life, especially in those who are solitary, is owing to their not having independence of mind enough to make them indifferent to the neglect which is too often the lot of age. The most obscure and despised individual who thus rises above her circumstances, and finds content within, is far more respectable, and enjoys a much more permanent and sterling species of happiness, than the most admired coquette, or the most richly bedizened dowager, who depends, for the maintenance of her happiness, like the meanest mendicants, on the crumbs of admiration and respect that are thrown to her by the surrounding crowd.

But I perceive that, like other old folks, I have wandered from my subject, and, forgetting that I am writing for the young, have been lecturing the old. However I am well persuaded that the same dispositions that are necessary to respectability and happiness at one period of life, are equally so at another: and she or he who would have a cheerful, peaceful, and respectable old age, must learn in youth to build happiness on a true foundation.

To return to the subject on which I set out, I will just say, that while I am so remarkably backward in taking offence, I hope I am equally reluctant to give it; and should be sincerely sorry if any remarks I have at present made should have such an effect on any of my readers. If however I may have unintentionally *hurt* any one, I humbly hope that they will prove that my advice has not been quite lost upon them, by a generous act of forgiveness towards the unknown offender; and that in future, as often as occasion may require, the same indulgence may be extended towards others: for truly when one comes impartially to consider the degree of uneasiness that the temper of which we have been speaking occasions, I doubt if one should find a very great deal to choose between a troublesome friend, and a troublesome enemy.

I am, my dear reader,
your humble servant, Dorothy

DOROTHY WORDSWORTH

DOROTHY WORDSWORTH (1771–1855) wrote letters, journals and accounts of her travels, and, occasionally, poetry. Susan M. Levin published for the first time all the known extant poems by Dorothy Wordsworth in an Appendix to *Dorothy Wordsworth and Romanticism* (1987). A few of these poems by Dorothy were included in her brother William's collections of poetry. Dorothy set up house with her brother, William, at Racedown, Dorset, in 1795, moving with him to Alfoxden in 1797. She remained with her brother after his marriage in 1802 to Mary Hutchinson, but she arranged to receive an annuity from another brother, Richard, so that she would be able to remain economically independent of the newly-weds. In her decision to keep house for William, who had already published one book of poetry, Dorothy placed herself at the hub of the 'Romantic' movement – or that part of it which is concerned with Nature. Among other prose works, Dorothy Wordsworth wrote but did not have published: *The Alfoxden Journal* (1798); *Journal of A Visit to Hamburgh and of A Journey from Hamburgh to Goslam* (1798); *The Grasmere Journal* (1800–3); *Recollections of a Tour Made in Scotland* (1803); *Excursion on the Banks of Ullswater* (November, 1805); *A Journal of a Tour on the Continent* (1820); *Journal of My Second Tour in Scotland* (1822); and *Journal of a Tour in the Isle of Man* (1828). Many of Dorothy's journals have been published posthumously: the Alfoxden journal (four volumes that she kept at Grasmere between May 1899 and December 1802), and later journals that she kept from 1824 to 1835, which included her travel writing as well as an account of her life at Rydal Mount to which William Wordsworth's family moved in 1813. She also wrote a piece of social history, *A Narrative Concerning George & Sarah Green* (ed. Ernest de Selincourt, 1936), and a children's story, 'Mary Jones and her Pet-Lamb' (?1805). Texts are from *The Letters of William and Dorothy Wordsworth: 2. The Middle*

Years, ed. Ernest de Selincourt, rev. Mary Moorman, vol. 2 (1969), pp. 23–4 and 85–6; and *Journals of Dorothy Wordsworth*, 2 vols, ed. Ernest de Selincourt (1941), vol. 2, pp. 7–31. Biographical information is from the *Journals of Dorothy Wordsworth*, ed. Mary Moorman (1971), and *Letters of Dorothy Wordsworth: A Selection*, ed. Alan G. Hill (1981).

FROM *LETTERS OF WILLIAM AND DOROTHY WORDSWORTH*

Letter to Lady Beaumont, 1806

Grasmere, Saturday afternoon
20 April

Many thanks, my dear Friend,* for your kind letter! You cannot
doubt but that it delighted us to hear of the pleasure you had
received from seeing my Brother; and it was very kind of you to
find a moment to write to me among your many engagements. I
am seated in a *shady* corner of the moss hut (for it fronts the
west and towards evening the sun shines full into it) and but
that Mr Crump's ruinous mansion (has my Brother told you
that one third of it is fallen down?) stares me in the face
whenever I look up there is not any object that is not cheerful
and in harmony with the sheltering mountains and quiet vale.
The lake is perfectly calm, two or three ploughs are at work, the
fields scattered over with sheep and lambs. Within three days
the flowers have sprung up by thousands. William's favourite,
the little celandine, glitters upon every bank, the fields are
becoming green, the buds bursting; and but three days ago
scarcely a trace of spring was to be seen. We have had two days
and nights of gentle rain with a South wind; and now that the
sun shines again the change seems almost miraculous. We are so
proud of it that we have scarcely been in the house ten minutes
together the whole day, and I, you see, have lost no time in
taking possession of our summer abode. Ever since my Brother
left us the weather has been unusually severe, much colder than
it was at Christmas; and it has been a very sickly time, and we
in our family have not escaped bad colds. John and Dorothy
were exceedingly poorly for several days. John is recovered
entirely and has been roaming about as happy as the young
lambs all this fine day, and we hope that Dorothy is in the way
of mending. I wish I could say the same of their Mother who
has a bad cough, which is particularly troublesome to her in her
present state; we trust however that, if the wind does not shift
to its old quarters in the North, she may soon get rid of it.

My Brother has received so much pleasure in your house, had

so many proofs of your affectionate regard that my heart is
overcome with gratitude! he has sent us the history of every day
that he has passed with you, and we are very happy in the
thought of his being now so near to you, so very near that it is
almost the same thing as if he were under your roof. I am truly
glad that my Brother's manuscript poems give you so much
pleasure – I was sure that you would be deeply impressed by the
Ode. The last time I read it over, I said: 'Lady Beaumont will
like this'. I long to know your opinion and Sir George's of
Benjamin, the Waggoner; I *think* you will be pleased with it, but
cannot be so sure of this – And you would persuade *me* that I
am capable of writing poems that might give pleasure to others
besides my own particular friends!! indeed, indeed you do not
know me thoroughly; you think far better of me than I deserve
– I must tell you the history of those two little things which
William in his fondness read to you. I happened to be writing a
letter one evening when he and my Sister were last at Park
house, I laid down the pen and thinking of little Johnny (then in
bed in the next room) I muttered a few lines of that address to
him about the Wind,* and having paper before me, wrote them
down, and went on till I had finished. The other lines I wrote in
the same way, and as William knows every thing that I do, I
showed them to him when he came home, and he was very much
pleased; but this I attributed to his partiality; yet because they
gave him pleasure and for the sake of the children I ventured to
hope that I might do something more at some time or other. Do
not think that I was ever bold enough to hope to compose verses
for the pleasure of grown persons. Descriptions, Sentiments, or
little stories for children was all I could be ambitious of doing,
and I did try one story, but failed so sadly that I was completely
discouraged. Believe me, since I received your letter I have made
several attempts (could I do less as you requested that I would
for your sake?) and have been obliged to give it up in despair;
and looking into my mind I find nothing there, even if I had the
gift of language and numbers, that I could have the vanity to
suppose could be of any use beyond our own fireside, or to
please, as in your case, a few partial friends; but I have no
command of language, no power of expressing my ideas, and no
one was ever more inapt at moulding words into regular metre.
I have often tried when I have been walking alone (muttering to
myself as is my Brother's custom) to express my feelings in

verse; feelings, and *ideas* such as they were, I have never wanted
at those times; but prose and rhyme and blank verse were
jumbled together and nothing ever came of it. As to those two
little things which I did write, I was very unwilling to place them
beside my Brother's poems, but he insisted upon it, and I was
obliged to submit; and though you have been pleased with them
I cannot but think that it was chiefly owing to the spirit which
William gave them in the reading and to your kindness for me. I
have said far more than enough on this subject, and am almost
at the end of my paper without having told you that Mrs
Coleridge and Hartley are at Grasmere. She desires me to say
that she intends writing to you in the course of a few days.
Hartley is a very interesting child, so like his Father that it is
quite affecting to observe him; his temper and many of his habits
are the very same. When you see my Brother pray tell him that
we shall write by next Tuesday's post, that we have received his
letter sent off last Tuesday, and that Johnny is well and Dorothy
much better. Adieu my good and dear Friend

Believe me affectionately yours
D. Wordsworth

Letter to Lady Beaumont, 1806

[Late September]

My dear Friend,
   I have put off writing to you for many days, hoping always
that the next post would bring us a letter from Coleridge
himself, from which some comfort might be gathered, and a
more accurate estimate formed of the state of his mind; but no
letter has arrived. I have, however, the satisfaction of telling you
that he is to be at home on the 29th of this month, he has
written to acquaint Mrs Coleridge with this, and has told her
that he has some notion of giving a course of Lectures in London
in the winter. This is all we know; I do not imagine he has
mentioned the subject of the lectures to Mrs C. Whatever his
plan may be, I confess I very much wish he may not put it in
practice, and for many reasons, first, because I fear his health
would suffer from late hours and being led too much into
company; and in the second place, I would fain see him address
the whole powers of his soul to some great work in prose or
verse, of which the effect would be permanent, and not personal

and transitory. I do not mean to say that much permanent good
may not be produced by communicating knowledge by means
of lectures, but a man is perpetually tempted to lower himself to
his hearers to bring them into sympathy with him, and no one
would be more likely to yield to such temptation than Coleridge;
therefore at every period of his life the objection would have
applied to his devoting himself to this employment; but at this
present time it seems almost necessary that he should have one
grand object before him which would turn his thoughts away in
a steady course from his own unhappy lot, and so prevent petty
irritations and distresses, and in the end produce a habit of
reconcilement and submission. – My dear friend, you will judge
how much we have suffered from anxiety and distress within
the few last weeks. We have long known how unfit Coleridge
and his wife were for each other; but we had hoped that his ill-
health, and the present need his children have of his care and
fatherly instructions, and the reflections of his own mind during
this long absence would have so wrought upon him that he
might have returned home with comfort, ready to partake of the
blessings of friendship, which he surely has in an abundant
degree, and to devote himself to his studies and his children. I
now trust he has brought himself into this state of mind; but as
we have had no letters from him since that miserable one which
we received a short time before my Brother mentioned the
subject to Sir George, I do not know what his views are. Poor
Soul! he had a struggle of many years, striving to bring
Mrs C. to a change of temper and something like communion
with him in his enjoyments: he is now, I trust, effectually
convinced that he has no power of this sort, and he has had so
long a time to know and feel this that I would gladly hope things
will not be so bad as he imagines when he finds himself once
again with his Children under his own roof. If he *can* make use
of the knowledge which he has of the utter impossibility of
producing powers and qualities of mind which are not in her,
or of much changing what is unsuitable to his disposition, I do
not think he will be unhappy; I am sure I think he ought not
to be *miserable*. While he imagined he had anything to hope for
no wonder that his perpetual disappointments made him so!
But suppose him once reconciled to that one great want, an
utter want of sympathy, I believe he may live in peace and quiet.
Mrs C. has many excellent properties; as you observe she is

unremitting in her attentions as a nurse to her Children, and indeed, I believe she would have made an excellent wife to many persons. Coleridge is as little fitted for her as she for him, and I am truly sorry for her. When we meet you at Coleorton* I trust we shall have been with Coleridge long enough to know what comfort he is likely to have. In the meantime I will say no more on this distressing subject unless some change should happen much for the better or the worse. I hope everything from the effect of my Brother's conversation upon Coleridge's mind; and bitterly do I regret that he did not at first go to London to meet him, as I think he might have roused him up and preserved him from much of the misery that he has endured. Now I must speak of the delight with which we look forward to seeing you. We think that nothing will prevent our accepting your kind offer;* for it is plain that Coleridge does not wish us to go to Keswick as he has not replied to that part of William's letter in which he spoke of our plans for the winter. We shall therefore prepare ourselves to be ready to set off at any time that you shall appoint, so as to be with you a few days before your departure from Coleorton; and happy indeed shall we be to turn our faces [MS. incomplete].

FROM *A JOURNAL OF A TOUR ON THE CONTINENT (1820)*

10 *July 1820, Monday.* We (William, Mary, and Dorothy Wordsworth) left the Rectory House, Lambeth, at a quarter before eight o'clock. Had the Union Coach to ourselves till within two stages of Canterbury, when two young ladies demanded inside places. One was obliged to mount beside the Coachman; the other seated herself with us, protesting that she would not for worlds have got on the outside: her Friend, unwilling to be seen in that situation at Canterbury, dismounted within a mile of the town, and *our* companion – very pretty, and superfine in delicacy – exclaimed from the coach-window, 'what! walk all the way by yourself! you will have a sad long dreary walk!' Yet she made no offer to accompany the forlorn pedestrian. Certainly there was nothing very unusual in this country-town-bred young Lady's notion of dreariness and a long

walk, and I should hardly have thought this incident of my journal worth preserving but for the ludicrous effect, at the time, of contrast with our own schemes and wishes; it being the object of our ambition to cross the Alps on foot! The Cathedral of Canterbury (described by Erasmus* as lifting itself up in 'such majesty towards heaven, that it strikes religion into the beholders from a distance') looks stately on the plain, when first seen from the gently descending road, and appeared to me a much finer building than in former times; and I felt, as I had often done during my last abode in London, that, whatever change, tending to melancholy, twenty years might have produced, they had called forth the capacity of enjoying the sight of ancient Buildings to which my youth was, comparatively, a stranger. Between London and Canterbury the scenes are varied and cheerful; first Blackheath, and its bordering villas, and shady trees – goats, asses, sheep, etc., pasturing at large near the houses. The Thames glorious – ships like castles, cutting their way as through green meadows, the river being concealed from the view – then it spreads out like a wide lake, scattered over with vessels.

At Rochester the spacious and naval Medway – bridge, bays and boats – Town and Castle on the hill. On as we travel, cherry-orchards (the pleasant labour of gathering going on, and baskets of ripe fruit under the trees) – Hop plantations – flower-gardens – neat or ornamented cottages and comfortable dwellings of larger size – no miserable huts! only *one* poor white-headed Boy ran after us begging. The light and elegant churchtower of Boughton and the village seen at the end of a long wide avenue to the left, and, all the way, villages among trees with steeple or spire. The neighbourhood of Canterbury is dignified by remembrances of Hooker,* whose *Ecclesiastical Polity* was principally composed at Bishops-Bourne, about three miles from that place, and he lies buried within the walls of the Parish Church. Had our mode of travelling allowed of such a pilgrimage we would gladly have turned aside to visit the spot, as Travellers often did, long after his death. Noticed a large Chalk Quarry near the way side – huts, labourers, and horses very picturesque under the white banks tinged with green or yellow and tufted with shrubs and flowers. When within a mile of Dover, saw crowds of people at a Cricket-match, the numerous combatants dressed in 'white-sleeved shirts', and it was in the very same field where, when we 'trod the grass of England' once again, twenty years ago, we had seen an Assemblage of Youths engaged in the same sport, so very like the present that all might have been the same!'*[1]

Arrived at Dover at 7 o'clock. A joyous meeting with Mr and Mrs Monkhouse, who on Saturday the 8th, their wedding day, had preceded us, accompanied by Miss Horrocks, and were to be our fellow-travellers.

11 July, Tuesday, Dover. We walked to the Castle before breakfast. The building, when you are close to it, appears even *sublime*, from its immense height and bulk; but it is not rich or beautiful in architecture. The old Warder stood in waiting upon the hill, to lead us forward. After ascending above a hundred stone steps, we were greeted by the slender tinkling of a Bell, a delicately wild sound in that place; it is fixed at the top of a pillar on which is inscribed a poetical petition in behalf of the prisoners confined above in the Castle; and, no doubt, some of those poor creatures were on the watch at one of the window niches to pull the string of the bell, a warning voice in aid of their rude rhymes,

> *Oh ye whose hours exempt from sorrow flow*
> *Behold the seat of pain and woe, etc, etc.*

The Warder was laborious in his descriptions of intelligible and unintelligible things, and, at parting seemed not over well satisfied with our poor shilling, which we considered as a tax *upon* a tax – our eyes not needing the aid of his loco-descriptive powers. He was an old man, had lived at Dover all his life, and had never had the curiosity to cross the Channel. After breakfast walked out again. The circular bay very fine, with fawn-coloured belt of sand girdling the blue waters, scattered over with ships and boats and surmounted by the lofty white cliffs. Great charges at the Inn, and poor attendance, yet civility enough and civility wherever you turn; but all for what is to come, wearisome demands, or entreaties for *every* service, or *no* service. The whole male population out of doors at Dover might seem to be employed in shoving this way, or that, the restless people, or the busy, or the curious, of these two great nations – nay, I must not say the *two* nations; for all the voyagers seem to be English. Sailed at ¼ past 10. Clear sunshine and a fresh breeze. *I* was

[1] See my brother's Sonnet. [Author's note]

first sick, Mr M. next; and Mary dropped away in a moment from pleasure and cheerfulness.

Landed on the shores of France at ½ past one. What shall I say of CALAIS? I looked about for what I remembered, and looked for new things, and in both quests was gratified. With one consent we stopped to gaze at a group – rather a *line* of women and girls, seated beside dirty fish-baskets under the old gateway and ramparts – their white nightcaps, brown and puckered faces, bright eyes etc. etc. very striking. The arrangements – how unlike those of a fish-market in the South of England! but the cleanly, tight dress of these females prevents all disgust in looking at *them*; however you may dislike the smells from their slovenly baskets, and even in the countenances of these fish-women, the very lowest of the people, there is a something of liveliness, of mental activity, interesting to me, an Englishwoman, fresh from home. Others however, if they have perceived, hardly remember this – and much of it may have been the gift of my own fancy. Every one is struck with the excessive ugliness (if I may apply the word to any *human* creatures) of the fish-women of Calais, and *that* no one can forget. Here are dull shops, quiet streets, a large Cathedral and a large *Place* or square with Town-hall. We had desired to be conducted to Dessin's Hotel, famous since the days of Sterne.* Convent-like, it turns its front from the street to a square enclosed by the buildings of the hotel – the square, a flower-garden laid out in formal beds – Our suite of rooms spacious, with showy, nay *elegant* furniture – shabby doors, lightsome summer windows carelessly fastened. The dinner (I record it as being our first meal in France) soup, turbot, boiled chickens, veal chops, potatoes, cauliflowers, spinach. Dessert – almonds, biscuits, currants, cherries. Chose Carriages in the decayed convent Chapel, Sterne's Remise. Drank tea late – 4 wax candles for which no charge was made (At Dover we had paid 3 shillings for the same) candle sticks tall and showy, with glass ornaments, like saucers at the top – no bedroom candle-sticks. Pleasant pretty *Femme de chambre* in snowwhite cap and jacket, with coloured petticoat – her keys by her side. She has lived seven years at this Hotel, and cannot speak a word of English – 'Nous sommes toujours occupées,* Madame'. 'The English language is very difficult, and one must have leisure to learn *any*thing.' Bought two old strong carriages for 1000 and 900 Francs.

Past 12 o'clock. I look out of my window and all round the square; the lights are extinguished. The stars are bright; no light to be seen but mine. On my bedroom door is inscribed 'Sterne's Room', and a print of him hangs over the fireplace. The walls painted in pannels, handsome carpets, chimney-piece marble-coloured, hearth red, bed-curtains white, sheets coarse, coverlet a mixture of cotton and woollen, beautifully white; but how clumsy all contrivances of braziers and smiths! The bell hangs on outside the wall, and gives a single, loud, dull stroke when pulled by the string, so that you must stand and pull four or five times, as if you were calling the people to prayers.

12 *July, Wednesday, Calais*. We rose at five, sunshine – and clear, but rather cold air. The Cathedral, a large edifice, not finely wrought, but the first effect is striking, from the size of the numerous pillars and arches, though they are paltry in the finishing – merely whitewashed and stuck over with bad pictures and tawdry images, yet the whole view at the entrance was affecting. Old men and women – *young* women and girls kneeling at their silent prayers, and some we espied, in obscure recesses, before a concealed crucifix, image, or altar. One grey-haired man I cannot forget, whose countenance bore the impression of worldly cares subdued, and peace in heavenly aspirations.

When we had advanced long and far, we heard a pattering voice and exclaimed 'There are prayers read somewhere' and discovered an inner Church (the quire) which a screen had concealed from us; and there stood the priest at the high Altar with two shabby little Boys, in school-day garb, in attendance. The Priest's dress, a striped muslin gown and a pinkish scarf. This scarf with some fumbling he *doffed*, spread on the Altar-table, and put on some other ornament as tawdry, – opened a little cupboard, suddenly knelt, and, in like haste, rose again – shut the door, re-opened it, and did the same two or three times. The only part of the vocal service which did not appear utterly contemptible from the careless manner in which it was gabbled over, and the intermixture of (to us) unmeaning ceremonies, was the chaunting, and that was pleasing; all appeared to join in it; and the worshippers in this inner temple were numerous; for the most part females, clad in long black or drab-coloured cloaks and white caps with broad borders: they generally wore ear-rings with large golden pendants. One figure I must not leave unnoticed, a squalid, ragged woman. She sat alone upon some steps at the side of the entrance to the quire: – there she sat, with a white dog beside her; no one was near, and the dog and she evidently belonged to each other, probably her *only* friend, for never was there a more wretchedly forlorn and miserable-looking human being: she did not notice us; but her rags, and her melancholy and sickly aspect drew a penny from me, and the change in the woman's skinny, doleful face is not to be imagined: it was brightened by a light and gracious smile: – the effect was almost as of something supernatural; – she bowed her body, waved her hand, and, with a politeness of gesture unknown in England in almost any station of life, beckoned that we might enter the church, where the people were kneeling upon chairs, of which there might be a thousand – *two* thousand – I cannot say how many – piled up in different parts of the Cathedral. At Calais we were amused in every street and at every turning... Wherever we look we see that we are not in our own country, and Calais is the same Calais it was twenty, fifty, I may say a *hundred* years ago. In all the every-day conveniences of life the French are unaccountably behind us. At a shop-door we noticed (among other Carpenter's goods) a child's chair which contained wood enough for half a dozen, and (hanging beside it) a bundle of semicircular fans made of rough chips, which we found were used instead of bellows. Enjoyed our breakfast at the Inn in a pleasant parlour looking upon the flower-and-fruit garden happily mingled with French taste and French formality. Went out to chat with *Madame* in the sunshine among the flowers, and nursed her two infants fresh from a plentiful washing in cold water (contrary to the French custom), and dressed loosely in white frocks in the English style; she herself sprightly, pretty and well-behaved and a perfect Frenchwoman. Her Husband came to us and they gave us bouquets ... My pretty Fille de Chambre, I found, was called Rosalie, a name well suited to the maiden and the place.

9 o'clock, Inn yard, Calais. Here I sit alone in the Voiture. Mr and Mrs M. and Miss H. at my right hand in theirs. W., M., and Mr Quillac[1] talking endlessly – there stands the fille de chambre, there the waiter with his napkin, and porters and

[1] The Master of the Inn – I believe of the family of the famous Monsieur Dessin. [Author's note]

other helpers with their gold ear-rings and leather or fur caps, by the half dozen: they expect nothing from us, for they have got their pay; but *there* they stand, as it seems in the pure spirit of sociability. The longest discourses will have an end, and W. and M. are preparing to join me. Off we drove, preceded by our friends, each postilion smacking his whip along the streets with a dexterity truly astonishing. Never before did I know the power of a clumsy whip, in concert with the rattling of wheels upon rough pavement! The effect was certainly not less upon us than upon the spectators, and we jolted away as merry as children – showed our passports – passed the gateways, drawbridges, and shabby soldiers, and, fresh to the feeling of being in a foreign land, drove briskly forward, watchful and gay. The country for many miles populous – this makes it amusing, though sandy and flat – no trees worth looking at singly *as* trees. Passed a Woman astride on an ass, two girls gaily dressed side by side on another ass, their faces turned different ways – clumsy carts with fruit and vegetables going to Calais – Women in carts – on foot – and some on horseback on large sheep-skin saddles with both feet upon a wooden stirrup; no corn cut, but much of it ripe – husbandry slovenly, but the abundance of flowers more than makes amends to the eye; the blue bells and poppies are most beautiful, like flowers in a garden; cottages of clay, white washed – one room – one window – one door – one chimney; within gay, hung with bright copper or brass vessels and ornamented with pictures – a lean, long-legged pig often tethered beside the door. Some cottages of larger size – rarely anything like a farm-house – never a Gentleman's house.

Changed horses at *Gravelines* in French Flanders, a wretched town; nothing to be seen worth the firing of a shot, and such a display of fortifications, moats and bridges! Bought a pound of cherries for six sous, probably twice as much as would have been demanded from French people; but the man of the House, noticing that Mrs M. took a fancy to his nice loaf of brown bread on the dinner-table, gave her a slice of it with true politeness. Country now more dull – few houses, and the women not so smartly dressed as the French at, or near Calais . . .

At the entrance of *Dunkirk*, we looked in vain for the *Superbe* of which the Postilion had given large promises. Here are gateways and drawbridges – a parade of strength with shabbiness and tendency to decay. Soldiers not spruce like ours, several

washing their linen in the moats. *Dunkirk*[1] is however a very
pretty town; and even lively to-day (being market day); there
was a curious mixture of commodities – pots, pans, earthen-
ware, baskets, old iron, broken keys, disabled horse-shoes (such
wares as you see in the dark windows in the alley leading to
Baldwin's Gardens) spread out on the ground, or on stalls, in
the large sunny market-place, where the houses have a much
smarter air than any at Calais. Dined at the Table d'Hote – very
amusing. Walked towards the sea-side in search of W. and M.,
and took up for my guide a lively little girl who now tried her
French, now her Flemish, to induce me to traffic with her for
her shells, and other curiosities which she had at home, she
employing herself with picking them up upon the sands. I was
much entertained with this Child, and her little artifices of
flattery and simplicity while she tried to give me a notion of the
poverty of her parents with their numerous family. She enlarged
on the wealth and grandeur of the English, and exclaimed 'Ah,
Madame! there is a great difference between the rich and the
poor!' All her time was spent in the streets or on the sea-shore;
she told me she had watched us get out of our carriages, and
described each of our party; and wherever we turned, the whole
afternoon, this little Wanderer was sure to cross our way, or to
be espied creeping after us. Her cunning, no doubt, makes her a
successful beggar, but a useless appendage of hers, a sickly girl,
who joined us in hopes that a little might fall to *her* share
(though she had not a word to say for it) pleaded with me as
powerfully for sous as my active, engaging little friend . . .

Half-past 10. The party gone to bed. This Salle, where I sit,
how unlike a parlour in an English inn! Yet the history of a sea-
fight, or a siege, painted on the walls, with the costumes of
Philip the Second, or even of our own time, would have better
suited my associations, with the names of Gravelines and
Dunkirk, than the story of Cupid and Psyche now before my
eyes, as large as life, on French paper! The paper is in pannels,
with big mirrors between, in gilt frames. With all this taste and
finery, and wax candles, and Brussels carpet, what a mixture of
troublesome awkwardness! They brought us a ponderous teapot

---

[1] At Dunkirk we see the first beginning of the Flemish style of Building – an
intermixture in the streets of gable-fronted houses, but not handsome in that
style which is so picturesque and admits of so much variety. [Author's note]

that would not pour out the tea: the latches (with metal enough to fasten up a dungeon) can hardly, by unpractised hands, be made to open and shut the doors. I have seen the diligence come into the yard and unload – heavy, dirty, dusty – a lap-dog walking about the top, like a panther in its cage, and viewing the gulf below. A monkey was an outside passenger when it departed.

13 July, Thursday, 5 o'clock, Dunkirk. Left at 20 minutes past 5; men, women, boys and girls in the street at this early hour. Our way along the bleak coast, towards Furnes, the towers of which place we had seen from the steeple of D., upon the plain at some distance from the coast. The morning cloudy, and cold – a fierce wind. We were twice stopped for toll on the dreary sands, and, on entering the dominions of the King of Holland, our luggage was examined. Meanwhile I sought shelter from the cold in a wretched hut, like a hovel of the lowlands of Scotland, – no fire, but the good woman soon lighted up a few sticks; two dirty beds, a sick woman lying in one of them. The family at breakfast; milk in a tea-kettle poured out into tea cups – brown bread and butter. *Furnes* a pretty Town on the same plan as Calais and Dunkirk, but much smaller. The Inn very large and such width and height of passages! ... Excellent breakfast, – eggs, honey, coffee, good bread, but indifferent tea. Passed from the old fashioned street, where was our Inn, through a handsome square to one of the churches, where a Priest was catechizing the children, and they questioned each other. The countenances of the women are more kindly, I think, than those of the French; but not so lively – their complexions fresher. I am alone waiting in the square for my companions, and, seated on the steps of a house, I take my pencil ... I will describe this Square – houses yellow, grey, white, and *there* is a *green* one! Yet the effect is not gaudy – half Grecian church, with Gothic spire; storks have built their nests, and are sitting upon the venerable tower of another church, a sight that pleasingly reminds us of our neighbourhood to Holland. The *Interior* of that which outwardly mimics the Grecian, is gothic and rather handsome in form, but white-washed, and bedaubed with tinsel, and dolls, and tortured images ... The Town Hall a handsome building with gable front, and blue-slated roof – the other houses are tiled. Bells continually tinkling. *There* goes a woman to her prayers, in a long black cloak, and bright blue stockings. *Here* comes a nicely-dressed old woman, leaning on her staff! Surely it is a blessing to the aged in Roman Catholic countries to have the churches always open for them, if it were only that it makes a variety in the course of a long day! How soothing, how natural to the aged, thus to withdraw from the stir of household cares, and occupations in which they can no longer take a part! and I must say (little as I have yet seen of this mode of worshipping God) I never beheld more of the expression of piety and earnest feeling than in some of the very old people in these churches. Every avenue of the square of this little town presents some picturesque continuation of buildings. All is old, and old-*fashioned*; nothing to complain of but a want of Dutch cleanliness, yet it does not obtrude on the eye, out of doors; the exterior is grave, decent, and quiet ...

Our ride of two stages was very pleasant, through a highly cultivated and productive country ... Dined at the little town of Ghistelles, eggs and bacon and omelet ... We go on through the same happy cultivated country – all whom we meet except the beggars well dressed, bright blue and red the prevailing colours – a single figure or group of figures, frequently gives a spirit to a line or bending of the road, to a cottage, a footpath, an embowered paddock, or a grove, transforming it into a cheerful picture, fitted with colouring such as a Flemish painter would have sketched.

We entered Bruges by a long gently-winding street and were so animated with pleasure in our hasty course that it seemed we too soon reached the Inn. W. and Mr M. walked out immediately, eager to view the City in the warm light of the setting sun. We had arrangements to make, and not very ready in speaking the two languages, German and French, and still less in understanding them when spoken, we felt *then*, (and long continued to feel) that a good work was performed when the business of allotting apartments to each was settled. After tea, with a lame boy for our guide, who was proudly qualified for the office, being able, as he said, to 'speak English', we set out on our walk. From the street where we lodged, came directly into the square or *Place*, presided over on one side by the Town Hall with a noble Tower, thence through ancient streets of lofty houses – no two alike in ornaments, hardly in colouring. They have mostly long gable fronts in the style of the old buildings in Glasgow ... Continued to walk through the silent town till ten o'clock – no carts, no chaises – a cloistral silence felt in every corner and every open space, yet the large square was scattered over with groups of people; or passengers walking to and fro, – no lights in the houses!

14 July, Friday, Bruges. At a little past 5, found our guide in waiting at the Inn door, who met us with a smile more easily understood than his English speech; he could however generally make us comprehend what he meant to say, yet I was obliged sometimes to resort to my sorry stock of German ... The morning was bright, sunshine and shade falling upon the lines of houses, and the out juttings of the more noble buildings. In the bright light of morning the same tender melancholy was over the city as in the sober time of twilight, yet with intervening images of rural life. A few Peasants were now entering the town and the rattling of a rustic cart prettily laden with vegetables fresh from the soil gave a gentle stirring to the fancy. Early as it was people of all ages were abroad, chiefly on their way to the churches; – the figure, gait, and motions of the women in harmony with the collegiate air of the streets, and the processions and solemnities of Catholic Worship. Such figures might have walked through these streets, two hundred years ago, streets bearing no stamp of progress or of decay. One might fancy that as the city had been built so it had remained. We first went to the church of St Salvador, a venerable Gothic edifice. Within the church, our walk between the lofty pillars was very solemn. We saw in perspective the marble floor scattered over, at irregular distances, with people of all ages – standing, or upon their knees, silent, yet making such motions as the order of their devotions prescribed, crossing themselves, beating their breasts, or telling their beads. Such the general appearance of the worshippers; but the gestures of some were more impassioned. One poor sickly man, I noticed, with outspread arms as if in an ecstasy of devotion; another, a venerable figure, near him, knelt upon one knee, supporting himself with a staff headed in the form of a cross. The different Altars on each side of the nave had their Priests; some employed as confessors, and others spattering over the prayers. We spent some time in admiring the quire, and every other part of this noble building, adorned as it is with statues, and pictures not in the paltry style of the churches at Calais and Furnes, but works of art that would be interesting *anywhere*, and much more so in these sacred places, where the wretched and the happy, the poor and the rich are alike invited to cast away wordly feelings, and may be elevated by the representations of scripture history, or of the sufferings and glory of martyrs and saints. Mass was beginning at the high Altar; the music was fine; and even the forms of the gaudy priests, whose various gesticulations (except from a natural respect for the sympathies of others) were fitted to raise in our minds any thoughts rather than those of devotion; even those Priests in their gaudy attire, with their young white-robed attendants, made a solemn appearance, while clouds of incense were ascending over their heads to the large crucifix above the Altar; and the 'pealing organ' sounded to the 'full-voiced quire'. There was a beautiful Nun in a grey garment with a long black scarf, white forehead band, belt, and rosary. Intent upon her devotions, she did not cast an eye towards us, and we stood to look at her. The faces of many of the women are handsome, but the steady grace, the chastened motions of their persons, and the mild seriousness of their countenances, are *most* remarkable.

Our guide had eagerly told us that to-day, being Friday, we might see the 'Blut von Jesus'*, happily preserved through the perils of the revoluton; and he had made a point of conducting us, soon after we entered the church, to the Altar, where a Priest was presenting, to all who came, the phial containing that precious relic. They knelt, and kissed it in quick succession, he with a little napkin wiping the phial after each kiss. We next went to the Cathedral, another superb Gothic structure, and visited again the small square where the ruins of a church remain, still adorned by two small towers . . .

We prepared with much regret to depart from Bruges at ten o'clock, wishing to see more of so interesting a place. The general effect upon the mind can never be forgotten. The race of the Great and Powerful by whom the noble public edifices were raised has passed away, yet the attire, the staid motions and demeanour of the present inhabitants are accordant with the stateliness of former ages; and the City remains as if self-sustained – no new houses to be seen,[1] no repairs going on! you might fancy that the sound of the Builder's hammer was never heard in these days!

[1] Observe, our stay was very short; but such was the impression on us – and such the appearance at that time. [Author's note]

Our journey in the voitures through the streets to the packet-boat was very droll. The postilion wore a white night-cap, had a full-blown rose stuck in his mouth, and was without coat. Thus attired and adorned, he smacked his whip through the suburbs in concert with the whip of Mr M.'s postilion, thus bringing the people out of their houses to look at us. From Furnes to Bruges we have travelled through a flat country, yet with an endless variety, produced by the various produce of a beautiful soil carefully cultivated. We had been told that the country between Ghent and Bruges was much of the same kind, only not so interesting; therefore we were not sorry to interpose the variety of the packet-boat to Ghent. Found it stationed at the end of the town, beside the bridge of the Canal ... The scene near the Bridge was pretty, – cheerful and sunny; but how different from the centre of the City! – a clatter of voices, vehement Beggars, fruit-sellers, and porters bearing in luggage ... When all was ready, [we] took our places on the deck of the vessel. The tinkling of a bell the signal for departure, and we glided gently away with motion only perceptible by the *eye*, looking at the retreating objects on the shore. The space on deck allotted to passengers was completely filled, the weather being so fine that no one wished to go below. Two nuns and a priest (his prayer-book in his hand), an English dandy, a handsome lady-like Flemish girl, dressed in an elegant gauze mob-cap with flowers, and robe *à la française*, were the most noticeable people ... Mary and I, withdrawing from the company, had placed ourselves in one of the *voitures* in the centre of the boat. The groups under the awning would make a lively picture. The priest, in his cocked hat, standing at his prayers, the pretty maiden in her cap and flowers, and *there* are the nuns. My brother and the nuns are very merry. *They* seem to have left their prayer-books at home, and one of them has a pamphlet in her hand that looks like a magazine. Low cottages, pretty and clean, close to the bank; a woman scouring a copper vessel, in white jacket, red cap, blue petticoat, and clean sailcloth apron; the flat country to be seen over the low banks of the canal, spires and towers, and sometimes a village may be descried among trees; many little public-houses to tempt a landing; near one I see a pleasant arbour, with seats aloft for smoking ... But the smell of dinner ascends from the cabin, and I hear them on deck talking of hunger and the good things we may expect

below. The nuns are merry; so is the priest, in his spectacles; the
Dandy recommends shoes, in preference to boots, as more
convenient. 'There is nobody that can clean either on the
Continent.' For my part, I think they clean *them* as well as
anything else, except their vessels for cookery; they cannot get
the dust out of a chair, or *rub* a table! . . . On descending to
dinner we perceived that our wordly wisdom was no match for
that of the Nuns and others of their country. Most of *us simple
English* were so tardy in obeying the summons that we found
vacant places only in the second cabin. We fared very well,
however, though the heat was a little oppressive. Three church
towers and the tall florid Gothic spire of the Cathedral of *Ghent*
appear at the distance of four miles, but nothing else to be seen
except cottages and their goings on, the banks being now so
high and steep . . . A busy scene when we reached the landing-
place, outside the city ramparts. Some were welcomed by friends
waiting on the shore and all in confusion seeking out their
luggage. The Nuns, bound to Brussels, to attend a 'grande Fête',
were not less anxious after their band-boxes than the rest . . .
Wm. and I remained till the carriages were safely landed, amid
a confusion of tongues, French, German, and English, and
inarticulate shoutings, such as belong to *all* nations. After
presenting our passport, we proceeded to an Inn, though we had
a long and intricate walk. Canals round the town, rows of trees,
fortifications converted into pleasure-grounds. We pass through
old and picturesque streets, with an intermixture of houses of a
later date, and showy shops; an appearance of commerce and
bustle, which makes the contrast with Bruges the more striking,
as the architecture of the ancient houses is of the same kind.

. . . After tea, walked through the city; the buildings, streets,
squares, all are picturesque; the houses, green, blue, pink,
yellow, with richest ornaments still varying. Strange it is that so
many and such strongly-contrasted colours should compose an
undiscordant whole. Towers and spires overlook the lofty
houses; and nothing is wanting at Ghent of venerable antiquity
to give to the mind the same melancholy composure, which
cannot but be felt in passing through the streets of Bruges; –
nothing but the impression that no change is going on, except
through the silent progress of time. *There* the very dresses of the
women might have been the same for hundreds of years. *Here*,
though the black cloak is prevalent, we see a mixture of all

kinds, from the dress of the English or French belle to that of
the poorest of our poor in a country town. The streets are full
of people; rude girls in dirty caps, and idle boys, ready with a
laugh for the passing stranger. Withal, here is an appearance of
wealth and commerce, – the heavy cart laden with merchandise,
and pleasure-carriages, post-chaises and coaches. At 9 o'clock
military music in the *Place d'Armes* – it is very spacious and
handsome, surrounded with large buildings; we sat upon stone
seats placed under rows of tall trees, to hear the music, till we
retired to our bedrooms at the very top of the huge hotel. Merry
chimes after ten o'clock – the square lighted.

15 July, Saturday, Ghent. Rose early . . . Again we walked
through the town, with still increasing admiration of the ancient
buildings. Sat on the steps of a house opposite to a small opening
or square (the butter market) (I can hardly endure to call a place
so dignified by such a name). The Cathedral spire overlooks it
in front, the prison Tower is to the left, and on the right is one
side of the Town-hall, the other side faces the street where we
were, which, being composed of large and old houses, is in
harmony with that ancient Building. The architecture is a
mixture of Gothic and Grecian (the three orders of pillars, one
above another), the Gothic part very rich. Laughter and rude
remarks of passengers in the street did not disturb us, sitting
upon the steps. Multitudes of swallows were wheeling round
the roof, regardless of carts and hammers, or whatever noise
was heard below, and the effect was indescribably interesting.
The restless motions and plaintive call of those little creatures
seemed to impart a stillness to every other object, and had the
power to lead the imagination gently on to the period when that
once superb but now decaying structure shall be 'lorded over
and possessed by nature'.* In every quarter of this once powerful
city are to be found buildings for public or private use (or the
remains of such) displaying the taste of former times . . . Having
long feasted our eyes on squares and streets (which often by the
bye reminded us of Oxford and made us say 'Oh that we could
transplant to Oxford that little bit, or that winding of a street!')
we went in search of public walks in the suburbs . . . We had
yet to seek a Table d'hote, our *Laquais de place* conducting us
from street to street; and no dinner, surely, was ever worth the
trouble we took. I had not been strong before, and was now
completely knocked up; and we had yet another journey to

make to the Hotel in the *Place d'Armes*, where, if the dinner hour had suited us, we might have dined, and thus filled up the time afterwards wasted in waiting for horses.

In this hotel what a curious conflict between French and Flemish propensities in matters of taste! In the passages, paintings and statues after the antique of Hebes and Apollos; and in the garden, a little pond about a yard and a half in diameter, a weeping willow bending over it, and under the shade of that tree, in the centre of the pond, a wooden painted statue of a Dutch or Flemish Boor looking ineffably sweet upon his mistress, and embracing her; – a living Duck tethered at the feet of the statues and alternately tormenting a miserable eel and itself with endeavours to escape from its bonds and prison. Had we chanced to espy the Hostess of the Hotel in this quaint rural retreat the picture would have been complete. She was a true Flemish figure, in the dress of the days of Holbein,* her symbol of office, a weighty bunch of keys, pendant from her portly waist.

We did not feel the same regret in departing from Ghent as from Bruges, though, if fine cities had been the main object of our tour, we could have been well amused there for many days. Switzerland was our end and aim; and if the season should fail us there we must return without the accomplishment of wishes cherished from the days of youth, when that romantic country was first shut out from the traveller. But at *Bruges* our fancy had been detained by objects so new to us, and so interesting, it seemed as if the Alps themselves could hardly give us anything better; yet Ghent is a finer city; and it is, perhaps, richer in ancient, and is certainly in *modern* buildings ... But at Bruges the pensive images of monastic life among the quiet goings-on of a thinly-peopled city were to us inexpressibly delightful – a cast of pensive grace over all, even the very children! We had four posts to travel to Brussels and did not set off till near four o'clock. Fertile country, at first very close and populous ... Arrived at *Alost* before sunset, two posts from Brussels and would have slept there, but the town was so full we could not procure beds ... *Alost* a rather shabbily-flashy town. Indifference of Innkeepers noticeable and boldness of women. Unreasonable demands made by the postilions, and Wm. at the Inn door looked as fierce as Buonaparte. When he came bustling up to us after his conflict M. and I said to each other 'They will think that B. himself is come back again to threaten this poor town.' A famous battle here. Ruins that remind us of the havoc. Rather open country – harvest beginning ... White butterflies were flitting over the green level, and perching upon the slender plants; it might have seemed that any *other* living thing would have been too heavy a burthen, and the plain was their own. Changed horses the last time in the dark.

I was roused from sleep at the gates of *Brussels*. The man who demanded our passports had the impudence to ask for money, the only demand of this kind. Mr M. was so generous as to give half a franc; and W., with grumbling, presented *two sous*. Light and shade very solemn upon the drawbridge. Passing through a heavy gate-way, we entered the City and drove through street after street, with a pleasure wholly new to us. Garlands of fresh boughs and flowers, in festoons, hung on each side; and the great height of the houses, especially in the narrow streets, (lighted as they were) gave a beautiful effect to the exhibition ... We stopped at the Hotel *de Belle Vue*, in the *Place Royale*, which looked like a square of palaces. It was past 11 o'clock; and although we had not long to wait for supper, there were so many arrangements to be made, and the chamber maids were so slow, that we did not get to bed till past one.

16 July, Sunday, Brussels. After breakfast, proceeded through the park, (a very large open space with shady walks, statues, fountains, pools, arbours, and seats, and surrounded by palaces and fine houses) to the Cathedral, which, though immensely large, was so filled with people that we could scarcely make our way so as, (by standing upon chairs for which we paid two sous each), to have a view of the Building over the multitudes of heads. The Priests, at high Mass, could not be seen; but the melody of human voices, accompanied by the organ, pierced through every recess; then came bursts of sound like thunder; and, at times, the solemn rousing of the trumpet. Powerful as was the effect of the music, the excessive heat and crowding after a short while overcame every other feeling, and we were glad to go into the open air. Our *Laquais de place* conducted us to the house of a shopkeeper, where, from a room in the attics, we might view the procession. It was close to one of the triangular openings with which most of the streets of Brussels terminate. To the right, we looked down the street along which the procession was to come, and, a little to the left below us, overlooked the triangle, in the centre of which was a fountain ornamented with three marble statues, three large urns at the corners, for the present occasion covered with moss, and a pillar in the midst, topped by a golden ball – the whole decorated with festoons of holly, and large roses made of paper, alternately red and yellow. In like manner the garlands were composed in all the streets through which the procession was to pass; but in some parts there were also young fir-trees stuck in the pavement, leaving a footway between *them* and the houses. Paintings were hung out by such as possessed them, – and ribbands and flags. The street where we were was lined with people assembled like ourselves in expectation, all in their best attire. Peasants to be distinguished by their short jackets, petticoats, in contrast, of scarlet or some other bright colour, crosses, or other ornament of gold or gilding; the bourgeoises, with black silk scarfs overhead, and reaching almost to their feet; ladies, a little too much of the French or English; little girls, with or without caps, and some in elegant white veils. The windows of all the houses open, and people seen at full length, or through doorways, sitting, or standing in patient expectation. It amused us to observe *them*, and the arrangements of their houses – which were even splendid, compared with those of persons of like condition in our own country – with an antique cast over all. Nor was it less amusing to note the groups or lines of people below us. Whether standing in the hot sunshine, or the shade, they appeared equally contented. Some approached the fountain – a sacred spot! – to drink of the pure waters, out of which rise the silent statues. The spot is sacred; for there, before the Priests arrived in the procession, incense was kindled in the urns, and a pause was made there with the canopy of the Host, while they continued chaunting the service.

But I am going too fast. The procession was, in its beginning, military, and its approach announced by sound of trumpets. Then came a troop of cavalry, four abreast, splendidly accoutred, dressed in blue and gold, and accompanied with a full band of music; next (I think) the Magistrates and constituted Authorities. But the *order* of the procession I do not recollect; only that the military, civil, and religious authorities and symbols were pleasingly combined, and the whole spectacle was beautiful. Long before the sound of the sacred service reached our ears, the *martial* music had died away in the distance, though there was no interruption in the line of the procession.

The contrast was very pleasing when the solemn chaunting came along the street, with the stream of banners; priests and choristers in their appropriate robes; and not the *least* pleasing part of it was a great number of young girls, two and two, all dressed in white frocks. It was a day made on purpose for this exhibition; the sun seemed to be feasting on the gorgeous colours and glittering banners; and there was no breeze to disturb garland or flower. When all was passed away, we returned to the Cathedral, which we found not so crowded as much to interrupt our view: yet the whole effect of the Interior was much injured by the decorations for the fête – especially by stiff orange-trees in tubs, placed between the pillars of the aisles. Though not equal to those of Bruges or Ghent, it is a very fine Gothic building, massy pillars and numerous statues, and windows of painted glass – an ornament which we have been so accustomed to in our own cathedrals that we lamented the want of it at G. and B.. . . .

Went through some modern streets, adjoining the park, to the assembly-room – very handsome – 17 lustres* – 14 huge mirrors – 14 marble Ionic pillars – scarlet sofas. The woman who has the care of the room told us of the ball given there by the Duchess of Richmond on the night of the beginning of the Battle of Waterloo,* from which some of our young officers hurried away in their dancing shoes, to meet the Enemy – and, of these, how *many* were brought back, in the course of a few hours, dead, dying, or wounded! She related, with lively gestures and in animated language, many affecting particulars of this kind, and of the agitation and terror of the city. Dined at the Table d'hôte – company of different nations, generally distinguishable by their dress and deportment, especially the Germans, whose pride seemed to lie in showing that they were subject to no restraint. They were thoroughly coarse in gesture, dress, and manners; but I must say that I was never before, nor have ever since been, so much struck with this. Two or three ate their dinner without coats. An elegant French-woman and her little boy sat at the head of our division of the table. Her address was in the best style of French ease combined with apparent modesty ... After dinner drove through the principal streets and markets. The Maison de Ville, surmounted by a beautiful spire, forms one side of a square where all the buildings are ancient, varied in architectural ornaments, and picturesque. Thence to the Allée verte, the Hyde Park of Brussels, streams of carriages of every description from the chariot of my Lord Anglais to the lowest of the Bourgeoisie (whose awkward vehicles were much more amusing) crammed like Johnny Gilpin's chaise* with whole families, from the grandmother to the babe at its Mother's breast. The Tandem of an English Buck was perfectly unmanageable, and certainly it produced the most *lively* amusement. On one side of the Drive a Fair was held; – smoking and drinking-booths – stalls of eatables and abundance of toys and trinkets. Returned through many streets – all the windows open; and we could view the insides of houses. Parties sitting near the windows, often card-playing within – two Priests engaged in that amusement – Ladies on the Balconies – shops open, but no appearance of business – pleasure the pursuit of young and old; but little to be *seen* of merriment, whether the pursuit was bustling and eager, or quiet and steady. To us this mode of spending Sunday appeared most melancholy, with all its 'gaités'.* Whatever serious or religious thoughts the morning's ceremonies might have raised in some minds, no such expression was now visible on the countenances of the many who passed before us; and I could not but think how wearied this crowd must go to bed at night! But the feverish quest after pleasure, or the listless gazing, did not cease when evening put a stop to the Fair. The City was to be illuminated, and we again set out to drive through the streets. In the centre of the Place Royale a cork-screw spire, spreading its light round the square and surrounded by crowds of gazers, was very beautiful ... Masses of fire, such as might have been viewed with dismay in times of war, upon the black towers of the Cathedral and of another old church, were even grand objects, and the long narrow streets of lofty houses, though poorly lighted, had a fantastic and romantic effect. Returned to our Inn at about 11 o'clock, and a little after midnight the splendid cork-screw spire had faded away, and all bustle and noise were over in the Square.

17 July, Monday, Brussels. A very hot morning ... Departed at a quarter past eleven for *Namur* by the way of Waterloo ... We do not travel far till we enter the Forest of Soignes, green tracks under the tall trees, – no very deep shade, not much undergrowth of thickets, yet I could not help thinking what a merciful shelter for the wounded soldier! Suddenly the small circular *church* of *Waterloo* with its portico and correspondent addition, on the opposite side, of quire or chancel is seen at a distance, appearing to terminate the vista of the road bordered irregularly by trees of the forest . . . Waterloo is a mean village; straggling on each side of the broad highway, children and poor people of all ages stood on the watch to conduct us to the church. Within the circle of its interior are found several mural monuments of our brave soldiers – long lists of naked names inscribed on marble slabs – not less moving than laboured epitaphs displaying the sorrow of surviving friends . . . Here we took up the very man who was Southey's* guide (Lacoste), whose name will make a figure in history. He bowed to us with French ceremony and liveliness, seeming proud, withal, to show himself as a sharer in the terrors of that time when Buonaparte's confusion and overthrow released him from unwilling service. He had been tied upon a horse as Buonaparte's guide through the country previous to the Battle, and was compelled to stay by his side till the moment of flight. This man mounted behind our carriage, and, halting in his story as we passed through the small village of St. Jean, he pointed to the left, saying 'there is my house, and that is my Wife', a fine looking woman, who stood within the threshold . . . He talked all the way with my Brother; but I could understand little till we got to the field of Battle, where we stood upon an elevation; and thence, looking round upon every memorable spot, by help of gesture and action, and the sounds, 'les Anglais, les Français' etc., I gathered up a small portion of the story, helped out by a few monuments erected to the memory of the slain; but all round there was no other visible record of slaughter; the wide fields were covered with luxuriant crops, – just as they had been before the battles, except that now the corn was nearly ripe, and *then* it was green. We stood upon grass, and corn fields where *heaps* of our countrymen lay buried beneath our feet. There was little to be seen; but much to be felt; – sorrow and sadness, and even something like horror breathed out of the ground as we stood upon it! The sky had been overshadowed by clouds during most of our journey; and now a storm threatened us, which helped with our own melancholy thoughts to cast a gloom over the open country, where few trees were to be seen except forests on the distant heights. The ruins of the severely contested chateau of Hougamont had been ridded away since the battle, and the injuries done to the farm-house repaired. Even these circumstances, natural and trivial as they were, suggested melancholy thoughts, by furnishing grounds for a charge of ingratitude against the course of things, that was thus hastily removing from the spot all vestiges of so momentous an event. Feeble barriers against this tendency are the few frail memorials erected in different parts of the field of battle! and we could not but anticipate the time, when through the flux and reflux of war, to which this part of the Continent has always been subject, or through some turn of popular passion, *these* also should fall; and 'Nature's universal robe of green, humanity's appointed shroud'* enwrap them: – and the very names of those whose valour they record be cast into shade, if not obliterated even in their own country, by the exploits of recent favourites in future ages.

We reached the beggarly little town of *Genappe* just before the bursting of a thunder storm; and there, in the worst of its fury, while torrents of rain were falling, with thunder and lightning and fearful darkness, we ate our dinner, in a room which had served as a shelter from worse storms. An active Flemish girl who waited on us, pointing to the door, said, 'There, at that very spot, died the French General'. The floor, she said, was covered with wounded and dying soldiers; and the wainscoat now bears the marks of bullets that had pierced through the walls. The house altogether gloomy suited the dismal stories of the horrors of those days. The bedrooms large, dark and low, yet I thought I could have slept there without discomfort, the beds were very clean, and I, not being well, felt as if I did not care how soon our day's journey was ended. When Sir George Beaumont was at this Inn, two years ago, there was a raven in the yard who, he was told, had been famous for his distinct articulation, and his loquacity, before the Battles, but the thunder of the cannon had so terrified him that he had never spoken since. Was the bird conscience-stricken? for in those miserable times he was seen more than once making his repast on human limbs. The rain over and the sky brightening, we departed soon after dinner.

At Quatre-bras a tall and bulky old man in a white night-cap was seated at the door of his house (a detached dwelling at the junction of four roads whence the hamlet has its name). He was nursing his grandchild ... We asked him several questions which he answered briefly, and as if with indifference; but at last, with a slow and stately step, came up to us, and showed us the spot (but a few yards off) where the Duke of Brunswick was killed. This man had stood his ground, he said, remaining in his own house during the whole of the Battle. 'Were you not afraid?' said I. 'No, I never was afraid: ceux qui ont peur n'ont point d'esprit.'* The earth was covered with flourishing crops. We noticed this to him – 'and so it was before the Battle – just the same' was his reply, – but the corn was then not ripened . . . Near 11 o'clock when we reached the gates of *Namur*. The Hotel large – Rooms large and widely parted – the doors, the windows, all of Brobdignag.* There is a church bell here, which is tolled only in the night – its monitory voice the grandest I had ever heard! It sounded while we were at tea, and all stopped to listen.

MARY LAMB

MARY LAMB (1764–1847) worked as a seamstress until, in a manic depressive episode, she killed her mother. Her brother, Charles, who was a clerk in the East India Office as well as a poet, dramatist and essayist, prevented her committal to an institution with the promise that he would look after her. She began jointly with her brother to write poetry and prose for children, at the invitation of the children's publisher, M. J. Godwin, the second wife of William Godwin. Mrs Godwin commissioned the Lambs to write *The King and Queen of Hearts* (by Charles Lamb), 1805; *Tales from Shakespeare* (two-thirds by Mary, and one-third by Charles), 1807; *The Adventures of Ulysses* (by Charles Lamb), 1808; *Mrs Leicester's School* (by Mary Lamb) and *Poetry for Children* (two-thirds by Mary and one-third by Charles), 1809; and *Prince Dorus* (by Charles Lamb), 1811. In her lifetime, none of Mary Lamb's works were attributed to her. 'On Needlework', her article on the plight of seamstresses, was first printed in *The British Lady's Magazine and Monthly Miscellany*, April 1815, under the pseudonym of 'Sempronia'. E. V. Lucas tries to explain this lack of attribution: 'Although Mary Lamb was the true author of the book [*Tales from Shakespeare*], as of *Mrs Leicester's School* and of *Poetry for Children*, her share being much greater than her brother's in all of these, she was not until many years later associated publicly with any of them. The *Tales* were attributed to Charles Lamb, presumably against his wish . . . and the other two books had no name attached to them at all. Why Mary Lamb preserved such strict anonymity we do not now know; but it was probably from a natural shrinking from any kind of publicity after the unhappy publicity which she had once gained by her misfortune [her matricide]' (*The Works of Charles and Mary Lamb*, ed. E. V. Lucas, vol. 3, *Poetry for Children*, 1903, p. 478). The text of 'On Needlework' comes from *The Works in Prose and Verse of Charles and Mary Lamb*, 2 vols, ed. Thomas Hutchinson

(1908), pp. 221–7. Biographical information comes from *The Works of Mary and Charles Lamb*, ed. E. V. Lucas, vol. 6, *Letters 1796–1820* (1905), Edmund Blunden's *Charles Lamb and His Contemporaries* (1934) and W. F. Courtney's *Young Charles Lamb* (1982).

ON NEEDLEWORK

In early life I passed eleven years in the exercise of my needle for a livelihood. Will you allow me to address your readers, among whom might perhaps be found some of the kind patronesses of my former humble labours, on a subject widely connected with female life – the state of needlework in this country.

To lighten the heavy burden which many ladies impose upon themselves is one object which I have in view: but I confess, my strongest motive is to excite attention towards the industrious sisterhood to which I once belonged.

From books I have been informed of the fact, upon which 'The British Lady's Magazine'* chiefly founds it pretensions, namely, that women have of late been rapidly advancing in intellectual improvement. Much may have been gained in this way, indirectly, for that class of females for whom I wish to plead. Needlework and intellectual improvement are naturally in a state of warfare. But I am afraid the root of the evil has not as yet been struck at. Workwomen of every description were never in so much distress for want of employment.

Among the present circle of my acquaintance I am proud to rank many that may truly be called respectable; nor do the female part of them, in their mental attainments, at all disprove the prevailing opinion of that intellectual progression which you have taken as the basis of your work; yet I affirm that I know not a single family where there is not some essential drawback to its comfort which may be traced to needlework *done at home*, as the phrase is for all needlework performed in a family by some of its own members, and for which no remuneration in money is received or expected.

In money alone, did I say? I would appeal to all the fair votaries of voluntary housewifery, whether, in the matter of conscience, any one of them ever thought she had done as much needlework as she ought to have done. Even fancy work, the fairest of the tribe! – how delightful the arrangement of her materials! the fixing upon her happiest pattern, how pleasing an anxiety! how cheerful the commencement of the labour she enjoins! But that lady must be a true lover of the art, and so industrious a pursuer of a predetermined purpose, that it were pity her energy should not have been directed to some wiser end, who can affirm she neither feels weariness during the execution of a fancy piece, nor takes more time than she had calculated for the performance.

Is it too bold an attempt to persuade your readers that it would prove an incalculable addition to general happiness, and the domestic comfort of both sexes, if needlework were never practised but for a remuneration in money? As nearly, however, as this desirable thing can be effected, so much more nearly will women be upon an equality with men, as far as respects the mere enjoyment of life. As far as that goes, I believe it is every woman's opinion that the condition of men is far superior to her own.

'They can do what they like,' we say. Do not these words generally mean, they have time to seek out whatever amusements suit their tastes? We dare not tell them we have no time to do this; for, if they should ask in what manner we dispose of our time, we should blush to enter upon a detail of the minutiæ which compose the sum of a woman's daily employment. Nay, many a lady who allows not herself one quarter of an hour's positive leisure during her waking hours, considers her own husband as the most industrious of men, if he steadily pursue his occupation till the hour of dinner, and will be perpetually lamenting her own idleness.

Real business and *real leisure* make up the portions of men's time – two sources of happiness which we certainly partake of in a very inferior degree. To the execution of employment, in which the faculties of the body or mind are called into busy action, there must be a consoling importance attached, which feminine duties (that generic term for all our business) cannot aspire to.

In the most meritorious discharges of those duties, the highest praise we can aim at is to be accounted the helpmates of *man*; who, in return for all he does for us, expects, and justly expects, us to do all in our power to soften and sweeten life.

In how many ways is a good woman employed, in thought or action, through the day, in order that her *good man* may be enabled to feel his leisure hours *real substantial holyday*, and perfect respite from the cares of business! Not the least part to be done to accomplish this end is to fit herself to become a conversational companion; that is to say, she has to study and understand the subjects on which he loves to talk. This part of our duty, if strictly performed, will be found by far our hardest part. The disadvantages we labour under from an education differing from a manly one make the hours in which we *sit and do nothing* in men's company too often any thing but a relaxation; although, as to pleasure and instruction, time so passed may be esteemed more or less delightful.

To make a man's home so desirable a place as to preclude his having a wish to pass his leisure hours at any fireside in preference to his own, I should humbly take to be the sum and substance of woman's domestic ambition. I would appeal to our *British ladies*, who are generally allowed to be the most zealous and successful of all women in the pursuit of this object, – I would appeal to them who have been most successful in the performance of this laudable service, in behalf of father, son, husband, or brother, whether an anxious desire to perform this duty well is not attended with enough of *mental* exertion, at least, to incline them to the opinion that women may be more properly ranked among the contributors to, than the partakers of, the undisturbed relaxation of man.

If a family be so well ordered that the master is never called in to its direction, and yet he perceives comfort and economy well attended to, the mistress of that family (especially if children form a part of it) has, I apprehend, as large a share of womanly employment as ought to satisfy her own sense of duty; even though the needle-book and thread-case were quite laid aside, and she cheerfully contributed her part to the slender gains of the corset-maker, the milliner, the dress-maker, the plain-worker, the embroidress, and all the numerous classifications of females supporting themselves by *needlework*, that great staple commodity which is alone appropriated to the self-supporting part of our sex.

Much has been said and written on the subject of men engrossing to themselves every occupation and calling. After many years of observation and reflection, I am obliged to acquiesce in the notion that it cannot well be ordered otherwise.

If at the birth of girls it were possible to foresee in what cases it would be their fortune to pass a single life, we should soon find trades wrested from their present occupiers, and transferred to the exclusive possession of our sex. The whole mechanical business of copying writings in the law department, for instance, might very soon be transferred with advantage to the poorer sort of women, who with very little teaching would soon beat their rivals of the other sex in facility and neatness. The parents of female children, who were known to be destined from their birth to maintain themselves through the whole course of their lives with like certainty as their sons are, would feel it a duty incumbent on themselves to strengthen the minds, and even the bodily constitutions, of their girls, so circumstanced, by an education which, without affronting the preconceived habits of society, might enable them to follow some occupation now considered above the capacity or too robust for the constitution of our sex. Plenty of resources would then lie open for single women to obtain an independent livelihood, when every parent would be upon the alert to encroach upon some employment, now engrossed by men, for such of their daughters as would then be exactly in the same predicament as their sons now are. Who, for instance, would lay by money to set up his sons in trade; give premiums, and in part maintain them through a long apprenticeship; or, which men of moderate incomes frequently do, strain every nerve in order to bring them up to a learned profession; if it were in a very high degree probable that, by the time they were twenty years of age, they would be taken from this trade or profession, and maintained during the remainder of their lives by the *person whom they should marry*. Yet this is precisely the situation in which every parent, whose income does not very much exceed the moderate, is placed with respect to his daughters.

Even where boys have gone through a laborious education, superinducing habits of steady attention, accompanied with the entire conviction that the business which they learn is to be the source of their future distinction, may it not be affirmed that the persevering industry required to accomplish this desirable end causes many a hard struggle in the minds of young men, even of the most hopeful disposition? What then must be the disadvantages under which a very young woman is placed who is required to learn a trade, from which she can never expect to reap any profit, but at the expense of losing that place in society, to the possession of which she may reasonably look forward, inasmuch as it is by far the most *common lot*, namely, the condition of a *happy* English wife?

As I desire to offer nothing to the consideration of your

readers but what, at least as far as my own observation goes, I consider as truths confirmed by experience, I will only say that, were I to follow the bent of my own speculative opinion, I should be inclined to persuade every female over whom I hoped to have any influence to contribute all the assistance in her power to those of her own sex who may need it, in the employments they at present occupy, rather than to force them into situations now filled wholly by men. With the mere exception of the profits which they have a right to derive from their needle, I would take nothing from the industry of man which he already possesses.

'A penny saved is a penny earned,' is a maxim not true, unless the penny be saved in the same time in which it might have been earned. I, who have known what it is to work for *money earned*, have since had much experience in working for *money saved*; and I consider, from the closest calculation I can make, that a *penny saved* in that way bears about a true proportion to a *farthing earned*. I am no advocate for women, who do not depend on themselves for a subsistence, proposing to themselves to *earn money*. My reasons for thinking it not advisable are too numerous to state – reasons deduced from authentic facts, and strict observations on domestic life in its various shades of comfort. But, if the females of a family, *nominally* supported by the other sex, find it necessary to add something to the common stock, why not endeavour to do something by which they may produce money *in its true shape*?

It would be an excellent plan, attended with very little trouble, to calculate every evening how much money has been saved by needlework *done in the family*, and compare the result with the daily portion of the yearly income. Nor would it be amiss to make a memorandum of the time passed in this way, adding also a guess as to what share it has taken up in the thoughts and conversation. This would be an easy mode of forming a true notion, and getting at the exact worth of this species of *home* industry, and perhaps might place it in a different light from any in which it has hitherto been the fashion to consider it.

Needlework, taken up as an amusement, may not be altogether unamusing. We are all pretty good judges of what entertains ourselves, but it is not so easy to pronounce upon what may contribute to the entertainment of others. At all events, let us not confuse the motives of economy with those of simple pastime. If *saving* be no object, and long habit have rendered needlework so delightful an avocation that we cannot think of relinquishing it, there are the good old contrivances in which our grand-dames were used to beguile and lose their time – knitting, knotting, netting, carpet working, and the like ingenious pursuits – those so-often-praised but tedious works, which are so long in the operation, that purchasing the labour has seldom been thought good economy, yet, by a certain fascination, they have been found to chain down the great to a self-imposed slavery, from which they considerately, or haughtily, excuse the needy. These may be esteemed lawful and lady-like amusements. But, if those works, more usually denominated useful, yield greater satisfaction, it might be a laudable scruple of conscience, and no bad test to herself of her own motive, if a lady, who had no absolute need, were to give the money so saved to poor needle-women belonging to those branches of employment from which she has borrowed these shares of pleasurable labour.

1815

MARY RUSSELL MITFORD

MARY RUSSELL MITFORD (1787–1855), poet and prose writer, was an only child who was born at Arlesford in Hampshire. Her mother had inherited money from her father Richard Russell, but she married a wastrel doctor of medicine, George Mitford, who was ten years younger, and who squandered both her inheritance and the £20,000 that their daughter won in a lottery in 1795. Neither mother nor daughter lost their affection for George Mitford throughout their decline from wealth to poverty. Mary Russell Mitford learned Latin, French, Italian, history, geography, and astronomy, as well as the feminine accomplishments of music, singing, and drawing. George Mitford established the family at Bertram House with the money from the lottery, but by 1820 they were forced because of financial losses to give up this prestigious home and move to a tenement at Three Miles Cross, near Reading, which was Mary Russell Mitford's home for thirty years. It was here that Mary Russell Mitford, always trying to recoup her father's losses through her prose writing, wrote the justly famed sketches that, after first appearing in *The Lady's Magazine*, formed the basis of the five-volume collection of sketches, *Our Village* (1824–32). She was awarded a literary pension of £100 per annum in 1837. Mitford also corresponded regularly with Sir William Elford (1749–1837) about literary and social matters of the day. By choice, Mitford never married. Mitford also published many prose essays as well as *Miscellaneous Poems* (1810). Biographical information comes from R. Brimley Johnson's 'Introduction' to *The Letters of Mary Russell Mitford* (1925), from which the text of the letter to Sir William Elford is taken (pp. 125–9). 'Our Village' comes from *Our Village: Sketches of Rural Character and Scenery*, 5th edn (1830), vol. 1, pp. 1–16.

Bertram House, 3 April 1815

Alas! my dear friend, you are mistaken – quite mistaken, I assure you. I am not going to be married. No such good luck, as papa says. I have not been courted, and I am not in love. So much for this question. If I ever should happen to be going to be married (elegant construction this!) I will then not fail to let you into the secret; but alas! alas! alas! 'In such a *then* I write a never.'

Pray have you read *The Lord of the Isles*?* I do not mean, as I once unwittingly did in the beginning of our correspondence, to draw you into the scrape of reading a poem; but, if you should by chance have looked at it, pray tell me how you like it. It is certainly a thousand times better than *Rokeby*, and yet it does not please me as Scott's poems used to do. I am afraid that I once admired him a great deal too much; and now am in some danger of liking him a great deal too little. Nothing is so violent as a rebound, either of the head or the heart. Once extinguished, enthusiasm and all the fire in Vesuvius* will never light it again. I fancy that the world is something of my mind in this respect, and begins to tire of its idol. Only the world is not half so honest, and instead of knocking down one piece of wood, contents itself with sticking up another right before it. 'It is not,' say all the gentle damsels of my acquaintance, 'that we like Scott* less – we only like Lord Byron* better.' Now I do not – I like Scott less – but Lord Byron less still. The only *modern* poet whom I like better and better is Campbell.*

I have told you that I would not put you in danger of being jingled into a fever by 'mincing poesy'; but I have found out, to my great satisfaction, that I shan't affront you by recommending a prose epic to your perusal; and I have lately been very much and very unexpectedly pleased with Lady Morgan's (*ci-devant* Miss Owenson) *O'Donnel*.* I had a great prejudice and dislike to this fair authoress ever since I read a certain description of which she was guilty, where part of a lady's dress is described as 'an apparent tissue of woven air', and really took up the book with an idea that nothing but nonsense could come from that quarter. I was, however, very much disappointed in my malicious expectations of laughing at her, and obliged to content myself with laughing with her. Her hero is very interesting – her heroine very amusing. There are some good characters, particularly a managing bustling woman of fashion; *et pour la bonne bouche** there is an Irish servant not much, if at all, inferior to the admirable Irishmen of Miss Edgeworth.*

À propos to novels, I have discovered that our great favourite, Miss Austen,* is my countrywoman; that mamma knew all her family very intimately; and that she herself is an old maid (I beg her pardon – I mean a young lady) with whom mamma before her marriage was acquainted. Mamma says that she was then the prettiest, silliest, most affected, husband-hunting butterfly she ever remembers; and a friend of mine, who visits her now, says that she has stiffened into the most perpendicular, precise, taciturn piece of 'single blessedness' that ever existed, and that, till *Pride and Prejudice* showed what a precious gem was hidden in that unbending case, she was no more regarded in society than a poker or a fire-screen, or any other thin upright piece of wood or iron that fills its corner in peace and quietness. The case is very different now; she is still a poker – but a poker of whom every one is afraid. It must be confessed that this silent observation from such an observer is rather formidable. Most writers are good-humoured chatterers – neither very wise nor very witty: – but nine times out of ten (at least in the few that I have known) unaffected and pleasant, and quite removing by their conversation any awe that may have been excited by their works. But a wit, a delineator of character, who does not talk, is terrific indeed!

After all, I do not know that I can quite vouch for this account, though the friend from whom I received it is truth itself; but her family connections must render her disagreeable to Miss Austen, since she is the sister-in-law of a gentleman who is at law with Miss A.'s brother for the greater part of his fortune. You must have remarked how much her stories hinge upon entailed estates; doubtless she has learnt to dislike entails. Her brother was adopted by Mr Knight, who left him his name and two much better legacies in an estate of five thousand a year in Kent, and another of nearly double the value in Hampshire; but it seems he forgot some ceremony – passing a fine, I think they call it – with regard to the Hampshire property, which Mr Baverstock has claimed in right of his mother, together with the

mesne rents, and is likely to be successful. Before I quite drop
the subject of novels, I must tell you that I am reading *Guy
Mannering** with great pleasure. I have not finished it nearly, so
that I speak of it now as any one would do that had read no
further than the second volume of the *Mysteries of Udolpho*,*
and that would be much better than one who had finished it. I
do not think that Walter Scott did write *Guy Mannering*; it is
not nearly so like him as *Waverley** was, and the motto is from
*The Lay.**

I am quite happy that you are of my opinion with regard to
Scripture heroes; I always think myself so safe when you agree
with me. It was, however, natural in Mr Haydon* to wish to
draw the bow of Ulysses* and try the subject which has engaged
all the great masters. Mr Eustace,* I think it is, who has objected
to the exaggerated expression of meekness which distinguishes
the Christ of the Italian painters. In those which I have seen I
should rather complain of the *entire absence* of the expression
of power – power latent, dormant, in repose, but still power –
still that power which could without exertion, with unaltered
calmness, heal the sick and raise the dead. It would be less
absurd to paint a sleeping Hercules* without the appearance of
strength, than to delineate our Saviour without the expression
of power. No one can so well supply this defect as Mr Haydon,
and he is very likely to have done it.

Always most affectionately yours,
M. R. M.

OUR VILLAGE

Of all situations for a constant residence, that which appears to
me most delightful is a little village far in the country: a small
neighbourhood, not of fine mansions finely peopled, but of
cottages and cottage-like houses, 'messuages* or tenements', as
a friend of mine calls such ignoble and nondescript dwellings,
with inhabitants whose faces are as familiar to us as the flowers
in our garden; a little world of our own, close-packed and
insulated like ants in an ant-hill, or bees in a hive, or sheep in a
fold, or nuns in a convent, or sailors in a ship; where we know
every one, are known to every one, interested in every one, and

authorized to hope that every one feels an interest in us. How pleasant it is to slide into these true-hearted feelings from the kindly and unconscious influence of habit, and to learn to know and to love the people about us, with all their peculiarities, just as we learn to know and to love the nooks and turns of the shady lanes and sunny commons that we pass every day. Even in books I like a confined locality, and so do the critics when they talk of the unities. Nothing is so tiresome as to be whirled half over Europe at the chariot wheels of a hero, to go to sleep at Vienna, and awaken at Madrid; it produces a real fatigue, a weariness of spirit. On the other hand, nothing is so delightful as to sit down in a country village in one of Miss Austen's delicious novels, quite sure before we leave it to become intimate with every spot and every person it contains; or to ramble with Mr White* over his own parish of Selborne, and form a friendship with the fields and coppices, as well as with the birds, mice, and squirrels, who inhabit them; or to sail with Robinson Crusoe to his island, and live there with him and his goats and his man Friday; – how much we dread any new comers, any fresh importation of savage or sailor! we never sympathise for a moment in our hero's want of company, and are quite grieved when he gets away; – or to be shipwrecked with Ferdinand on that other lovelier island – the island of Prospero, and Miranda, and Caliban, and Ariel,* and nobody else, none of Dryden's* exotic inventions; – that is best of all. And a small neighbourhood is as good in sober waking reality as in poetry or prose; a village neighbourhood, such as this Berkshire hamlet in which I write, a long, straggling, winding street at the bottom of a fine eminence, with a road through it, always abounding in carts, horsemen, and carriages, and lately enlivened by a stage-coach from B—— to S——, which passed through about ten days ago, and will I suppose return some time or other. There are coaches of all varieties now-a-days; perhaps this may be intended for a monthly diligence, or a fortnight fly. Will you walk with me through our village, courteous reader? The journey is not long. We will begin at the lower end, and proceed up the hill.

The tidy, square, red cottage on the right hand, with the long well-stocked garden by the side of the road, belongs to a retired publican from a neighbouring town; a substantial person with a comely wife; one who piques himself on independence and idleness, talks politics, reads newspapers, hates the minister, and

cries out for reform. He introduced into our peaceful vicinage
the rebellious innovation of an illumination on the queen's
acquittal. Remonstrance and persuasion were in vain; he talked
of liberty and broken windows – so we all lighted up. Oh! how
he shone that night with candles and laurel, and white bows,
and gold paper, and a transparency (originally designed for a
pocket-handkerchief) with a flaming portrait of her Majesty,
hatted and feathered, in red ochre. He had no rival in the village,
that we all acknowledged; the very bonfire was less splendid;
the little boys reserved their best crackers to be expended in his
honour, and he gave them full sixpence more than any one else.
He would like an illumination once a month; for it must not be
concealed that, in spite of gardening, of newspaper reading, of
jaunting about in his little cart, and frequenting both church
and meeting, our worthy neighbour begins to feel the weariness
of idleness. He hangs over his gate, and tries to entice passengers
to stop and chat; he volunteers little jobs all round, smokes
cherry-trees to cure the blight, and traces and blows up all the
wasp-nests in the parish. I have seen a great many wasps in our
garden to-day, and shall enchant him with the intelligence. He
even assists his wife in her sweepings and dustings. Poor man!
he is a very respectable person, and would be a very happy one,
if he would add a little employment to his dignity. It would be
the salt of life to him.

Next to his house, though parted from it by another long
garden with a new arbour at the end, is the pretty dwelling of
the shoemaker, a pale, sickly-looking, black-haired man, the
very model of sober industry. There he sits in his little shop
from early morning till late at night. An earthquake would
hardly stir him: the illumination did not. He stuck immoveably
to his last, from the first lighting up, through the long blaze and
the slow decay, till his large solitary candle was the only light in
the place. One cannot conceive any thing more perfect than the
contempt which the man of transparencies and the man of shoes
must have felt for each other on that evening. There was at least
as much vanity in the sturdy industry as in the strenuous
idleness, for our shoemaker is a man of substance, he employs
three journeymen, two lame, and one a dwarf, so that his shop
looks like an hospital; he has purchased the lease of his
commodious dwelling, some even say that he has bought it out
and out; and he has only one pretty daughter, a light, delicate,

fair-haired girl of fourteen, the champion, protectress, and playfellow of every brat under three years old, whom she jumps, dances, dandles, and feeds all day long. A very attractive person is that child-loving girl. I have never seen any one in her station who possessed so thoroughly that undefinable charm, the lady-look. See her on a Sunday in her simplicity and her white frock, and she might pass for an earl's daughter. She likes flowers too, and has a profusion of white stocks under her window, as pure and delicate as herself.

The first house on the opposite side of the way is the blacksmith's; a gloomy dwelling, where the sun never seems to shine; dark and smoky within and without, like a forge. The blacksmith is a high officer in our little state, nothing less than a constable; but, alas! alas! when tumults arise, and the constable is called for, he will commonly be found in the thickest of the fray. Lucky would it be for his wife and her eight children if there were no public-house in the land: an inveterate inclination to enter those bewitching doors is Mr Constable's only fault.

Next to this official dwelling is a spruce brick tenement, red, high, and narrow, boasting, one above another, three sash-windows, the only sash-windows in the village, with a clematis on one side and a rose on the other, tall and narrow like itself. That slender mansion has a fine genteel look. The little parlour seems made for Hogarth's old maid and her stunted footboy; for tea and card-parties, – it would just hold one table; for the rustle of faded silks, and the splendour of old china; for the delight of four by honours, and a little snug quiet scandal between the deals; for affected gentility and real starvation. This should have been its destiny; but fate has been unpropitious; it belongs to a plump, merry, bustling dame, with four fat, rosy, noisy children, the very essence of vulgarity and plenty.

Then comes the village shop, like other village shops, multi-farious as a bazaar; a repository for bread, shoes, tea, cheese, tape, ribands, and bacon; for every thing, in short, except the one particular thing which you happen to want at the moment, and will be sure not to find. The people are civil and thriving, and frugal withal; they have let the upper part of their house to two young women (one of them is a pretty blue-eyed girl) who teach little children their A B C, and make caps and gowns for their mammas, – parcel schoolmistress, parcel mantua-maker. I believe they find adorning the body a more profitable vocation than adorning the mind.

Divided from the shop by a narrow yard, and opposite the shoemaker's, is a habitation of whose inmates I shall say nothing. A cottage – no – a miniature house, with many additions, little odds and ends of places, pantries, and what not; all angles, and of a charming in-and-outness; a little bricked court before one half, and a little flower-yard before the other; the walls, old and weather-stained, covered with hollyhocks, roses, honeysuckles, and a great apricot-tree; the casements full of geraniums: (ah, there is our superb white cat peeping out from amongst them!) the closets (our landlord has the assurance to call them rooms) full of contrivances and corner-cupboards; and the little garden behind full of common flowers, tulips, pinks, larkspurs, peonies, stocks, and carnations, with an arbour of privet, not unlike a sentry-box, where one lives in a delicious green light, and looks out on the gayest of all gay flower-beds. That house was built on purpose to show in what an exceedingly small compass comfort may be packed. Well, I will loiter there no longer.

The next tenement is a place of importance, the Rose inn; a white-washed building, retired from the road behind its fine swinging sign, with a little bow-window room coming out on one side, and forming, with our stable on the other, a sort of open square, which is the constant resort of carts, waggons, and return chaises. There are two carts there now, and mine host is serving them with beer in his eternal red waistcoat. He is a thriving man and a portly, as his waistcoat attests, which has been twice let out within this twelvemonth. Our landlord has a stirring wife, a hopeful son, and a daughter, the belle of the village; not so pretty as the fair nymph of the shoe-shop, and far less elegant, but ten times as fine; all curl-papers in the morning, like a porcupine, all curls in the afternoon, like a poodle, with more flounces than curl-papers, and more lovers than curls. Miss Phœbe is fitter for town than country; and, to do her justice, she has a consciousness of that fitness, and turns her steps town-ward as often as she can. She is gone to B—— to-day with her last and principal lover, a recruiting serjeant – a man as tall as Serjeant Kite, and as impudent. Some day or other he will carry off Miss Phœbe.

In a line with the bow-window room is a low garden-wall,

belonging to a house under repair: – the white house opposite the collar-maker's shop, with four lime-trees before it, and a waggon-load of bricks at the door. That house is the plaything of a wealthy, well-meaning, whimsical person, who lives about a mile off. He has a passion for brick and mortar, and, being too wise to meddle with his own residence, diverts himself with altering and re-altering, improving and re-improving, doing and undoing here. It is a perfect Penelope's web.* Carpenters and bricklayers have been at work for these eighteen months, and yet I sometimes stand and wonder whether any thing has really been done. One exploit in last June was, however, by no means equivocal. Our good neighbour fancied that the limes shaded the rooms, and made them dark, (there was not a creature in the house but the workmen,) so he had all the leaves stripped from every tree. There they stood, poor miserable skeletons, as bare as Christmas under the glowing midsummer sun. Nature revenged herself, in her own sweet and gracious manner; fresh leaves sprang out, and at nearly Christmas the foliage was as brilliant as when the outrage was committed.

Next door lives a carpenter, 'famed ten miles round, and worthy all his fame,' – few cabinet-makers surpass him, with his excellent wife, and their little daughter Lizzy, the plaything and queen of the village, a child three years old according to the register, but six in size and strength and intellect, in power and in self-will. She manages everybody in the place, her school-mistress included; turns the wheeler's children out of their own little cart, and makes them draw her; seduces cakes and lolly-pops from the very shop window; makes the lazy carry her, the silent talk to her, the grave romp with her; does any thing she pleases; is absolutely irresistible. Her chief attraction lies in her exceeding power of loving, and her firm reliance on the love and indulgence of others. How impossible it would be to disappoint the dear little girl when she runs to meet you, slides her pretty hand into yours, looks up gladly in your face, and says, 'Come!' You must go: you cannot help it. Another part of her charm is her singular beauty. Together with a good deal of the character of Napoleon, she has something of his square, sturdy, upright form, with the finest limbs in the world, a complexion purely English, a round laughing face, sunburnt and rosy, large merry blue eyes, curling brown hair, and a wonderful play of counten-ance. She has the imperial attitudes too, and loves to stand with her hands behind her, or folded over her bosom; and sometimes, when she has a little touch of shyness, she clasps them together on the top of her head, pressing down her shining curls, and looking so exquisitely pretty! Yes, Lizzy is queen of the village! She has but one rival in her dominions, a certain white greyhound called May-flower, much her friend, who resembles her in beauty and strength, in playfulness, and almost in sagacity, and reigns over the animal world as she over the human. They are both coming with me, Lizzy and Lizzy's 'pretty May'. We are now at the end of the street; a cross lane, a rope-walk, shaded with limes and oaks, and a cool clear pond overhung with elms, lead us to the bottom of the hill. There is still one house round the corner, ending in a picturesque wheeler's shop. The dwelling-house is more ambitious. Look at the fine flowered window-blinds, the green door with the brass knocker, and the somewhat prim but very civil person, who is sending off a labouring man with sirs and curtsies enough for a prince of the blood. Those are the curate's lodgings – apartments his landlady would call them: he lives with his own family four miles off, but once or twice a week he comes to his neat little parlour to write sermons, to marry, or to bury, as the case may require. Never were better or kinder people than his host and hostess: and there is a reflection of clerical importance about them, since their connection with the Church, which is quite edifying – a decorum, a gravity, a solemn politeness. Oh, to see the worthy wheeler carry the gown after his lodger on a Sunday, nicely pinned up in his wife's best handkerchief – or to hear him rebuke a squalling child or a squabbling woman! The curate is nothing to him. He is fit to be perpetual churchwarden.

We must now cross the lane into the shady rope-walk. That pretty white cottage opposite, which stands straggling at the end of the village in a garden full of flowers, belongs to our mason, the shortest of men, and his handsome, tall wife: he, a dwarf, with the voice of a giant; one starts when he begins to talk as if he were shouting through a speaking trumpet; she, the sister, daughter, and grand-daughter, of a long line of gardeners, and no contemptible one herself. It is very magnanimous in me not to hate her: for she beats me in my own way, in chrysanthemums, and dahlias, and the like gauds. Her plants are sure to live; mine have a sad trick of dying, perhaps because I love them, 'not wisely, but too well', and kill them with over-kindness. Half-way up the hill is another detached cottage, the residence of an officer, and his beautiful family. That eldest boy, who is hanging over the gate, and looking with such intense childish admiration at my Lizzy, might be a model for a Cupid.

How pleasantly the road winds up the hill, with its broad green borders and hedge-rows so thickly timbered! How finely the evening sun falls on that sandy excavated bank, and touches the farm-house on the top of the eminence! and how clearly defined and relieved is the figure of the man who is just coming down! It is poor John Evans, the gardener – an excellent gardener till about ten years ago, when he lost his wife, and became insane. He was sent to St Luke's, and dismissed as cured; but his power was gone and his strength; he could no longer manage a garden, nor submit to the restraint, nor encounter the fatigue of regular employment; so he retreated to the workhouse, the pensioner and factotum of the village, amongst whom he divides his services. His mind often wanders, intent on some fantastic and impracticable plan, and lost to present objects; but he is perfectly harmless, and full of a childlike simplicity, a smiling contentedness, a most touching gratitude. Every one is kind to John Evans, for there is that about him which must be loved; and his unprotectedness, his utter defencelessness, have an irresistible claim on every better feeling. I know nobody who inspires so deep and tender a pity; he improves all around him. He is useful, too, to the extent of his little power; will do any thing, but loves gardening best, and still piques himself on his old arts of pruning fruit-trees, and raising cucumbers. He is the happiest of men just now, for he has the management of a melon bed – a melon bed! – fie! What a grand pompous name was that for three melon plants under a hand-light! John Evans is sure that they will succeed. We shall see: as the chancellor said, 'I doubt.'

We are now on the very brow of the eminence, close to the Hill-house and its beautiful garden. On the outer edge of the paling, hanging over the bank that skirts the road, is an old thorn – such a thorn! The long sprays covered with snowy blossoms, so graceful, so elegant, so lightsome, and yet so rich! There only wants a pool under the thorn to give a still lovelier reflection, quivering and trembling, like a tuft of feathers, whiter and greener than the life, and more prettily mixed with the bright blue sky. There should indeed be a pool; but on the dark grass-plat, under the high bank, which is crowned by that magnificent plume, there is something that does almost as well, – Lizzy and May-flower in the midst of a game at romps, 'making a sun-shine in the shady place'; Lizzy rolling, laughing, clapping her hands, and glowing like a rose; May-flower playing about her like summer lightning, dazzling the eyes with her sudden turns, her leaps, her bounds, her attacks and her escapes. She darts round the lovely little girl, with the same momentary touch that the swallow skims over the water, and has exactly the same power of flight, the same matchless ease and strength and grace. What a pretty picture they would make; what a pretty foreground they do make to the real landscape! The road winding down the hill with a slight bend, like that in the High-street at Oxford; a waggon slowly ascending, and a horseman passing it at a full trot – (ah! Lizzy, May-flower will certainly desert you to have a gambol with that blood-horse!) half-way down, just at the turn, the red cottage of the lieutenant, covered with vines, the very image of comfort and content; farther down, on the opposite side, the small white dwelling of the little mason; then the limes and the rope-walk; then the village street, peeping through the trees, whose clustering tops hide all but the chimneys, and various roofs of the houses, and here and there some angle of a wall: farther on, the elegant town of B——, with its fine old church-towers and spires; the whole view shut in by a range of chalky hills; and over every part of the picture, trees so profusely scattered, that it appears like a woodland scene, with glades and villages intermixed. The trees are of all kinds and all hues, chiefly the finely-shaped elm, of so deep and bright a green, the tips of whose high outer branches drop down with such a crisp and garland-like richness, and the oak, whose stately form is just now so splendidly adorned by the sunny colouring of the young leaves. Turning again up the hill, we find ourselves on that peculiar charm of English scenery, a green common, divided by the road; the right side fringed by hedge-rows and trees, with cottages and farm-houses irregularly placed, and terminated by a double avenue of noble oaks; the left, prettier still, dappled by bright pools of water, and islands of cottages and cottage-gardens, and sinking gradually down to corn-fields and meadows, and an old farm-house, with pointed roofs and clustered chimneys, looking out from its blooming orchard, and backed by woody hills. The common is itself the prettiest part of the prospect; half covered with low furze, whose golden blossoms reflect so intensely the last beams of the setting sun, and alive with cows and sheep, and two sets of cricketers: one of young men, surrounded with spectators, some standing, some sitting, some stretched on the grass, all taking a delighted interest in the game; the other, a merry group of little boys, at a humble distance, for whom even cricket is scarcely lively enough, shouting, leaping, and enjoying themselves to their hearts' content. But cricketers and country boys are too important persons in our village to be talked of merely as figures in the landscape. They deserve an individual introduction – an essay to themselves – and they shall have it. No fear of forgetting the good-humoured faces that meet us in our walks every day.

1824

MARY SHELLEY

MARY SHELLEY (née Godwin) (1797–1851) was the daughter of Mary Wollstonecraft and William Godwin, who at the age of seventeen eloped with Percy Bysshe Shelley (1792–1822), the poet and freethinker. Mary Godwin's stepsister, Claire Clairmont, who was sixteen, accompanied them on a brief tour of Europe, which came to an end when they ran out of money. (See entry on Claire Clairmont.) Because Shelley espoused the notion of 'free love', that is of having a sexual relationship outside his marriage, he and Mary Godwin had a child, William, before he married her after the suicide of his first wife Harriet (née Westbrook). Mary Godwin Shelley's literary inclination, which was encouraged early in life, came to fruition through her liaison and subsequent marriage to Percy Bysshe Shelley. Her first work, *History of a Six Weeks' Tour* (1817) was published jointly with him. In it she used her journal record, two of her letters, and two of Shelley's letters as well as his poem, 'Mont Blanc'. Subsequently, she wrote *Frankenstein* (1818); *Rambles in Germany and Italy* (1844); two dramas, *Prosperine* (1820, published 1832) and *Midas* (1820, published 1822); *Lives* (1835–9); and short stories, poems, essays, translations, and reviews. She also became P. B. Shelley's editor after his death in 1822, annotating his *Posthumous Poems* (1822), *Poetical Works* (1839), and *Essays, Letters* (1840). Texts of the letters to Fanny Imlay are from *History of a Six Weeks' Tour* (1817), pp. 85–106; the essay, 'Ghosts', is from *The London Magazine*, 9, March 1824, pp. 253–6; the text of the letter to Maria Gisborne is from the British Library MS (Ashley 5022). Biographical information comes from *The Letters of Mary Wollstonecraft [Godwin] Shelley*, vol. 1, ed. Betty T. Bennett (Baltimore London: The Johns Hopkins University Press, 1980).

Letter 1:
17 May 1816

Hôtel de Secheron, Geneva,
17 May 1816

We arrived at Paris on the 8th of this month, and were detained
two days for the purpose of obtaining the various signatures
necessary to our passports, the French government having
become much more circumspect since the escape of Lavalette.*
We had no letters of introduction, or any friend in that city, and
were therefore confined to our hotel, where we were obliged to
hire apartments for the week, although when we first arrived we
expected to be detained one night only; for in Paris there are no
houses where you can be accommodated with apartments by
the day.

The manners of the French are interesting, although less
attractive, at least to Englishmen, than before the last invasion
of the Allies:* the discontent and sullenness of their minds
perpetually betrays itself. Nor is it wonderful that they should
regard the subjects of a government which fills their country
with hostile garrisons, and sustains a detested dynasty on the
throne, with an acrimony and indignation of which that govern-
ment alone is the proper object. This feeling is honourable to
the French, and encouraging to all those of every nation in
Europe who have a fellow feeling with the oppressed, and who
cherish an unconquerable hope that the cause of liberty must at
length prevail.

Our route after Paris, as far as Troyes, lay through the same
uninteresting tract of country which we had traversed on foot
nearly two years before, but on quitting Troyes we left the road
leading to Neufchâtel, to follow that which was to conduct us
to Geneva. We entered Dijon on the third evening after our
departure from Paris, and passing through Dôle, arrived at
Poligny. This town is built at the foot of Jura, which rises
abruptly from a plain of vast extent. The rocks of the mountain
overhang the houses. Some difficulty in procuring horses

detained us here until the evening closed in, when we proceeded, by the light of a stormy moon, to Champagnolles, a little village situated in the depth of the mountains. The road was serpentine and exceedingly steep, and was overhung on one side by half distinguished precipices, whilst the other was a gulf, filled by the darkness of the driving clouds. The dashing of the invisible mountain streams announced to us that we had quitted the plains of France, as we slowly ascended, amidst a violent storm of wind and rain, to Champagnolles, where we arrived at twelve o'clock, the fourth night after our departure from Paris.

The next morning we proceeded, still ascending among the ravines and vallies of the mountain. The scenery perpetually grows more wonderful and sublime: pine forests of impenetrable thickness, and untrodden, nay, inaccessible expanse spread on every side. Sometimes the dark woods descending, follow the route into the vallies, the distorted trees struggling with knotted roots between the most barren clefts; sometimes the road winds high into the regions of frost, and then the forests become scattered, and the branches of the trees are loaded with snow, and half of the enormous pines themselves buried in the wavy drifts. The spring, as the inhabitants informed us, was unusually late, and indeed the cold was excessive; as we ascended the mountains, the same clouds which rained on us in the vallies poured forth large flakes of snow thick and fast. The sun occasionally shone through these showers, and illuminated the magnificent ravines of the mountains, whose gigantic pines were some laden with snow, some wreathed round by the lines of scattered and lingering vapour; others darting their dark spires into the sunny sky, brilliantly clear and azure.

As the evening advanced, and we ascended higher, the snow, which we had beheld whitening the overhanging rocks, now encroached upon our road, and it snowed fast as we entered the village of Les Rousses, where we were threatened by the apparent necessity of passing the night in a bad inn and dirty beds. For from that place there are two roads to Geneva; one by Nion, in the Swiss territory, where the mountain route is shorter, and comparatively easy at that time of the year, when the road is for several leagues covered with snow of an enormous depth; the other road lay through Gex, and was too circuitous and dangerous to be attempted at so late an hour in the day. Our passport, however, was for Gex, and we were told that we could not change its destination; but all these police laws, so severe in themselves, are to be softened by bribery, and this difficulty was at length overcome. We hired four horses, and ten men to support the carriage, and departed from Les Rousses at six in the evening, when the sun had already far descended, and the snow pelting against the windows of our carriage, assisted the coming darkness to deprive us of the view of the lake of Geneva and the far distant Alps.

The prospect around, however, was sufficiently sublime to command our attention – never was scene more awfully desolate. The trees in these regions are incredibly large, and stand in scattered clumps over the white wilderness; the vast expanse of snow was chequered only by these gigantic pines, and the poles that marked our road: no river or rock-encircled lawn relieved the eye, by adding the picturesque to the sublime. The natural silence of that uninhabited desert contrasted strangely with the voices of the men who conducted us, who, with animated tones and gestures, called to one another in a *patois* composed of French and Italian, creating disturbance, where but for them, there was none.

To what a different scene are we now arrived! To the warm sunshine and to the humming of sun-loving insects. From the windows of our hotel we see the lovely lake, blue as the heavens which it reflects, and sparkling with golden beams. The opposite shore is sloping, and covered with vines, which however do not so early in the season· add to the beauty of the prospect. Gentlemen's seats are scattered over these banks, behind which rise the various ridges of black mountains, and towering far above, in the midst of its snowy Alps, the majestic Mont Blanc, highest and queen of all. Such is the view reflected by the lake; it is a bright summer scene without any of that sacred solitude and deep seclusion that delighted us at Lucerne.

We have not yet found out any very agreeable walks, but you know our attachment to water excursions. We have hired a boat, and every evening at about six o'clock we sail on the lake, which is delightful, whether we glide over a glassy surface or are speeded along by a strong wind. The waves of this lake never afflict me with that sickness that deprives me of all enjoyment in a sea voyage; on the contrary, the tossing of our boat raises my spirits and inspires me with unusual hilarity. Twilight here is of short duration, but we at present enjoy the benefit of an increasing moon, and seldom return until ten o'clock, when, as we approach the shore, we are saluted by the delightful scent of flowers and new mown grass, and the chirp of the grasshoppers, and the song of the evening birds.

We do not enter into society here, yet our time passes swiftly and delightfully. We read Latin and Italian during the heats of noon, and when the sun declines we walk in the garden of the hotel, looking at the rabbits, relieving fallen cockchaffers, and watching the motions of a myriad of lizards, who inhabit a southern wall of the garden. You know that we have just escaped from the gloom of winter and of London; and coming to this delightful spot during this divine weather, I feel as happy as a new-fledged bird, and hardly care what twig I fly to, so that I may try my new-found wings. A more experienced bird may be more difficult in its choice of a bower; but in my present temper of mind, the budding flowers, the fresh grass of spring, and the happy creatures about me that live and enjoy these pleasures, are quite enough to afford me exquisite delight, even though clouds should shut out Mont Blanc from my sight. Adieu!

M.

Letter 2: 1 June 1816

Coligny–Geneva–Plainpalais

Campagne C******, near Coligny,
1 June

You will perceive from my date that we have changed our residence since my last letter. We now inhabit a little cottage on the opposite shore of the lake, and have exchanged the view of Mont Blanc and her snowy *aiguilles** for the dark frowning Jura, behind whose range we every evening see the sun sink, and darkness approaches our valley from behind the Alps, which are then tinged by that glowing rose-like hue which is observed in England to attend on the clouds of an autumnal sky when daylight is almost gone. The lake is at our feet, and a little harbour contains our boat, in which we still enjoy our evening excursions on the water. Unfortunately we do not now enjoy those brilliant skies that hailed us on our first arrival to this country. An almost perpetual rain confines us principally to the house; but when the sun bursts forth it is with a splendour and heat unknown in

England. The thunder storms that visit us are grander and more terrific than I have ever seen before. We watch them as they approach from the opposite side of the lake, observing the lightning play among the clouds in various parts of the heavens, and dart in jagged figures upon the piny heights of Jura, dark with the shadow of the overhanging cloud, while perhaps the sun is shining cheerily upon us. One night we *enjoyed* a finer storm than I had ever before beheld. The lake was lit up – the pines on Jura made visible, and all the scene illuminated for an instant, when a pitchy blackness succeeded, and the thunder came in frightful bursts over our heads amid the darkness.

But while I still dwell on the country around Geneva, you will expect me to say something of the town itself: there is nothing, however, in it that can repay you for the trouble of walking over its rough stones. The houses are high, the streets narrow, many of them on the ascent, and no public building of any beauty to attract your eye, or any architecture to gratify your taste. The town is surrounded by a wall, the three gates of which are shut exactly at ten o'clock, when no bribery (as in France) can open them. To the south of the town is the promenade of the Genevese, a grassy plain planted with a few trees, and called Plainpalais. Here a small obelisk is erected to the glory of Rousseau, and here (such is the mutability of human life) the magistrates, the successors of those who exiled him from his native country, were shot by the populace during that revolution, which his writings mainly contributed to mature, and which, notwithstanding the temporary bloodshed and injustice with which it was polluted, has produced enduring benefits to mankind, which all the chicanery of statesmen, nor even the great conspiracy of kings, can entirely render vain. From respect to the memory of their predecessors, none of the present magistrates ever walk in Plainpalais. Another Sunday recreation for the citizens is an excursion to the top of Mont Salève. This hill is within a league of the town, and rises perpendicularly from the cultivated plain. It is ascended on the other side, and I should judge from its situation that your toil is rewarded by a delightful view of the course of the Rhone and Arve, and of the shores of the lake. We have not yet visited it.

There is more equality of classes here than in England. This occasions a greater freedom and refinement of manners among the lower orders than we meet with in our own country. I fancy

the haughty English ladies are greatly disgusted with this conse-
quence of republican institutions, for the Genevese servants
complain very much of their *scolding*, an exercise of the tongue,
I believe, perfectly unknown here. The peasants of Switzerland
may not however emulate the vivacity and grace of the French.
They are more cleanly, but they are slow and inapt. I know a
girl of twenty, who although she had lived all her life among
vineyards, could not inform me during what month the vintage
took place, and I discovered she was utterly ignorant of the
order in which the months succeed to one another. She would
not have been surprised if I had talked of the burning sun and
delicious fruits of December, or of the frosts of July. Yet she is
by no means deficient in understanding.

The Genevese are also much inclined to puritanism. It is true
that from habit they dance on a Sunday, but as soon as the
French government was abolished in the town, the magistrates
ordered the theatre to be closed, and measures were taken to
pull down the building.

We have latterly enjoyed fine weather, and nothing is more
pleasant than to listen to the evening song of the vine-dressers.
They are all women, and most of them have harmonious
although masculine voices. The theme of their ballads consists
of shepherds, love, flocks, and the sons of kings who fall in love
with beautiful shepherdesses. Their tunes are monotonous, but
it is sweet to hear them in the stillness of evening, while we are
enjoying the sight of the setting sun, either from the hill behind
our house or from the lake.

Such are our pleasures here, which would be greatly increased
if the season had been more favourable, for they chiefly consist
in such enjoyments as sunshine and gentle breezes bestow. We
have not yet made any excursion in the environs of the town,
but we have planned several, when you shall again hear of us;
and we will endeavour, by the magic of words, to transport the
ethereal part of you to the neighbourhood of the Alps, and
mountain streams, and forests, which, while they clothe the
former, darken the latter with their vast shadows. Adieu!

M.

ON GHOSTS

> I look for ghosts – but none will force
> Their way to me; 'tis falsely said
> That there was ever intercourse
> Between the living and the dead – Wordsworth*

What a different earth do we inhabit from that on which our forefathers dwelt! The antediluvian world, strode over by mammoths, preyed upon by the megatherion, and peopled by the offspring of the Sons of God, is a better type of the earth of Homer, Herodotus, and Plato,* than the hedged-in cornfields and measured hills of the present day. The globe was then encircled by a wall which paled in the bodies of men, whilst their feathered thoughts soared over the boundary; it had a brink, and in the deep profound which it overhung, men's imaginations, eagle-winged, dived and flew, and brought home strange tales to their believing auditors. Deep caverns harboured giants; cloudlike birds cast their shadows upon the plains; while far out at sea lay islands of bliss, the fair paradise of Atlantis* or El Dorado* sparkling with untold jewels. Where are they now? The Fortunate Isles* have lost the glory that spread a halo round them; for who deems himself nearer to the golden age, because he touches at the Canaries* on his voyage to India? Our only riddle is the rise of the Niger,* the interior of New Holland,* our only terra incognita; and our sole mare incognitum,* the north-west passage. But these are tame wonders, lions in leash; we do not invest Mungo Park,* or the Captain of the *Hecla*,* with divine attributes; no one fancies that the waters of the unknown river bubble up from hell's fountains, no strange and weird power is supposed to guide the ice-berg, nor do we fable that a stray pick-pocket from Botany Bay* has found the gardens of the Hesperides* within the circuit of the Blue Mountains.* What have we left to dream about? The clouds are no longer the charioted servants of the sun, nor does he any more hath his glowing brow in the bath of Thetis;* the rainbow has ceased to be the messenger of the Gods, and thunder is no longer their awful voice, warning man of that which is to come. We have the sun which has been weighed and measured, but not understood; we have the assemblage of the planets, the congregation of the stars, and the yet unshackled ministration of the winds: – such is the list of our ignorance.

Nor is the empire of the imagination less bounded in its own proper creations, than in those which were bestowed on it by the poor blind eyes of our ancestors. What has become of enchantresses with their palaces of crystal and dungeons of palpable darkness? What of fairies and their wands? What of witches and their familiars? and, last, what of ghosts, with beckoning hands and fleeting shapes, which quelled the soldier's brave heart, and made the murderer disclose to the astonished noon the veiled work of midnight? These which were realities to our forefathers, in our wiser age –

> – Characterless are grated
> To dusty nothing.

Yet is it true that we do not believe in ghosts? There used to be several traditionary tales repeated, with their authorities, enough to stagger us when we consigned them to that place where that is which 'is as though it had never been'. But these are gone out of fashion. Brutus's dream* has become a deception of his over-heated brain, Lord Lyttleton's vision* is called a cheat; and one by one these inhabitants of deserted houses, moonlight glades, misty mountain tops, and midnight church-yards, have been ejected from their immemorial seats, and small thrill is felt when the dead majesty of Denmark blanches the cheek and unsettles the reason of his philosophic son.*

But do none of us believe in ghosts? If this question be read at noon-day, when –

> Every little corner, nook, and hole,
> Is penetrated with the insolent light –

at such a time derision is seated on the features of my reader. But let it be twelve at night in a lone house; take up, I beseech you, the story of the Bleeding Nun; or of the Statue, to which the bridegroom gave the wedding ring, and she came in the dead of night to claim him, tall, white, and cold; or of the Grandsire, who with shadowy form and breathless lips stood over the couch and kissed the foreheads of his sleeping grandchildren, and thus doomed them to their fated death; and let all these details be assisted by solitude, flapping curtains, rushing wind, a long and dusky passage, an half open door – O, then truly, another answer may be given, and many will request leave to sleep upon it, before they decide whether there be such a thing as a ghost in the world, or out of the world, if that phraseology be more spiritual. What is the meaning of this feeling?

For my own part, I never saw a ghost except once in a dream. I feared it in my sleep; I awoke trembling, and lights and the speech of others could hardly dissipate my fear. Some years ago I lost a friend, and a few months afterwards visited the house where I had last seen him. It was deserted, and though in the midst of a city, its vast halls and spacious apartments occasioned the same sense of loneliness as if it had been situated on an uninhabited heath. I walked through the vacant chambers by twilight, and none save I awakened the echoes of their pavement. The far mountains (visible from the upper windows) had lost their tinge of sunset; the tranquil atmosphere grew leaden coloured as the golden stars appeared in the firmament; no wind ruffled the shrunk-up river which crawled lazily through the deepest channel of its wide and empty bed; the chimes of the Ave Maria had ceased, and the bell hung moveless in the open belfry: beauty invested a reposing world, and awe was inspired by beauty only. I walked through the rooms filled with sensations of the most poignant grief. He had been there; his living frame had been caged by those walls, his breath had mingled with that atmosphere, his step had been on those stones, I thought: – the earth is a tomb, the gaudy sky a vault, we but walking corpses. The wind rising in the east rushed through the open casements, making them shake; – methought, I heard, I felt – I know not what – but I trembled. To have seen him but for a moment, I would have knelt until the stones had been worn by the impress, so I told myself, and so I knew a moment after, but then I trembled, awe-struck and fearful. Wherefore? There is something beyond us of which we are ignorant. The sun drawing up the vaporous air makes a void, and the wind rushes in to fill it, – thus beyond our soul's ken there is an empty space; and our hopes and fears, in gentle gales or terrific whirlwinds, occupy the vacuum; and if it does no more, it bestows on the feeling heart a belief that influences do exist to watch and guard us, though they be impalpable to the coarser faculties.

I have heard that when Coleridge* was asked if he believed in ghosts, – he replied that he had seen too many to put any trust in their reality; and the person of the most lively imagination that I ever knew echoed this reply. But these were not real ghosts (pardon, unbelievers, my mode of speech) that they saw; they were shadows, phantoms unreal; that while they appalled the senses, yet carried no other feeling to the mind of others than delusion, and were viewed as we might view an optical deception which we see to be true with our eyes, and know to be false with our understandings. I speak of other shapes. The returning bride, who claims the fidelity of her betrothed; the murdered man who shakes to remorse the murderer's heart; ghosts that lift the curtains at the foot of your bed as the clock chimes one; who rise all pale and ghastly from the church-yard and haunt their ancient abodes; who, spoken to, reply; and whose cold unearthly touch makes the hair stand stark upon the head; the true old-fashioned, foretelling, flitting, gliding ghost, – who has seen such a one?

I have known two persons who at broad daylight have owned that they believed in ghosts, for that they had seen one. One of these was an Englishman, and the other an Italian. The former had lost a friend he dearly loved, who for a while appeared to him nightly, gently stroking his cheek and spreading a serene calm over his mind. He did not fear the appearance, although he was somewhat awe-stricken as each night it glided into his chamber, and,

> Ponsi del letto in su la sponda manca.*

This visitation continued for several weeks, when by some accident he altered his residence, and then he saw it no more. Such a tale may easily be explained away; – but several years had passed, and he, a man of strong and virile intellect, said that 'he had seen a ghost.'

The Italian was a noble, a soldier, and by no means addicted to superstition: he had served in Napoleon's armies from early youth, and had been to Russia, had fought and bled, and been rewarded, and he unhesitatingly, and with deep belief, recounted his story.

This Chevalier, a young, and (somewhat a miraculous incident) a gallant Italian, was engaged in a duel with a brother officer, and wounded him in the arm. The subject of the duel was frivolous; and distressed therefore at its consequences he attended on his youthful adversary during his consequent illness, so that when the latter recovered they became firm and dear friends. They were quartered together at Milan, where the youth fell desperately in love with the wife of a musician, who disdained his passion, so that it preyed on his spirits and his health; he absented himself from all amusements, avoided all his brother officers, and his only consolation was to pour his love-sick plaints into the ear of the Chevalier, who strove in vain to inspire him either with indifference towards the fair disdainer, or to inculcate lessons of fortitude and heroism. As a last resource he urged him to ask leave of absence; and to seek, either in change of scene, or the amusement of hunting, some diversion to his passion. One evening the youth came to the Chevalier, and said, 'Well, I have asked leave of absence, and am to have it early to-morrow morning, so lend me your fowling-piece and cartridges, for I shall go to hunt for a fortnight.' The Chevalier gave him what he asked; among the shot there were a few bullets. 'I will take these also,' said the youth, 'to secure myself against the attack of any wolf, for I mean to bury myself in the woods.'

Although he had obtained that for which he came, the youth still lingered. He talked of the cruelty of his lady, lamented that she would not even permit him a hopeless attendance, but that she inexorably banished him from her sight, 'so that,' said he, 'I have no hope but in oblivion.' At length he rose to depart. He took the Chevalier's hand and said, 'You will see her tomorrow, you will speak to her, and hear her speak; tell her, I entreat you, that our conversation to-night has been concerning her, and that her name was the last that I spoke.' 'Yes, yes,' cried the Chevalier, 'I will say any thing you please; but you must not talk of her any more, you must forget her.' The youth embraced his friend with warmth, but the latter saw nothing more in it than the effects of his affection, combined with his melancholy at absenting himself from his mistress, whose name, joined to a tender farewell, was the last sound that he uttered.

When the Chevalier was on guard that night, he heard the report of a gun. He was at first troubled and agitated by it, but afterwards thought no more of it, and when relieved from guard went to bed, although he passed a restless, sleepless night. Early in the morning some one knocked at his door. It was a soldier, who said that he had got the young officer's leave of absence, and had taken it to his house; a servant had admitted him, and he had gone up stairs, but the room door of the officer was locked, and no one answered to his knocking, but something oozed through from under the door that looked like blood. The Chevalier, agitated and frightened at this account, hurried to his friend's house, burst open the door, and found him stretched on the ground – he had blown out his brains, and the body lay a headless trunk, cold, and stiff.

The shock and grief which the Chevalier experienced in consequence of this catastrophe produced a fever which lasted for some days. When he got well, he obtained leave of absence, and went into the country to try to divert his mind. One evening at moonlight, he was returning home from a walk, and passed through a lane with a hedge on both sides, so high that he could not see over them. The night was balmy; the bushes gleamed with fireflies, brighter than the stars which the moon had veiled with her silver light. Suddenly he heard a rustling near him, and the figure of his friend issued from the hedge and stood before him, mutilated as he had seen him after his death. This figure he saw several times, always in the same place. It was impalpable to the touch, motionless, except in its advance, and made no sign when it was addressed. Once the Chevalier took a friend with him to the spot. The same rustling was heard, the same shadow stept forth, his companion fled in horror, but the Chevalier stayed, vainly endeavouring to discover what called his friend from his quiet tomb, and if any act of his might give repose to the restless shade.

Such are my two stories, and I record them the more willingly, since they occurred to men, and to individuals distinguished the one for courage and the other for sagacity. I will conclude my 'modern instances', with a story told by M. G. Lewis,* not probably so authentic as these, but perhaps more amusing. I relate it as nearly as possible in his own words.

'A gentleman journeying towards the house of a friend, who lived on the skirts of an extensive forest, in the east of Germany, lost his way. He wandered for some time among the trees, when he saw a light at a distance. On approaching it he was surprised to observe that it proceeded from the interior of a ruined monastery. Before he knocked at the gate he thought it proper to look through the window. He saw a number of cats assembled round a small grave, four of whom were at that moment letting down a coffin with a crown upon it. The gentleman startled at

this unusual sight, and, imagining that he had arrived at the
retreats of fiends or witches, mounted his horse and rode away
with the utmost precipitation. He arrived at his friend's house
at a late hour, who sat up waiting for him. On his arrival his
friend questioned him as to the cause of the traces of agitation
visible in his face. He began to recount his adventures after
much hesitation, knowing that it was scarcely possible that his
friend should give faith to his relation. No sooner had he
mentioned the coffin with the crown upon it, than his friend's
cat, who seemed to have been lying asleep before the fire, leaped
up, crying out, 'Then I am king of the cats;' and then scrambled
up his chimney, and was never seen more.

LETTER TO MARIA GISBORNE*

Pisa, 15 August 1822

I said in a letter to Peacock,* my dear Mrs Gisborne, that I
would send you some account of the last miserable months of
my disastrous life.* From day to day I have put this off, but I
will now endeavour to fulfill my design. The scene of my
existence is closed & though there be no pleasure in retracing
the scenes that have preceded the event which has crushed my
hopes yet there seems to be a necessity in doing so, and I obey
the impulse that urges me. I wrote to you either at the end of
May or the beginning of June. I described to you the place we
were living in: – Our desolate house,* the beauty yet strangeness
of the scenery and the delight Shelley took in all this – he never
was in better health or spirits than during this time. I was not
well in body or mind. My nerves were wound up to the utmost
irritation, and the sense of misfortune hung over my spirits. No
words can tell you how I hated our house & the country about
it. Shelley reproached me for this – his health was good & the
place was quite after his own heart – What could I answer – that
the people were wild & hateful, that though the country was
beautiful yet I liked a more *countryfied* place, that there was
great difficulty in living – that all our Tuscans would leave us,
& that the very jargon of these *Genovese* was disgusting – This
was all I had to say but no words could describe my feelings –
the beauty of the woods made me weep & shudder – so

vehement was my feeling of dislike that I used to rejoice when
the winds & waves permitted me to go out in the boat so that I
was not obliged to take my usual walk among tree shaded paths,
allies of vine festooned trees – all that before I doated on – &
that now weighed on me. My only moments of peace were on
board that unhappy boat, when lying down with my head on
his knee I shut my eyes & felt the wind & our swift motion
alone. My ill health might account for much of this – bathing in
the sea somewhat relieved me – but on the 8th of June (I think
it was) I was threatened with a miscarriage, & after a week of
great ill health on Sunday the 16th this took place at eight in the
morning. I was so ill that for seven hours I lay nearly lifeless –
kept from fainting by brandy, vinegar eau de Cologne etc. – at
length ice was brought to our solitude – it came before the
doctor so Claire* & Jane* were afraid of using it but Shelley
overruled them & by an unsparing application of it I was
restored. They all thought & so did I at one time that I was
about to die – I hardly wish that I had, my own Shelley could
never have lived without me, the sense of eternal misfortune
would have pressed too heavily upon him, & what would have
become of my poor babe?* My convalescence was slow and
during it a strange occurrence happened to retard it. But first I
must describe our house to you. The floor on which we lived
was thus

5	7		3
	2	
6		4
	1	

1 is a terrace that went the
whole length of our house &
was precipitous to the sea. 2
the large dining hall – 3, a
private staircase. 4 my bed-
room 5 Mrs Williams's bed-
room, 6 Shelley's & 7 the
entrance from the great stair-
case. Now to return. As I said
Shelley was at first in perfect
health but having over
fatigued himself one day, & and then the fright my illness gave
him caused a return of nervous sensations & visions as bad as
in his worst times. I think it was the Saturday after my illness
while yet unable to walk I was confined to my bed – in the
middle of the night I was awoke by hearing him scream & come
rushing into my room; I was sure that he was asleep & tried to

waken him by calling on him, but he continued to scream which
inspired me with such a panic that I jumped out of bed & ran
across the hall to Mrs W.'s room where I fell through weakness,
though I was so frightened that I got up again immediately – she
let me in & Williams went to S. who had been wakened by my
getting out of bed – he said that he had not been asleep & that
it was a vision that he saw that had frightened him – But as he
declared that he had not screamed it was certainly a dream &
no waking vision – What had frightened him was this – He
dreamt that lying as he did in bed Edward* & Jane came into
him, they were in the most horrible condition, their bodies
lacerated – their bones starting through their skin, the faces pale
yet stained with blood, they could hardly walk, but Edward was
the weakest & Jane was supporting him – Edward said – 'Get
up, Shelley, the sea is flooding the house & it is all coming
down.' S. got up, he thought, & went to the window that looked
on the terrace & the sea & thought he saw the sea rushing in.
Suddenly his vision changed & he saw the figure of himself
strangling me, that had made him rush into my room, yet fearful
of frightening me he dared not approach the bed, when my
jumping out awoke him, or as he phrased it caused his vision to
vanish. All this was frightful enough, & talking it over the next
morning he told me that he had had many visions lately – he
had seen the figure of himself which met him as he walked on
the terrace & said to him – 'How long do you mean to be
content' – No very terrific words & certainly not prophetic of
what has occurred. But Shelley had often seen these figures when
ill; but the strangest thing is that Mrs W. saw him. Now Jane
though a woman of sensibility, has not much imagination & is
not in the slightest degree nervous – neither in dreams or
otherwise. She was standing one day, the day before I was taken
ill, at a window that looked on the Terrace with Trelawny* – it
was day – she saw as she thought Shelley pass by the window,
as he often was then, without a coat or jacket – he passed again
– now as he passed both times the same way – and as from the
side towards which he went each time there was no way to get
back except past the window again (except over a wall twenty
feet from the ground) she was struck at seeing him pass twice
thus & looked out & seeing him no more she cried – 'Good
God can Shelley have leapt from the wall? Where can he be
gone?' Shelley, said Trelawny – 'No Shelley has past – What do

you mean?' Trelawny says that she trembled exceedingly when
she heard this & it proved indeed that Shelley had never been
on the terrace & was far off at the time she saw him. Well we
thought no more of these things & I slowly got better. Having
heard from Hunt* that he had sailed from Genoa, on Monday
July 1st S., Edward & Captain Roberts (the Gent. who built our
boat) departed in our boat for Leghorn to receive him – I was
then just better, had begun to crawl from my bedroom to the
terrace; but bad spirits succeeded to ill health, and this departure
of Shelley's seemed to add insufferably to my misery. I could not
endure that he should go – I called him back two or three times,
& told him that if I did not see him soon I would go to Pisa
with the child – I cried bitterly when he went away. They went
& Jane, Claire & I remained alone with the children – I could
not walk out, & though I gradually gathered strength it was
slowly & my ill spirits increased; in my letters to him I entreated
him to return – 'the feeling that some misfortune would happen,'
I said, 'haunted me': I feared for the child, for the idea of danger
connected with him never struck me – When Jane & Claire took
their evening walk I used to patrol the terrace, oppressed with
wretchedness, yet gazing on the most beautiful scene in the
world. This Gulf of Spezia is subdivided into many small bays
of which ours was far the most beautiful – the two horns of the
bay (so to express myself) were wood covered promontories
crowned with castles – at the foot of these on the furthest was
Lerici on the nearest Sanᵗ Arenzo – Lerici being above a mile by
land from us & San Arenzo about a hundred or two yards –
trees covered the hills that enclosed this bay & then beautiful
groups were picturesquely contrasted with the rocks, the castle
and the town – the sea lay far extended in front while to the
west we saw the promontory & islands which formed one of
the extreme boundaries of the Gulf – to see the sun set upon this
scene, the stars shine & the moon rise was a sight of wondrous
beauty, but to me it added only to my wretchedness – I repeated
to myself all that another would have said to console me, &
told myself the tale of love, peace & competence which I enjoyed
– but I answered myself by tears – did not my William* die? &
did I hold my Percy by a firmer tenure? – Yet I thought when
he, when my Shelley returns I shall be happy – he will comfort
me, if my boy be ill he will restore him & encourage me. I had a
letter or two from Shelley mentioning the difficulties he had in

establishing the Hunts & that he was unable to fix the time of
his return. Thus a week past. On Monday 8th Jane had a letter
from Edward, dated Saturday, he said that he waited at Leghorn
for S. who was at Pisa. That S's return was certain, 'but' he
continued, 'if he should not come by Monday I will come in a
felucca, & you may expect me Tuesday evening at furthest'.
This was Monday, the fatal Monday, but with us it was stormy
all day & we did not at all suppose that they could put to sea.
At twelve at night we had a thunderstorm; Tuesday it rained all
day & was calm – the sky wept on their graves – on Wednesday
– the wind was fair from Leghorn & in the evening several
feluccas arrived thence – one brought word that they had sailed
Monday, but we did not believe them – Thursday was another
day of fair wind & when twelve at night came & we did not see
the tall sails of the little boat double the promontory before us
we began to fear not the truth, but some illness – some
disagreeable news for their detention. Jane got so uneasy that
she determined to proceed the next day to Leghorn in a boat to
see what was the matter – Friday came & with it a heavy sea &
bad wind – Jane however resolved to be rowed to Leghorn (since
no boat could sail) and busied herself in preparations – I wished
her to wait for letters, since Friday was letter day – she would
not – but the sea detained her, the swell rose so that no boat
would venture out – At 12 at noon our letters came – there was
one from Hunt to Shelley, it said – 'pray write to tell us how
you got home, for they say that you had bad weather after you
sailed Monday & we are anxious' – the paper fell from me – I
trembled all over – Jane read it – 'Then it is all over!' she said.
'No, my dear Jane,' I cried, 'it is not all over, but this suspense
is dreadful – come with me, we will go to Leghorn, we will post
to be swift & learn our fate.' We crossed to Lerici, despair in
our hearts; they raised our spirits there by telling us that no
accident had been heard of & that it must have been known &c
– but still our fear was great – & without resting we posted to
Pisa. It must have been fearful to see us – two poor, wild, aghast
creatures – driving (like Matilda)* towards the *sea* to learn if we
were to be for ever doomed to misery. I knew that Hunt was at
Pisa at Lord Byron's house but I thought that L. B. was at
Leghorn. I settled that we should drive to Casa Lanfranchi that
I should get out & ask the fearful question of Hunt, 'do you
know any thing of Shelley?' On entering Pisa the idea of seeing

Hunt for the first time for four years under such circumstances,
& asking him such a question was so terrific to me that it was
with difficulty that I prevented myself from going into convul-
sions – my struggles were dreadful – they knocked at the door
& some one called out 'Chi è?' it was the Guiccioli's* maid. L.
B. was in Pisa – Hunt was in bed, so I was to see L. B. instead
of him – This was a great relief to me; I staggered up stairs – the
Guiccioli came to meet me smiling while I could hardly say –
'Where is he – Sapete alcuna cosa di Shelley' – They knew
nothing – he had left Pisa on Sunday – on Monday he had sailed
– there had been bad weather Monday afternoon – more they
knew not. Both L. B. & the lady have told me since – that on
that terrific evening I looked more like a ghost than a woman –
light seemed to emanate from my features, my face was very
white. I looked like marble – Alas. I had risen almost from a bed
of sickness for this journey – I had travelled all day – it was now
12 at night – & we, refusing to rest, proceeded to Leghorn – not
in despair – no, for then we must have died; but with sufficient
hope to keep up the agitation of the spirits which was all my
life. It was past two in the morning when we arrived – They
took us to the wrong inn – neither Trelawny or Captain Roberts
were there nor did we exactly know where they were so we were
obliged to wait until daylight. We threw ourselves drest on our
beds & slept a little but at 6 o'clock we went to one or two inns
to ask for one or the other of these gentlemen. We found
Roberts at the Globe. He came down to us with a face which
seemed to tell us that the worst was true, and here we learned
all that had occurred during the week they had been absent from
us, & under what circumstances they had departed on their
return. – Shelley had past most of the time at Pisa – arranging
the affairs of the Hunts – & screwing L. B.'s mind to the sticking
place about the journal. He had found this a difficult task at
first but at length he had succeeded to his heart's content with
both points. Mrs Mason* said that she saw him in better health
and spirits than she had ever known him, when he took leave of
her Sunday July 7th. His face burnt by the sun, & his heart light
that he had succeeded in rendering the Hunts' tolerably comfort-
able. Edward had remained at Leghorn. On Monday July 8th
during the morning they were employed in buying many things
– eatables etc. for our solitude. There had been a thunderstorm
early but about noon the weather was fine & the wind right fair

for Lerici – They were impatient to be gone. Roberts said, 'Stay
until tomorrow to see if the weather is settled; & S. might have
staid but Edward was in so great an anxiety to reach home –
saying they would get there in seven hours with that wind – that
they sailed! S. being in one of those extravagant fits of good
spirits in which you have sometimes seen him. Roberts went out
to the end of the mole & watched them out of sight – they sailed
at one & went off at the rate of about 7 knots – About three –
Roberts, who was still on the mole – saw wind coming from the
Gulf – or rather what the Italians call a temporale anxious to
know how the boat would weather the storm, he got leave to go
up the tower & with the glass discovered them about ten miles
out at sea, off Via Reggio, they were taking in their topsails –
'The haze of the storm,' he said, 'hid them from me & I saw
them no more – when the storm cleared I looked again fancying
that I should see them on their return to us – but there was no
boat on the sea.' – This then was all we knew, yet we did not
despair – they might have been driven over to Corsica & not
knowing the coast & gone god knows where. Reports favoured
this belief. – it was even said that they had been seen in the Gulf
– We resolved to return with all possible speed – We sent a
courier to go from tower to tower along the coast to know if
any thing had been seen or found, & at 9 a.m. we quitted
Leghorn – stopped but one moment at Pisa & proceeded
towards Lerici. When at 2 miles from Via Reggio we rode down
to that town to know if they knew any thing – here our calamity
first began to break on us – a little boat & a water cask had
been found five miles off – they had manufactured a *piccolissima
lancia* of thin planks stitched by a shoemaker just to let them
run on shore without wetting themselves as our boat drew 4 feet
water. – the description of that found tallied with this – but then
this boat was very cumbersome & in bad weather they might
have been easily led to throw it overboard – the cask frightened
me most – but the same reason might in some sort be given for
that. I must tell you that Jane & I were not now alone –
Trelawny accompanied us back to our home. We journeyed on
& reached the Magra about ½ past ten p.m. I cannot describe
to you what I felt in the first moment when, fording this river, I
felt the water splash about our wheels – I was suffocated – I
gasped for breath – I thought I should have gone into convul-
sions, I struggled violently that Jane might not perceive it –

looking down the river I saw the two great lights burning at the *foce* – A voice from within me seemed to cry aloud that is his grave. After passing the river I gradually recovered. Arriving at Lerici we were obliged to cross our little bay in a boat – San Arenzo was illuminated for a festa – what a scene – the roaring sea – the scirocco wind – the lights of the town towards which we rowed – & our own desolate hearts – that coloured all with a shroud – we landed; nothing had been heard of them. This was Saturday July 13, & thus we waited until Thursday July 25th thrown about by hope & fear. We sent messengers along the coast towards Genoa & to Via Reggio – nothing had been found more than the *lancetta*; reports were brought us – we hoped – & yet to tell you all the agony we endured during those 12 days would be to make you conceive a universe of pain – each moment intolerable & giving place to one still worse. The people of the country too added to one's discomfort – they are like wild savages – on festas the men & women & children in different bands – the sexes always separate – pass the whole night in dancing on the sands close to our door running into the sea then back again & screaming all the time one perpetual air – the most detestable in the world – then the scirocco perpetually blew & the sea for ever moaned their dirge. On Thursday 25th Trelawny left us to go to Leghorn to see what was doing or what could be done. On Friday I was very ill but as evening came on I said to Jane – 'If anything had been found on the coast Trelawny would have returned to let us know. He has not returned so I hope.' About 7 o'clock p.m. he did return – all was over – all was quiet now, they had been found washed on shore – Well all this was to be endured.

Well what more have I to say? The next day we returned to Pisa. And here we are still – days pass away – one after another – & we live thus. We are all together – we shall quit Italy together. Jane must proceed to London – if letters do not alter my views I shall remain in Paris. – Thus we live – Seeing the Hunts now & then. Poor Hunt has suffered terribly as you may guess. Lord Byron is very kind to me & comes with the Guiccioli to see me often.

Today – this day – the sun shining in the sky – they are gone to the desolate sea coast to perform the last offices to their earthly remains. Hunt, L. B. & Trelawny. The quarantine laws would not permit us to remove them sooner – & now only on

condition that we burn them to ashes. That I do not dislike –
His rest shall be at Rome beside my child* – where one day I
also shall join them – Adonais* is not Keats's it is his own elegy
– he bids you there go to Rome. – I have seen the spot where he
now lies – the sticks that mark the spot where the sands cover
him – he shall not be there it is too near Via Reggio – They are
now about this fearful office – & I live!

One more circumstance I will mention. As I said he took leave
of Mrs Mason in high spirits on Sunday – 'Never,' said she, 'did
I see him look happier than the last glance I had of his
countenance.' On Monday he was lost – on Monday night she
dreamt – that she was somewhere – she knew not where & he
came looking very pale & fearfully melancholy – she said to him
– 'You look ill, you are tired, sit down & eat.' 'No,' he replied,
'I shall never eat more; I have not a *soldo* left in the world.' –
'Nonsense,' said she, 'this is no inn – you need not pay – ' –
'Perhaps,' he answered, 'it is the worse for that.' Then she awoke
& going to sleep again she dreamt that my Percy was dead &
she awoke crying bitterly & felt so miserable – that she said to
herself – 'why if the little boy should die I should not feel it in
this manner.' She was so struck with these dreams that she
mentioned them to her servant the next day – saying she hoped
all was well with us.

Well here is my story – the last story I shall have to tell – all
that might have been bright in my life is now despoiled – I shall
live to improve myself, to take care of my child, & render myself
worthy to join him. soon my weary pilgrimage will begin – I rest
now – but soon I must leave Italy – & then – there is an end of
all despair. Adieu I hope you are well & happy. I have an idea
that while he was at Pisa that he received a letter from you that
I have never seen – so not knowing where to direct I shall send
this letter to Peacock – I shall send it open – he may be glad to
read it –

                         Your's ever truly Mary WS. – Pisa
I shall probably write to you soon again.

I have left out a material circumstance – A Fishing boat saw
them go down – It was about 4 in the afternoon – they saw the
boy at mast head, when baffling winds struck the sails, they had
looked away a moment & looking again the boat was gone –
This is their story but there is little doubt that these men might
have saved them, at least Edward who could swim. They could

not they said get near her – but 3 quarters of an hour after passed over the spot where they had seen her – they protested no wreck of her was visible, but Roberts going on board their boat found several spars belonging to her. – perhaps they let them perish to obtain these. Trelawny thinks he can get her up, since another fisherman thinks that he has found the spot where she lies, having drifted near shore. Trelawny does this to know perhaps the cause of her wreck – but I care little about it.

CLAIRE CLAIRMONT

CLAIRE CLAIRMONT (1798–1879) is reported to have been born illegitimately to Mary Vial (also known as Clairmont). Mrs Clairmont married William Godwin in 1802, which brought together four children: Jane (later known as Claire), her older brother, Charles Clairmont, Fanny Imlay (the illegitimate daughter of Mary Wollstonecraft and Gilbert Imlay), and Mary (Wollstonecraft) Godwin. Mary (Vial) Clairmont's and William Godwin's son, William, was born in 1803. In 1805, Mrs Godwin took advantage of the new market for children's books by becoming a publisher of books for juveniles. Thus Claire Clairmont grew up in a literary environment in which her natural and step-parents were engaged in the production of literary texts as their source of income. Claire and the other children, for example, accompanied William Godwin to literary events such as Samuel Taylor Coleridge's lectures on Shakespeare and Milton at the London Philosophical Society in 1811. In 1812, William Godwin took Claire and Fanny to meet Harriet and Percy Bysshe Shelley. By 1813, Shelley had become intimate with Mary [Wollstonecraft] Godwin, and, despite William Godwin's remonstrations to his daughter and stepdaughter, Mary and Claire ran off with Shelley to the Continent in July 1814. By mid-September that year, all three returned to London because Shelley had run out of money. By 1816, the three embarked for the Continent again, partly to seek out Lord Byron in Geneva, because Claire thought herself to be pregnant by him. She had a child, Allegra, whom Byron acknowledged as his, and for whom he took financial and legal responsibility. Claire accused him of neglecting their child after Byron had placed her in a convent where Allegra died at the age of twelve. Claire Clairmont's *Journal*, which survives from mid-August 1814, records her early naïveté which gradually becomes transformed into an informed wordliness. After P. B. Shelley's death in 1822, she became a governess for various families, travelling

throughout Europe. The text comes from *The Journals of Claire
Clairmont*, ed. Marion Kingston Stocking (1968), pp. 182–4,
and biographical information comes from the same source.

Wednesday, 8 November [1820]

Caricatures for Albe.* He, sitting at writing poetry, the words *Oh! faithless Woman*; round the room, hearts are strewed, inscribed, *We died for love of you.* Another – he catching a lady by her waist, his face turned towards her, his other hand extended holding a club stick in the act of giving a blow to a man who is escaping. From his mouth

> The maid I love, the man I hate –
> I'll kiss her lips and break his Pate.

Three more to be called Lord Byron's Morning, Noon & Night: the first he looking at the sky, a sun brightly shining – saying 'Come I feel quite bold and cheerful – there is no God'; the second towards evening, a grey tint spread over the face of Nature, the sun behind a cloud, a shower of rain falling, a dinner table in the distance covered with a profusion of dishes, he, with a wallop, says, 'What a change I feel in me after dinner; where we see design we suppose a designer; I'll be a Deist; I am a Deist.' The third – evening – candles just lighted, all dark without the windows, a cup of green tea on the table: and trees agitated much by wind beating against the panes, also thunder & lightning. He says 'God bless me! suppose there should be a God – it is as well to stand in his good graces. Let me say prayers. I'll say my prayers tonight, & write to Murray* to put in a touch concerning blowing of the last Trumpet.' Pistols are on the table, also daggers, bullets, and Turkish scimitars.

Another to be called Lord Byron's receipt for writing pathetic Poetry. He sitting drinking spirits, playing with his white mustachios. His mistress, the Fornara opposite him drinking coffee. Fumes coming from her mouth, over which is written garlic; these curling, direct themselves towards his English footman who is just then entering the room & he is knocked backward – Lord B. is writing. He says, 'Imprimis to be a great pathetic poet. 1st. Prepare a small colony, then dispatch the mother by worrying & cruelty to her grave; afterwards to neglect & ill treat the children – to have as many & as dirty mistresses as can be found; from their embraces to catch horrible diseases, thus a tolerable quantity of discontent and remorse being prepared, to give it vent on paper, & to remember particularly to rail against learned women. This is my infallible receipt by which I have made so much money.'

The last his Death. He, dead, extended on his bed, covered all but his breast, which many wigged doctors are cutting open to find out (as one may be saying) what was the extraordinary disease of which this great man died. His heart laid bare, they find an immense capital I grown on its surface – and which had begun to pierce the breast. They are all astonished. One says, 'A new disease.' Another, 'I never had a case of this kind before.' A third, 'What medicines would have been proper?' The fourth holding up his finger, 'A desert island.'

Caricature for poor Shelley. He looking very sweet and smiling. A little Jesus Christ playing about the room. He says, 'I will quietly murder that little child.'

Another. Himself & God Almighty. He says, 'If you please, God Almighty, I had rather be damned with Plato & Lord Bacon than go to Heaven with Paley & Malthus.'* God Almighty, 'It shall be quite as you please, pray don't stand upon ceremony.' Shelley's three aversions: God Almighty, Lord Chancellor & Didactic Poetry.

FRANCES TROLLOPE

FRANCES TROLLOPE (née Milton) (1780–1863), who became
an author late in life, was born at Stapleton, near Bristol. In
1809, she married Thomas Anthony Trollope, a barrister, who
lost his money through mismanagement. The family emigrated
to Cincinnati in 1827 in an attempt to retrieve the family
fortunes, but their attempts at commerce failed, and Frances
Trollope began to write in order to make money. She used her
experiences in America for her first book, *Domestic Manners of
the Americans* (1832), which was a success in Europe, but not
in America. She wrote other semi-sociological works of a similar
nature about countries in Europe. She also wrote a large number
of popular novels, but in the writing of fiction, she was surpassed
by her son, Anthony Trollope. She was widowed in 1835, and
settled in Florence, Italy, where she died. Biographical infor-
mation comes from DNB, and the text from *Domestic Manners
of the Americans*, Vol. 2, 2nd Edn, 1832, pp. 40–57.

Chapter 22, Small Landed Proprietors – Slavery

I now, for the first time since I crossed the mountains,* found myself sufficiently at leisure to look deliberately round, and mark the different aspects of men and things in a region which, though bearing the same name, and calling itself the same land, was, in many respects, as different from the one I had left, as Amsterdam from St Petersburg. There every man was straining, and struggling, and striving for himself (heaven knows!) Here every white man was waited upon, more or less, by a slave. There, the newly-cleared lands, rich with the vegetable manure accumulated for ages, demanded the slightest labour to return the richest produce; where the plough entered, crops the most abundant followed; but where it came not, no spot of native verdure, no native fruits, no native flowers cheered the eye; all was close, dark, stifling forest. Here the soil had long ago yielded its first fruits; much that had been cleared and cultivated for tobacco (the most exhausting of crops) by the English, required careful and laborious husbandry to produce any return; and much was left as sheep-walks. It was in these spots that the natural bounty of the soil and climate was displayed by the innumerable wild fruits and flowers which made every dingle and bushy dell seem a garden.

On entering the cottages I found also a great difference in the manner of living. Here, indeed, there were few cottages without a slave, but there were fewer still that had their beef-steak and onions for breakfast, dinner, and supper. The herrings of the bountiful Potomac* supply their place. These are excellent 'relish', as they call it, when salted, and, if I mistake not, are sold at a dollar and a half per thousand. Whiskey, however, flows every where at the same fatally cheap rate of twenty cents (about one shilling) the gallon, and its hideous effects are visible on the countenance of every man you meet.

The class of people the most completely unlike any existing in England, are those who, farming their own freehold estates, and often possessing several slaves, yet live with as few of the refinements, and I think I may say, with as few of the comforts of life, as the very poorest English peasant. When in Maryland, I went into the houses of several of these small proprietors, and remained long enough, and looked and listened sufficiently, to obtain a tolerably correct idea of their manner of living.

One of these families consisted of a young man, his wife, two children, a female slave, and two young lads, slaves also. The farm belonged to the wife, and, I was told, consisted of about three hundred acres of indifferent land, but all cleared. The house was built of wood, and looked as if the three slaves might have overturned it, had they pushed hard against the gable end. It contained one room, of about twelve feet square, and another adjoining it, hardly larger than a closet; this second chamber was the lodging-room of the white part of the family. Above these rooms was a loft, without windows, where I was told the 'staying company' who visited them, were lodged. Near this mansion was a 'shanty', a black hole, without any window, which served as kitchen and all other offices, and also as the lodging of the blacks.

We were invited to take tea with this family, and readily consented to do so. The furniture of the room was one heavy huge table, and about six wooden chairs. When we arrived the lady was in rather a dusky dishabille, but she vehemently urged us to be seated, and then retired to the closet-chamber above mentioned, whence she continued to address to us from behind the door, all kinds of 'genteel country visiting talk', and at length emerged upon us in a smart new dress.

Her female slave set out the great table, and placed upon it cups of the very coarsest blue ware, a little brown sugar in one, and a tiny drop of milk in another, no butter, though the lady assured us she had a '*deary*' and two cows. Instead of butter, she 'hoped we would fix a little relish with our crackers', in ancient English, eat salt meat and dry biscuits. Such was the fare, and for guests that certainly were intended to be honoured. I could not help recalling the delicious repasts which I remembered to have enjoyed at little dairy farms in England, not *possessed*, but rented, and at high rents too; where the clean, fresh-coloured, bustling mistress herself skimmed the delicious cream, herself spread the yellow butter on the delightful brown loaf, and placed her curds, and her junket, and all the delicate treasures of her dairy before us, and then, with hospitable pride, placed herself at her board, and added the more delicate 'relish' of good tea and good cream. I remembered all this, and did not think the difference atoned for, by the dignity of having my cup handed to me by a slave. The lady I now visited, however, greatly surpassed my quondam friends in the refinement of her conversation. She ambled through the whole time the visit lasted, in a sort of elegantly mincing familiar style of gossip, which, I think, she was imitating from some novel, for I was told she was a great novel reader, and left all household occupations to be performed by her slaves. To say she addressed us in a tone of equality, will give no adequate idea of her manner; I am persuaded that no misgiving on the subject ever entered her head. She told us that their estate was her divi-*dend* of her father's property. She had married a first cousin, who was as fine a gentleman as she was a lady, and as idle, preferring hunting (as they called shooting) to any other occupation. The consequence was, that but a very small portion of the divi-*dend* was cultivated, and their poverty was extreme. The slaves, particularly the lads, were considerably more than half naked, but the air of dignity with which, in the midst of all this misery, the lanky lady said to one of the young negroes, 'Attend to your young master, Lycurgus', must have been heard to be conceived in the full extent of its mock heroic.

Another dwelling of one of these landed proprietors was a hovel as wretched as the one above described, but there was more industry within it. The gentleman, indeed, was himself one of the numerous tribe of regular whiskey drinkers, and was rarely capable of any work; but he had a family of twelve children, who, with their skeleton mother, worked much harder than I ever saw negroes do. They were, accordingly, much less elegant and much less poor than the heiress; yet they lived with no appearance of comfort, and with, I believe, nothing beyond the necessaries of life. One proof of this was, that the worthless father would not suffer them to raise, even by their own labour, any garden vegetables, and they lived upon their fat pork, salt fish, and corn bread, summer and winter, without variation. This, I found, was frequently the case among the farmers. The luxury of whiskey is more appreciated by the men than all the green delicacies from the garden, and if all the ready money goes for that and their darling chewing tobacco, none can be spent by the wife for garden seeds; and as far as my observation

extended, I never saw any American *ménage* where the toast
and no toast question, would have been decided in favour of the
lady.

There are some small farmers who hold their lands as tenants,
but these are by no means numerous: they do not pay their rent
in money, but by making over a third of the produce to the
owner; a mode of paying rent, considerably more advantageous
to the tenant than the landlord; but the difficulty of obtaining
money in payment, excepting for mere retail articles, is very
great in all American transactions. 'I can pay in pro-*duce*', is the
offer which I was assured is constantly made on all occasions,
and if rejected, 'Then I guess we can't deal,' is the usual
rejoinder. This statement does not, of course, include the great
merchants of great cities, but refers to the mass of the people
scattered over the country; it has, indeed, been my object, in
speaking of the customs of the people, to give an idea of what
they are *generally*.

The effect produced upon English people by the sight of
slavery in every direction is very new, and not very agreeable,
and it is not the less painfully felt from hearing upon every
breeze the mocking words, 'All men are born free and equal.'
One must be in the heart of American slavery, fully to appreciate
that wonderfully fine passage in Moore's Epistle to Lord Vis-
count Forbes, which describes perhaps more faithfully, as well
as more powerfully, the political state of America, than any
thing that has ever been written upon it . . .*

The condition of domestic slaves, however, does not generally
appear to be bad; but the ugly feature is, that should it be so,
they have no power to change it. I have seen much kind attention
bestowed upon the health of slaves; but it is on these occasions
impossible to forget, that did this attention fail, a valuable piece
of property would be endangered. Unhappily the slaves, too,
know this, and the consequence is, that real kindly feeling very
rarely can exist between the parties. It is said that slaves born in
a family are attached to the children of it, who have grown up
with them. This may be the case where the petty acts of infant
tyranny have not been sufficient to conquer the kindly feeling
naturally produced by long and early association: and this sort
of attachment may last as long as the slave can be kept in that
state of profound ignorance which precludes reflection. The law
of Virginia has taken care of this. The State legislators may truly

be said to be 'wiser in their generation than the children of light,' and they ensure their safety by forbidding light to enter among them. By the law of Virginia it is penal to teach any slave to read, and it is penal to be aiding and abetting in the act of instructing them. This law speaks volumes. Domestic slaves are, generally speaking, tolerably well fed, and decently clothed; and the mode in which they are lodged seems a matter of great indifference to them. They are rarely exposed to the lash, and they are carefully nursed in sickness. These are the favourable features of their situation. The sad one is, that they *may* be sent to *the south* and sold. This is the dread of all the slaves north of Louisiana. The sugar plantations, and more than all, the rice grounds of Georgia and the Carolinas, are the terror of American negroes; and well they may be, for they open an early grave to thousands; and to *avoid loss* it is needful to make their previous labour pay their value.

There is something in the system of breeding and rearing negroes in the Northern States, for the express purpose of sending them to be sold in the South, that strikes painfully against every feeling of justice, mercy, or common humanity. During my residence in America I became perfectly persuaded that the state of a domestic slave in a gentleman's family was preferable to that of a hired American 'help', both because they are more cared for and valued, and because their condition being born with them, their spirits do not struggle against it with that pining discontent which seems the lot of all free servants in America. But the case is widely different with such as, in their own persons, or those of their children, 'loved in vain', are exposed to the dreadful traffic above mentioned. In what is their condition better than that of the kidnapped negroes on the coast of Africa? Of the horror in which this enforced migration is held I had a strong proof during our stay in Virginia. The father of a young slave, who belonged to the lady with whom we boarded, was destined to this fate, and within an hour after it was made known to him, he sharpened the hatchet with which he had been felling timber, and with his right hand severed his left from the wrist.

But this is a subject on which I do not mean to dilate; it has been lately treated most judiciously by a far abler hand.[1] Its

[1] See Captain Hall's *Travels in America*.

effects on the moral feelings and external manners of the people
are all I wish to observe upon, and these are unquestionably
most injurious. The same man who beards his wealthier and
more educated neighbour with the bullying boast, 'I'm as good
as you', turns to his slave, and knocks him down, if the furrow
he has ploughed, or the log he has felled, please not this stickler
for equality. There is a glaring falsehood on the very surface of
such a man's principles that is revolting. It is not among the
higher classes that the possession of slaves produces the worst
effects. Among the poorer class of landholders, who are often as
profoundly ignorant as the negroes they own, the effect of this
plenary power over males and females is most demoralising; and
the kind of coarse, not to say brutal, authority which is
exercised, furnishes the most disgusting moral spectacle I ever
witnessed. In all ranks, however, it appeared to me that the
greatest and best feelings of the human heart were paralyzed by
the relative positions of slave and owner. The characters, the
hearts of children, are irretrievably injured by it. In Virginia we
boarded for some time in a family consisting of a widow and
her four daughters, and I there witnessed a scene strongly
indicative of the effect I have mentioned. A young female slave,
about eight years of age, had found on the shelf of a cupboard a
biscuit, temptingly buttered, of which she had eaten a consider-
able portion before she was observed. The butter had been
copiously sprinkled with arsenic for the destruction of rats, and
had been thus most incautiously placed by one of the young
ladies of the family. As soon as the circumstance was known,
the lady of the house came to consult me as to what had best be
done for the poor child; I immediately mixed a large cup of
mustard and water (the most rapid of all emetics) and got the
little girl to swallow it. The desired effect was instantly pro-
duced, but the poor child, partly from nausea, and partly from
the terror of hearing her death proclaimed by half a dozen voices
round her, trembled so violently that I thought she would fall. I
sat down in the court where we were standing, and, as a matter
of course, took the little sufferer in my lap. I observed a general
titter among the white members of the family, while the black
stood aloof, and looked stupefied. The youngest of the family, a
little girl about the age of the young slave, after gazing at me for
a few moments in utter astonishment, exclaimed, 'My! If Mrs
Trollope has not taken her in her lap, and wiped her nasty

mouth! Why I would not have touched her mouth for two hundred dollars!'

The little slave was laid on a bed, and I returned to my own apartments; some time afterwards I sent to enquire for her, and learnt that she was in great pain. I immediately went myself to enquire farther, when another young lady of the family, the one by whose imprudence the accident had occurred, met my anxious enquiries with ill-suppressed mirth – told me they had sent for the doctor – and then burst into uncontrollable laughter. The idea of really sympathising in the sufferings of a slave appeared to them as absurd as weeping over a calf that had been slaughtered by the butcher. The daughters of my hostess were as lovely as features and complexion could make them; but the neutralizing effect of this total want of feeling upon youth and beauty, must be witnessed, to be conceived.

There seems in general a strong feeling throughout America, that none of the negro race can be trusted, and as fear, according to their notions, is the only principle by which a slave can be actuated, it is not wonderful if the imputation be just. But I am persuaded that were a different mode of moral treatment pursued, most important and beneficial consequences would result from it. Negroes are very sensible to kindness, and might, I think, be rendered more profitably obedient by the practice of it towards them, than by any other mode of discipline whatever. To emancipate them entirely throughout the Union cannot, I conceive, be thought of, consistently with the safety of the country; but were the possibility of amelioration taken into the consideration of the legislature, with all the wisdom, justice, and mercy, that could be brought to bear upon it, the negro population of the Union might cease to be a terror, and their situation no longer be a subject either of indignation or of pity.

I observed every where throughout the slave States that all articles which can be taken and consumed are constantly locked up, and in large families, where the extent of the establishment multiplies the number of keys, these are deposited in a basket, and consigned to the care of a little negress, who is constantly seen following her mistress's steps with this basket on her arm, and this, not only that the keys may be always at hand, but because, should they be out of sight one moment, that moment would infallibly be employed for purposes of plunder. It seemed to me in this instance, as in many others, that the close personal attendance of these sable shadows, must be very annoying; but whenever I mentioned it, I was assured that no such feeling existed, and that use rendered them almost unconscious of their presence.

I had, indeed, frequent opportunities of observing this habitual indifference to the presence of their slaves. They talk of them, of their condition, of their faculties, of their conduct, exactly as if they were incapable of hearing. I once saw a young lady, who, when seated at table between a male and a female, was induced by her modesty to intrude on the chair of her female neighbour to avoid the indelicacy of touching the elbow of *a man*. I once saw this very young lady lacing her stays with the most perfect composure before a negro footman. A Virginian gentleman told me that ever since he had married, he had been accustomed to have a negro girl sleep in the same chamber with himself and his wife. I asked for what purpose this nocturnal attendance was necessary? 'Good heaven!' was the reply, 'if I wanted a glass of water during the night, what would become of me?'

1832

NOTES

Mary Wollstonecraft

Reading
p. 5 'are made ... fools': Alexander Pope, *An Essay on Criticism* (1719), ll. 26–7.
p. 5 the *Adventurer*: (1752–4) was a periodical for which Samuel Johnson, among others, wrote essays.
p. 6 'words of thundering sound': Oliver Goldsmith, *The Deserted Village* (1770), ll. 211–14.
p. 6 'how it shall ... clothed': Matthew 6:31.
p. 7 A woman may ... family: MW maintained this non-separatist feminist view of gender roles in marriage throughout her life. In *A Vindication of the Rights of Woman* (1792), she suggests again that one of the main reasons for giving women an education which is equal to that of men is so that women can become 'companions' to their husbands as well as educators of their children.

From the Analytical Review, *Articles XXV, XVII*
MW reviewed books regularly for the *Analytical Review* (1788–97), which was founded by her publisher, Joseph Johnson, and Thomas Christie. This monthly periodical consisted of reviews of works that were of general interest. Of MW's varied reviews in the fields of religion, moral philosophy, travel, music and education, the most interesting are those of sentimental novels. She very often satirized the failings of these 'lady novelists' who she thought were corrupting other young women with false notions of the nature of heterosexual love.

ARTICLE XXV
This satirical review typifies MW's attitudes to the fiction of 'lady novelists' which she thought fostered to ill effect the romantic longings of young women.

ARTICLE XVII
This brief review shows how MW distanced herself from the difficulties of uneducated women.

A Vindication of the Rights of Woman

p. 11 adjust ... the beam: reference to the twenty-year war of European countries against France after the French Revolution.

p. 11 Fabricius: a Roman consul from 282 to 278 BC, remarkable for his frugality.

p. 11 Washington: George Washington (1732–99) returned to farming after military victories.

p. 12 to bubble: to trick

p. 12 Milk of human kindness: *Macbeth*, I.v.18.

p. 12 Cerberus: in Greek mythology, guarded the entrance to Hell.

p. 14 'How ... camp': Rousseau, *Emilius*, vol. IV, Ch. v, p. 13. Rousseau is referring to the incompatibility of nursing and soldiering, suggesting that women cannot take up the latter career.

p. 16 to suckle ... beer: *Othello*, II.i.160.

p. 16 *accoucheur*: male midwife.

p. 16 'that shape hath none': John Milton, *Paradise Lost*, II, 667.

p. 17 'the lily ... plow-share.': Fénelon, *The Adventures of Telemachus*, trs. Isaac Littlebury (1699), vol. 1, p. 153.

Letter to Joseph Johnson

Wollstonecraft had travelled to Paris after her abortive passion for the artist, Henry Fuseli, had come to an end. But she seems to have lived in Paris in order to write about the progress of the French Revolution.

Letters Written during a Short Residence in Sweden, Norway, and Denmark

LETTER 4

p. 21 You: MW addressed these letters, which were intended for publication, to her lover, Gilbert Imlay, for whom she was executing a business commission connected with the disappearance of his ship, the *Maria and Margaretha*.

p. 22 human face divine: an allusion to a passage from John Milton, *Paradise Lost*, III, l. 44.

LETTER 7

p. 22 fruit of their labour: Norway had been united politically with Denmark since 1397.

p. 23 Christiania: Oslo.

p. 23 the Prince Royal: the future King Frederick VI (1768–1839).

p. 24 reship: MW means that Norwegian ships could not land their cargoes in Norway, but had to sail on to unload them in Denmark. She compared this Norwegian subordination to Denmark to the 'painful subordination of Ireland [to England]' at that time.

p. 25   Quistram: this battle formed part of the Norwegian invasion of Sweden in 1788.

p. 27   Bernstof: Andreas Peter Bernstof (1735–97), Foreign Minister.

p. 28   university in Norway: the first university of Norway was established at Oslo in 1811.

p. 29   nice, *clean* **state:** Windsor Castle had been restored under George III.

p. 30   first of England: James I (1566–1625).

Letter on the Present Character of the French Nation

This letter was intended to form part of a series, but MW finished only this one. William Godwin published this letter after her death in *Posthumous Works of the Author of A Vindication of the Rights of Woman* (1798). The main interest of this letter lies in MW's intimation in the last paragraph of her disillusion with the supposedly liberating effects of the French Revolution. Her mannered style in which she addresses an imagined recipient should be compared with the more straightforward letter-writing mode that she adopts in her letters to Joseph Johnson and Gilbert Imlay.

Letters to Gilbert Imlay

This numbered series of personal letters was first published in *Posthumous Works of the Author of A Vindication of the Rights of Woman*, ed. William Godwin (1798). Wollstonecraft met the American entrepreneur, Gilbert Imlay, in Paris and lived with him periodically. She had one child, Fanny Imlay, by him. Wollstonecraft at first stayed in Paris when Imlay travelled to Le Havre, but she joined him for a short time until he travelled to London in pursuit of business speculations. Wollstonecraft's letters are a poignant record of a woman who gradually realizes that her lover no longer wants her. According to Ralph Wardle, Wollstonecraft retrieved her letters from Imlay when their affair finally ended.

LETTER 69

Wollstonecraft wrote this letter on the eve of her attempt to commit suicide by drowning herself in the Thames. *The Times* (24 October 1795) reports a woman's attempt at suicide by jumping off Putney Bridge on 10 October and Ralph Wardle suggests that this woman was very likely to have been Wollstonecraft (*Letters*, p. 317). Wollstonecraft was saved by a passerby.

p. 35 **forced from her:** she had discovered from the cook that Imlay kept a mistress.

LETTER 70

p. 37 **accept it:** Wollstonecraft refused to let Imlay support her or her child, Fanny.

LETTER 71

p. 37 **perfectly free:** although MW insists that Imlay is now free, she continues to upbraid him in subsequent letters.

LETTER 74

p. 38 **Mr——:** possibly Joseph Johnson, her friend and publisher, or Thomas Christie (1761–96), co-editor of the *Analytical Review*, and friend to both Imlay and MW. MW stayed at the Christies' home until she recovered from her near-drowning.

p. 38 **let——:** possibly the maid, Marguerite, who is to bring MW's belongings from Imlay to the lodgings which MW has taken near to Thomas and Rebecca Christie's home.

p. 38 **transact your business:** Imlay transacts business with Thomas Christie.

LETTER 75

p. 38 **letters you returned:** MW has had her letters to Imlay returned to her.

p. 39 **Paris:** William Godwin claims that Imlay and his new mistress had retreated to Paris.

LETTER 76

p. 41 **Money was lavished away:** MW implies that, even if she were to agree to take his money, Imlay's promises of financial support are hollow.

Anna Seward

Letter 5

p. 46 **Josiah Wedgwood:** (1730–95), a famous English potter, whose products were named after him.

p. 47 **Mr Day's ... Negro':** Thomas Day (1848–89) published his poem, 'The Dying Negro', to great acclaim in 1773.

p. 47 **Sir Joseph Banks:** (1743–1820), English botanist, accompanied Captain Cook on his expedition around the world in 1768–71.

NOTES   255

p. 47   **Captain Cook:** Captain James Cook (1728–79), English navigator, was killed on his last voyage around the north coast of America (1776–9).

p. 48   **Cowley's:** Abraham Cowley (1618–67) introduced the vogue for the rhetorical ode in irregular verse.

p. 48   **Mr Bently:** Richard Bentley (1794–1871), publisher, was also a reviewer of poetry for the *Monthly Review*.

p. 48   **Lactilla:** Ann Yearsley (1752–1806) was a dairymaid and milkseller who became a poet and novelist. She was the protégée of Hannah More (1745–1833), with whom she fell out over the money she earned from subscriptions to her first volume of poetry. 'A Poem on the Inhumanity of the Slave-Trade' was published in 1788 after Hannah More's poem 'Slavery' in that same year.

p. 48   **Aonian employments:** the writing of poetry. Aonia, in Greek mythology, was sacred to the Muses, forming part of Boeotia near Mt. Helicon.

Letter 61

p. 49   **Your charming ... present:** Helen Maria Williams, *A Poem on the Bill Lately Passed for Regulating the Slave Trade* (1788).

p. 49   **the Allegro, Il Penseroso:** poems by John Milton (1608–74).

p. 49   **Gray's ... Odin:** Thomas Gray (1716–71).

p. 49   **Mrs Siddons:** Mrs Sarah Siddons (1755–1831).

p. 49   **Law of Lombardy:** reference to Robert Jephson's play, *Julia, or the Italian Lover*, performed by John Philip Kemble (1757–1823) and Mrs Siddons at Drury Lane in 1787.

p. 49   **Mr Jephson:** Robert Jephson (1736–1803).

p. 49   **Mrs Piozzi:** Hester Lynch Thrale Piozzi (1741–1821).

p. 49   **Della Crusca's Diversity:** the Della Cruscan school of poetry was inaugurated by Robert Merry (1755–98).

p. 49   **Mr Hayley:** William Hayley (1745–1820), poet.

p. 49   **Mrs Smith's:** Charlotte Smith (1749–1806) helped to re-establish the use of the sonnet form in English poetry. Her *Elegiac Sonnets* (1787) soon went into a fifth edition (1789).

p. 50   **Dryden:** John Dryden (1631–1700).

p. 50   **Lord Lyttleton [sic]:** George Lyttelton (1709–73).

Letter 66

p. 50   **Sir Walter Scott:** (1771–1832), poet, novelist, and dramatist.

p. 50   **young prodigy of the theatre:** William Henry West Betty

(1791–1870) was a precocious actor who played Romeo, Hamlet, and Prince Arthur at the age of twelve.

p. 51   **David Garrick:** (1717–79), a famous actor and dramatist.

p. 51   **Old Betty:** Henry Betty's father.

p. 51   **Kemble:** John Philip Kemble (1757–1823), actor.

p. 52   **Gil Blas':** Alain René Le Sage (1668–1747), *The Adventures of Gil Blas of Santillane* (1715–35). This picaresque romance is set in Spain.

p. 52   **Garrick's Abel Drugger:** a character in Ben Jonson's *The Alchemist* (1610), was one of Garrick's most famous parts.

p. 52   **Hibernian:** Irish

p. 52   **Essex:** the Earl of Essex (1566–1601).

p. 52   **Wordsworth:** William Wordsworth (1770–1850).

p. 52   **the poet Lee:** Nathaniel Lee (?1653–92) was a playwright who wrote dramas in blank verse. He became 'mad' and was confined to Bedlam from 1684 to 1689.

p. 52   **volumes of his:** *Lyrical Ballads* (3rd edn, 1802).

p. 53   **an ode of Coleridge's:** 'Dejection: An Ode, Written April 4, 1892'.

p. 53   **Southey:** Robert Southey (1774–1843) published *Madoc* in 1805.

Catherine Macaulay

Letter 14

p. 57   **Plutarch's … translation:** Plutarch (*c.* AD 46–*c.* 120) wrote *Parallel Lives* about 23 Greeks and 23 Romans. John and William Langhorne made an English translation in 1770.

p. 57   **Lowth's introduction:** Robert Lowth (1710–87) treated the language of the Bible as poetry.

p. 58   **Dr Samuel Johnson's:** (1709–84), founder-editor of *The Rambler* (1750–52), most of which he wrote himself.

p. 58   **Livy's … original:** Livy (Titus Livius) (57 BC–AD 17), Roman historian.

p. 58   **Dion … English:** Dion Cassius (*c.* 155–*c.* 230), Greek historian; Sallust (86–34 BC), Roman historian; Tacitus (*c.* 55–120), Roman historian; Adam Ferguson (1723–1816), Scottish historian, wrote *History of the Roman Republic* (1782); Edward Gibbon (1737–94) wrote *History of the Decline and Fall of the Roman Empire* (1776–88).

p. 58   **Cicero … Seneca:** Cicero (106–43 BC), Roman man of letters;

Epictetus (born *c.* AD 50), Stoic philosopher; and Seneca the Younger (*c.* 5 BC–AD 65), moral philosopher.

p. 58 Fenelon's Telemachus: François de Salignac de la Mothe-Fénelon (1651–1715), French divine and author of *Les Aventures de Télémaque* (1699).

p. 58 Rollin's Belles Lettres: Charles Rollin (1661–1741), French historian, was author of *Traité des études* (1726–31).

p. 58 Addison's Cato: Joseph Addison (1672–1719) was author of the acclaimed tragedy, *Cato*.

p. 58 Steele's Conscious Lovers: Sir Richard Steele (1672–1729), playwright, wrote *inter alia The Conscious Lovers*, first produced in 1722.

p. 58 Milton: John Milton (1608–74), poet.

p. 58 Pope: Alexander Pope (1688–1744), poet, wrote *Eloisa to Abelard* (1717).

p. 58 Boileau: Nicolas Boileau (1636–1711), French critic and poet.

p. 58 Corneille ... works: Pierre Corneille (1606–84); Jean **Racine** (1639–99); **Molière** (pseudonym of Jean-Baptiste **Poquelin** (1622–73); and **Voltaire** (pseudonym of François Marie Arouet) (1694–1778) were all French dramatists.

p. 58 Terence: (*c.* 190–59 BC), a Roman dramatist, wrote comedies.

p. 58 Martial: (*c.* AD 40–104) wrote epigrams on Roman manners.

p. 58 Virgil's ... Georgics: Virgil (70–19 BC), Roman poet, wrote the epic poem, *The Aeneid*, and *The Georgics*, a didactic poem.

p. 60 Cellarius: unidentified.

p. 60 Ferguson's astronomy: James Ferguson (1710–76), Scottish astronomer, wrote *Astronomy Explained upon Newton's Principles* (1756).

p. 60 Pliny: Pliny the Elder (AD 23–79) wrote *Historia Naturalis*.

p. 60 Buffon: Georges Louis Leclerc de Buffon (1707–88), French naturalist, wrote the pioneer work, *Histoire Naturelle* (1749–88).

Letter 15

p. 61 trips to Scotland: allusion to elopements to Gretna Green.

p. 61 Cervantes ... Fielding: Miguel de Cervantes, *Don Quixote* (1605–15); Alain René Le Sage, *The Adventures of Gil Blas of Santillane* (1715–35); Henry Fielding, *The History of the Adventures of Joseph Andrews* (1742).

p. 62 Cyrus's Travels: Madeleine de Scudéry (1607–1701) wrote

French heroic romances, the most famous of which is *Artamène, ou le grand Cyrus* (10 vols, 1649–53).

p. 62 Pamela: Samuel Richardson, *Pamela* (1740–41).

p. 62 Clarissa Harlow: Samuel Richardson, *Clarissa Harlow* (1747–8).

p. 63 Sir Charles Grandison: Samuel Richardson, *The History of Sir Charles Grandison* (1753–4).

p. 63 the Cecilia of Miss Burney: Fanny Burney, *Cecilia* (1782).

Letter 22

p. 66 Addison: Joseph Addison (1672–1719), poet and politician, was a contributor to Steele's *Tatler*, part-editor of the *Spectator*, and author of the acclaimed tragedy, *Cato*.

p. 67 Chesterfield: Philip Dormer Stanhope Chesterfield (1694–1773), politician and diplomat, wrote a volume, *Letters*, to his 'natural' son that was published by his son's widow in 1774.

Helen Maria Williams

Letter 4

p. 71 'A la Bastille ... resterons pas': 'To the Bastille – but we shall not remain there.'

p. 71 Man ... weep: *Measure for Measure*, II,ii,117–22 (*Complete Works*, ed. W. J. Craig, OUP 1980).

p. 72 Henry ... in vain: Henry IV (1553–1610) undertook a siege of Paris in 1590.

p. 72 Monsieur de Launay: Bernard René Jordan de Launay (1740–89) was governor of the Bastille (1776–89).

p. 72 'Il nous faut ... enfants.': 'We must have bread for our children.'

p. 73 *Négociant*: a businessman

p. 73 '*Qui va là*?: 'Who goes there?'

p. 73 '*Madame ... Nation!*': 'Madam, for this poor devil, who has been killed for the Nation! – Sir, for this unfortunate dog, who has been killed for the Nation!'

p. 73 *Messieurs, ... nourrira.*' 'Gentlemen, you have rendered me one great service; render me another – kill me! for I know not where to go.' – 'Come along, come along; the Nation will provide for you.'

Mary Hays

No. 3

p. 76 Say . . . fail?: Unidentified.

p. 76 Plutus: Plutus was the son of Demeter and the god of wealth in Greek mythology.

p. 77 Ephesians: boon companions.

p. 78 Let him . . . fear: unidentified.

p. 78 Persian Letters: *Les Lettre Persanes* (1721, Eng. trs. Ozell, 1722), by Charles Montesquieu (1689–1755), is a satirical novel in the form of letters by a Persian visitor to Paris.

p. 79 Dr Priestley: Joseph Priestley (1733–1804) was a Presbyterian minister, philosopher and chemist who discovered oxygen.

p. 79 Mrs Glasse's Art of Cookery: Hannah Glasse, *The Art of Cookery Made Plain and Easy* (1747).

p. 79 Fitzosborne's . . . Letters: unidentified.

p. 80 Mr Robinson: Robert Robinson (1727–91) was a dissenting minister who published several pamphlets.

p. 80 Happy . . . chain: unidentified.

Improvements Suggested in Female Education

p. 81 the strictures of A, B, and C,: the author is referring to her earlier essay-letter which comprised 'a defence of the talents of women' and which had aroused some controversy in the 'Miscellany' columns of the *Monthly Magazine*.

p. 81 Procrustes: in Greek legend, he was a thief in Attica who was reputed to tie his victims to a bed. If their legs were too long, he cut them off; if too short, he stretched them until they fitted the length of the bed.

p. 82 Hume: David (1711–76), philosopher, wrote *Enquiry Concerning Human Understanding* (1748)

p. 82 Rousseau: Jean-Jacques (1712–78) expressed his views on the education of women in various works, including the novel *Emile* (1762).

Anna Barbauld

On the Origin and Progress of Novel-Writing

p. 91 Clarissa: *Clarissa: or The History of a Young Lady* (1747–9), 8 vols, is an epistolary novel by Samuel Richardson (1689–1761).

p. 91   *Cecilia*: *Cecilia: or Memoirs of an Heiress* (1782) is a novel by
Fanny Burney (1752–1840).

p. 92   *The Vicar of Wakefield*: (1766), a novel by Oliver Goldsmith
(?1730–74).

p. 92   *The Fool of Quality*: (1765–70), 5 vols, a novel by Henry
Brooke (1703–83).

p. 92   Burney: Fanny Burney (1752–1840).

p. 92   Edgeworth: Maria Edgeworth (1768–1849) was an educational
author and novelist.

p. 92   *Harrels:* the Harrels are characters in Fanny Burney's
Cecilia.

pp. 92–3   Vice ... embrace: Alexander Pope (1688–1744), *An Essay
on Criticism*, ll. 217–20.

p. 93   Rousseau: Jean-Jacques Rousseau (1712–78), author of *Julie:
or la Nouvelle Heloise* (1761), a novel. Rousseau also wrote works of
political philosophy, moral theology, educational theory and
autobiography.

p. 93   Madame de Staël: (1766–1817), a literary critic and novelist,
who wrote *Delphine* (1802) and *Corinne* (1807).

p. 94   All ... life: unidentified.

p. 94   Miss Byron: Miss Harriet Byron, the heroine of *Sir Charles
Grandison* (1754), a novel by Samuel Richardson (1689–1761).

p. 95   *Gil Blas*: (1715–35), a French novel by Alain René Le Sage
(1668–1747), which was translated into English in 1749 by Tobias
Smollett (1721–71).

p. 95   *Tom Jones*: *The History of Tom Jones* (1749) is a novel by
Henry Fielding (1707–54).

p. 95   *Sophia*: Sophia Western was the heroine of *The History of Tom
Jones*.

p. 95   *Amelia*: (1751), a novel by Henry Fielding in which Captain
Billy Booth is the hero.

p. 96   *Zeluco*: (1786), a novel by Dr John Moore (1729–1802).

p. 96   Crebillon: Claude-Prosper Jolyot de Crébillon (1707–77) was
the author of tales and dialogues which might have appeared to be
encouraging licentiousness.

p. 96   Louvet: Jean-Baptiste Louvet de Couvray (1760–97) was the
author of *Les Amours du Chevalier de Faublas* (1789–90).

p. 96   D'Arblay: Fanny Burney (1752–1840) was a novelist and diarist
who married General d'Arblay in 1793.

p. 96   Inchbald: Mrs Elizabeth Inchbald, née Simpson (1753–1821),
was a novelist, dramatist, and actress.

p. 96   **Radcliffe:** Mrs Ann Radcliffe (1764–1823) was a novelist and travel-writer.

Joanna Baillie

This excerpt is part of a much longer introduction to *Plays on the Passions*.

Hannah More

Strictures on the Modern System of Female Education

p. 106   **Euclid:** the geometrician who lived in Alexandria in the reign of Ptolemy (323–283 BC), told Ptolemy that there was no 'royal road' to geometry.

p. 111   **Watts's:** Isaac Watts (1674–1748) wrote doctrinal treatises and educational manuals as well as hymns.

p. 111   **Duncan's . . . Logic:** John Duncan (1721–1808) wrote religious philosophy and verse.

p. 111   **Mr Locke's . . . Understanding:** John Locke (1632–1704) wrote *Essay Concerning Human Understanding* (1690).

p. 111   **Bishop Butler's Analogy:** Joseph Butler (1692–1752) wrote *Analogy of Religion Natural and Revealed* (1736).

p. 114   **Alexander:** Alexander the Great (356–23 BC), King of Macedonia, popularized the civilization of Greece.

p. 114   **Corregio [sic]::** Antonio Correggio (c. 1494–1534) was an Italian artist.

p. 114   **Another . . . another!:** *Macbeth*, IV.i, 112–24.

Unprofitable Reading

p. 116   **Dr Johnson:** Dr Samuel Johnson (1709–84), scholar and wit, is famous for his original *Dictionary of the English Language*.

p. 116   **Tom Jones:** *Tom Jones, A Foundling* (1749), the novel by Henry Fielding (1707–54), explored the question of freeing oneself from artificial restraints.

p. 116   **Rousseau's Heloise:** *La Nouvelle Héloïse* (1761) by Jean-Jacques Rousseau (1712–78) also explored the question of people freeing themselves from artificial restraints.

p. 117   **That . . . is the shame:** unidentified.

p. 118   **Doctors' Commons:** this alludes to the Ecclesiastical and Admiralty courts in which, *inter alia*, divorce proceedings took place.

p. 118   **profligate and infidel poet**: possibly a reference to Lord George Gordon Byron (1788–1824) or John Wilmot Rochester (1648–80), Restoration poet and libertine.

p. 118   **Milton ... Beattie**: John Milton (1604–74); Edmund Spenser (?1552–99); William Cowper (1731–1800); Edward Young (1683–1765); James Thomson (1834–82); Oliver Goldsmith (?1730–74); Thomas Gray (1716–71); and James Beattie (1735–1803) are all English literary authors.

p. 119   **the wits of Charles's days**: a reference to some of the plays of the Restoration period such as William Wycherley's *The Country Wife* (1675).

p. 119   **'teach ... down?'**: Deuteronomy 11:19.

Mary Robinson

Letter to the Women of England ...

p. 122   **'The Rights of Woman'**: Mary Wollstonecraft, *A Vindication of the Rights of Woman* (1792).

p. 124   **Ruin ... fame**: unidentified.

p. 126   **Sévigné**: Mme de Sévigné (1626–96) was a French writer whose published *Letters* were well known.

p. 126   **Stephano**: a drunken butler in Shakespeare's *The Tempest*.

p. 127   **Socrates**: Socrates (before 469–399 BC) was married to Xantippe [Zantippe] who was reputed to be shrewish.

p. 127   **Demosthenes ... Brutus**: Demosthenes (*c.* 373–22 BC), Pythagoras (6th century BC), Leontius, Eustathius (12th century AD), and Marcus Junius Brutus (85–42 BC), were Greek thinkers, politicians or classical scholars. The author suggests that their British counterparts would prefer an 'unlettered' mistress to an educated woman (see next note).

p. 127   **Theano ... Portia**: Theano, Themiste, Cornelia, Sosipatra, and Portia [Porcia] are wives or mothers of famous Greek or classical scholars.

p. 127   **Cicero**: Marcus Tullius Cicero (106–43 BC).

Memoirs

p. 128   **At the period ... fabric**: General Thomas Fairfax (1612–71) and his revolutionary 'scratch Army' defeated Charles I at Naseby and stormed Bristol, capturing the occupied city from Prince Rupert (1619–82) and his Royalist forces (1645).

p. 131   Pope's Lines ... Lady: Alexander Pope (1688–1744).

p. 131   Mason's Elegy ... Coventry: William Mason (1724–97).

p. 131   Gay: John Gay (1685–1732). ''Twas when the seas were roaring' is a ballad in his first play, *What D'ye Call It?* (1715).

p. 131   Lord Lyttelton: George Lyttelton (1709–73).

p. 131   the lady ... celebrated: Hannah More (1745–1833).

p. 132   that great actor: William Powell (1735–69).

Fanny Burney

Diary and Letters (1802)

p. 138   *'vite ... en effet'*: 'Madame, take your place in the coach, because there's an English gentleman, who is certainly going to take the best place! – indeed.'

p. 139   the Castle and Shakspeare's Cliff: Dover cliffs and castle.

p. 141   *'Vite! ... arrêtée!'*: 'Quickly! Quickly! Look for it, or you will be arrested!'

p. 143   *'Mais, Madame, ... alors peut-être – '*: 'But, Madame, have you anything new?/ Yes, Monsieur./Some petticoats?/ Many, Monsieur./ Some cotton stockings?/Several, Monsieur./Well! Madame, everything will be seized./But, Monsieur, what if it's not for sale, but just for wearing?/ It's all the same, Madame, everything will be seized./Eh! but what's to be done then?/ It's necessary, Madame, to tip generously; and if you are very sure that none of it's for sale, then perhaps ...'

p. 143   restoration ... *Décade*: Napoleon had restored Sundays as holy days.

p. 144   Robespierre: Maximilien Marie Isidore de Robespierre (1758–94), one of the French revolutionaries, was guillotined himself in 1794 during the aftermath of factional in-fighting.

Diary and Letters (1815)

p. 145   A more terrific ... imagined: the Battle of Waterloo had just taken place.

p. 146   Jacobins: French political radicals.

p. 148   Blücher: Gebhard Leberecht von Blücher (1742–1819) led the Prussians against Napoleon and with Wellington at the Battle of Waterloo.

p. 148   *'Suivez ... bras!'*: 'Follow quickly, my children! or tomorrow we will still be at arms!'

p. 148   the Duke of Wellington: Arthur Wellesley, 1st Duke of Wel-

lington (1769–1852) led the army that totally routed the French, led by
Napoleon, on 18 June 1815 at Waterloo.

Jane Taylor

Letter to Miss S.L.C.
p. 150 **famous victory':** at the Battle of Trafalgar in 1805, the English
fleet defeated the French, but Viscount Horatio Nelson (1758–1805),
who led the attack, was killed in the battle.

The Troublesome Friend
p. 152 Jane Taylor, under the pseudonym of QQ, wrote this spoof
letter for the *Youth's Magazine*.

To Whomsoever It May Concern
p. 155 This letter was made up by Jane Taylor in response to her
pseudonymous letter, 'The Troublesome Friend', in the previous issue
of *Youth's Magazine*.

Dorothy Wordsworth

Letter to Lady Beaumont, April 1806
p. 163 **my dear Friend:** Lady Beaumont and Sir George Howland
Beaumont (1753–1827) were patrons of the arts and friends of the
Wordsworths.
p. 164 **address … Wind:** See Dorothy Wordsworth's 'Address to a
Child During a Boisterous Winter Evening', in *Women Romantic Poets:
An Anthology, 1785–1832*, ed. Jennifer Breen, pp. 128–9.

Letter to Lady Beaumont, September 1806
p. 167 **Coleorton:** the home of Lady and Sir George Beaumont.
p. 167 **kind offer:** the Beaumonts loaned their Hall Farm at Coleorton
to the Wordsworths for a time.

A Journal of a Tour on the Continent (1820)
Dorothy Wordsworth toured Belgium, Holland, France, Switzerland
and Germany with her brother, William, his wife, Mary, and their
cousins, Mr and Mrs Monkhouse and Miss Horrocks. This excerpt
describes their journey from Canterbury to Dover and thence to Calais
and Brussels.

p. 168   Erasmus: Desiderius (1466–1536), a humanist Dutch scholar, who, through his writings, helped to prepare the way for the Reformation.

p. 168   Hooker: Richard (1554?–1600), wrote a defence of the Church of England entitled *Of the Laws of Ecclesiastical Politie*.

p. 169   have been the same': 'Here on our native soil' is the first line of William Wordsworth's sonnet, 'Composed in the Valley near Dover, on the Day of Landing' (1802, pub. 1807).

p. 170   Sterne: Laurence (1713–68), novelist, had travelled in that area (cf. *A Sentimental Journey*, 1768).

p. 170   'Nous sommes toujours occupées': 'We are always busy.'

p. 178   'Blut von Jesus': blood of Jesus.

p. 181   'lorded over and possessed by nature': William Wordsworth, *The Prelude* (1805), Book 6, ll. 520–21.

p. 182   Holbein: Hans, the Younger (1497/8–1543), a Swiss artist who in *c.* 1536 was Court painter to Henry VIII.

p. 185   lustres: chandeliers.

p. 185   Battle of Waterloo: Wellington (1769–1852) led the army that totally routed the French, headed by Napoleon Bonaparte, on 18 June 1815 at Waterloo.

p. 186   Johnny Gilpin's chaise: alludes to William Cowper's ballad, 'The Diverting History of John Gilpin' (1782).

p. 186   gaités: jollities.

p. 187   Southey's: Robert (1774–1843), poet and friend of the Wordsworths.

p. 188   'Nature's ... shroud': William Wordsworth, *The Excursion*, Book 7, ll. 997–8.

p. 189   'ceux qui ont peur n'ont point d'esprit': 'those who are afraid have no spirit'.

p. 189   Brobdignag: an allusion to Jonathan Swift's *Gulliver's Travels* (1726), a satiric novel in which Brobdignag is a land of giants in comparison to the hero, Gulliver.

Mary Lamb

On Needlework

p. 193   'The British Lady's Magazine: this essay was first published in *The British Lady's Magazine and Monthly Miscellany*, April 1815, under the pseudonym Sempronia.

Mary Russell Mitford

Letter to Sir William Elford

p. 200   **Sir William Elford**: Sir William Elford (1749–1837), banker, politician, and amateur artist, corresponded with Mary Russell Mitford regularly about literary matters until his death.

p. 200   *The Lord of the Isles*: a ballad by Sir Walter Scott (1771–1832) published in 1815.

p. 200   **Vesuvius**: a famous volcano at Pompeii, Italy.

p. 200   **Scott**: Sir Walter Scott published popular verse until 1817, and novels anonymously from 1814.

p. 200   **Lord Byron**: Lord George Gordon Byron (1788–1824), poet.

p. 200   **Campbell**: Thomas Campbell (1777–1844) had by then published two popular books of poetry: *The Pleasures of Hope* (1799) and *Gertrude of Wyoming* (1809).

p. 200   **Lady Morgan's ... O'Donnel**: Lady Morgan, née Sydney Owenson (1776–1859), novelist, poet, biographer and memoiriste, published her novel, *O'Donnell*, in 1815.

p. 201   *et pour la bonne bouche*: and as a tit-bit.

p. 201   **Miss Edgeworth**: Maria Edgeworth (1768–1849), essayist, novelist, and children's writer, was interested in the education of girls and women.

p. 201   **Miss Austen**: Jane Austen (1775–1817) had by then published *Sense and Sensibility* (1811), *Pride and Prejudice* (1813), and *Mansfield Park* (1814). See David Cecil, *A Portrait of Jane Austen* (1978), for his comments on Mitford's letter (pp. 67 and 136).

p. 202   *Guy Mannering*: a novel by Sir Walter Scott that he at first published anonymously (1815).

p. 202   *Mysteries of Udolpho*: a Gothic romance by Ann Radcliffe (1764–1823) published in 1794.

p. 202   *Waverley*: the first of Sir Walter Scott's novels (1814).

p. 202   *The Lay*: *The Lay of the Last Minstrel* (1805) is Scott's earliest romance in ballad form.

p. 202   **Mr Haydon**: Benjamin Robert Haydon (1786–1846) painted biblical and classical subjects.

p. 202   **the bow of Ulysses**: Ulysses was said to have won the challenge of stringing his own bow and hitting the target above the skill of his rivals. Mitford is implying that Haydon is extremely talented at biblical subjects.

p. 202   **Mr Eustace**: unidentified.

p. 202 **Hercules:** Hercules in Greek mythology was noted for his strength.

Our Village

This essay draws on Mitford's observation of the village of Three Miles Cross, near Reading, where she lived.

p. 202 **messuages:** 'a dwelling-house with its outbuildings, courtyard and adjacent land assigned to its use' (OED).

p. 203 **Mr White:** Gilbert White (1720–93), *Natural History and Antiquities of Selborne* (1789).

p. 203 **that other . . . Ariel:** the island in Shakespeare's *The Tempest*.

p. 203 **Dryden's:** John Dryden (1631–1700), English poet and dramatist.

p. 204 **Penelope's web:** an allusion to a labour that is never finished, from the story of the unfinished shroud of Ulysses' wife, Penelope, which she undid each night in order to put off accepting the offer of any of her importunate suitors.

Mary Shelley

Letters

These two letters are thought to have been addressed to Fanny Imlay. They were written during the second journey made by Mary Godwin and P. B. Shelley to France with their son, William. Claire Clairmont accompanied them again as she had done when Godwin and Shelley eloped and travelled to the Continent in 1814. Mary Godwin's journal of the 1814 travels forms the basis of the first part of *History of a Six Weeks' Tour*, in the second half of which she used these two letters.

LETTER, 17 MAY 1816

p. 214 **Lavalette:** Le comte de La Vallette (1769–1830) had escaped from prison in 1815 and left France with the help of three Englishmen.

p. 214 **the last . . . of the Allies:** Mary Godwin is comparing her 1814 journey with her present one, which takes place just after Napoleon I and France had been finally defeated by the English (led by Wellington) and Prussian armies at the Battle of Waterloo.

LETTER, 1 JUNE 1816

p. 217 *aiguilles:* pointed peaks

On Ghosts

p. 220o   **Wordsworth:** William Wordsworth, 'The Affliction of Margaret' (?1804, pub. 1807), Stanza 9.

p. 220   **Homer, Herodotus, and Plato:** early Greek thinkers and writers.

p. 220   **Atlantis:** fabulous island which was reputed to be the centre of an empire dominating part of Europe and Africa.

p. 220   **El Dorado:** fabulous city or country which was said to abound in gold.

p. 220   **The Fortunate Isles:** in Greek and Roman legend, the souls of the virtuous were said to go to these isles after death.

p. 220   **the Canaries:** the Canary Islands in the Atlantic, off Spain.

p. 220   **Niger:** the major river in West Africa.

p. 220   **New Holland:** the original European name for Australia.

p. 220   **mare incognitum:** unknown sea.

p. 220   **Mungo Park:** Park (1771–1806) explored the course of the Niger and subsequently wrote *Travels in the Interior of Africa* (1799).

p. 220   **Captain of the *Hecla*:** unidentified.

p. 220   **Botany Bay:** British convicts and settlers first landed with the military at this Sydney cove during the settlement of Australia.

p. 220   **Hesperides:** in Greek legend, these were nymphs who guarded the golden apples of Hera on the day of her marriage with Zeus.

p. 220   **Blue Mountains:** mountain range near Sydney.

p. 220   **Thetis:** mythological sea deity who was the mother of Achilles.

p. 221   **Brutus's dream:** Brutus and Cassius plotted to kill Julius Caesar, Roman dictator in Shakespeare's play, *Julius Caesar.*

p. 221   **Lord Lyttleton's [*sic*] vision:** Lyttelton wrote *Dialogues of the Dead* (1760).

p. 221   **philosophic son:** central protagonist in Shakespeare's play, *Hamlet.*

p. 222   **Coleridge:** Samuel Taylor Coleridge (1772–1834), poet and essayist.

p. 223   **Ponsi ... manca:** unidentified but refers to the ghost's seeming presence beside the Englishman's bedside.

p. 225   **M. G. Lewis:** Matthew Gregory Lewis (1775–1818) (see *The Journals of Mary Shelley*: 1814–44, vol. 1, ed. Paula R. Feldman and Diana Scott-Kilvert, 1987, p. 129).

Letter to Maria Gisborne

p. 226   **Maria Gisborne:** (1770–1836) had nursed Mary Godwin immediately after her mother's death in 1797 when Mary Godwin was ten days old. The Shelleys had made friends with Maria and her second husband, John Gisborne, when the Shelleys moved to Italy in 1818.

p. 226   Peacock: Thomas Love Peacock (1785–1866), author of the satires, *Headlong Hall* (1816), *Nightmare Abbey* (1818) and *Crochet Castle* (1831).

p. 226   disastrous life: Percy Bysshe Shelley was drowned in a boating accident on 8 July 1822.

p. 226   desolate house: Casa Magni at San Terenzo near Lerici on the Bay of Spezia.

p. 227   Claire: Claire Clairmont (1798–1879).

p. 227   Jane: Jane Williams was a friend of the Shelleys.

p. 227   my poor babe: Percy Florence Shelley, who was born in 1819.

p. 228   Edward: Jane Williams's husband.

p. 228   Trelawny: Edward John Trelawny (1792–1881) was a friend of the Shelleys.

p. 229   Hunt: Leigh Hunt (1784–1859), essayist and editor, visited Byron in Italy to inaugurate a new journal, *The Liberal* (4 issues, 1822).

p. 229   William: (1816–19) the son of Mary and Percy Shelley.

p. 230   Matilda: Mary Shelley is referring to her own novel *Matilda* (written 1819).

p. 231   the Guiccioli's: Lord Byron's mistress, Countess Teresa Guiccioli.

p. 231   Mrs Mason: formerly Lady Mountcashel (1772–1835) who changed her name when she left her husband. Mary Wollstonecraft had taught her when she was a governess, and thus Mrs Mason befriended the Shelleys and Claire Clairmont in Pisa where she lived with her lover, George William Tighe.

p. 234   my child: William was buried at Rome.

p. 234   Adonais: Percy Shelley's elegy (1821) to the poet, John Keats (1795–1821).

Claire Clairmont

Journal

p. 239   Albe: Albe is Lord Byron, nicknamed thus by Mary and P. B. Shelley.

p. 239   Murray: John Murray, Byron's publisher.

p. 240   'If you ... Malthus: Clairmont is satirizing Shelley's bravado in adopting radical thinkers who seem to him to be humanist rather than coldly utilitarian. See Shelley's preface to *Prometheus Unbound* (1820): 'For my part I had rather be damned with Plato and Lord Bacon, than go to Heaven with Paley and Malthus.'

Frances Trollope

Small Landed Proprietors – Slavery

p. 242   **crossed the mountains:** Trollope is travelling in America and has crossed from Maryland into Virginia.

p. 242   **Potomac:** the Potomac river forms the border between Maryland and Virginia.

p. 245   **upon it …:** she quotes a passage on slavery from a poem, 'Epistle to Lord Viscount Forbes', by Thomas Moore (1779–1852).

THE AUTHORS AND THEIR CRITICS

The following extract from Germaine Greer's essay on the need for informed scholarship in women's literary studies is an early one of its kind:

> In the relentless course of the polarizing activity which assigns to each sex its proper domain, language has always appeared to be peculiarly female. Little girls develop verbal skills more swiftly and earlier than little boys and continue to out-talk and out-write them until puberty. Words are the classic weapon of the female who is considered able to *nag* a man to *death*. In all fields except that of the literary establishment, where they can only command the demotic written word rather than the arcane dialect of the masculine ruling class, women have held their own or even dominated.
>
> Occasionally women have been moved to protest against their exclusion from the mastery of the rhetoric of the ruling class, but it has also been clear that to be constrained to write in the vernacular may actually be a source of strength; the stultifying rules of the intellectual establishment do not apply to the living language of the people. The form such writing takes is likely to be organic, growing out of the intrinsic pressure of the ideas being developed and the use to which they are being put. For that reason, such writing is also likely to be misunderstood, reviled, and consigned to obscurity by the educated elite, if not during its own time and popularity, then soon after.
>
> Like the living language itself, the vast bulk of multifarious utterance of women has died with the people who produced it, either because it was never written down at all, or because it remained unpublished, or because it was published in ephemeral form, or because it perished with the fashions which allowed it momentarily to thrive. Dead though it may be, however, women's utterance underlies our present day literary activities as the coral rock supports the living reef.

Nowadays most of the literature studied even in our haughtiest academic institutions is demotic literature. The novel, which so many distinguished academics now expound in place of Homer and Virgil, is a literary form pioneered by women, produced under the pressure of female influence and published to beguile the leisure of the literate but uneducated daughters of the middle class. It is also the medium in which women have excelled, and yet, even so, many of the women who dominated the literary marketplace in their own lifetimes have now sunk into the aggregate of forgotten literary activity.

There are good reasons for investigating the vast mass of female product which is our inheritance. The first is simply that it is our inheritance: to understand it is to gain a clearer idea of who we are, or, in current jargon, where we are coming from. Most of it, letters, diaries, and other occasional writing, was not set down in the hope of immortality. Most of it does not assume the posture of the writer addressing (his) public but remains the unaffected discourse between self and self or self and a familiar friend. Such writing can help to illuminate the other side of the coin struck by official historians in the same way that demographic and sociological research in our own time has revolutionized the concept of history itself. We may choose to call it 'herstory' but we ought also to see how clearly our alternative version of history is related to the other forms which tell the story of exploration, conquest, colony, and empire from the point of view of the subject peoples.

We are now gradually realizing that if we are to learn the lessons that history holds for a future which will be more or less democratic and cooperative, we must uncover the past of the masses. We need to know the form and pressure of the daily life of past ages more than we need to know the terms of treaties and the bloodlines of monarchs. It was women who set down the minutiae of the joys and sorrows of ordinary people, their idealism, their skepticism, their heroism, and their wisdom. Nothing has shocked us into as stark an awareness of the cost of the settlement of the United States and the building up of the richest country in the world as the uncomplaining records kept by pioneer women.

There is much even in such writing which we cannot understand. We do not at once recognize the patterns which have governed these women's perception and their selection of details, their irony, their self-censorship, the hints which were nudges to women of their own kind, about sex, about abortion, about sabotage and rebellion. Twentieth-century females, admitted under sufferance to the masculine intellectual establishment, are not necessarily equipped with the correct ciphers to decode all kinds of *écriture féminine*. In our anxiety to be admitted to the competitive establishment we temporarily lost sight of the import- ance of the alternative female society and its contrasting cultural values, and because that culture was organic and had to be kept alive by continuity of practice, it fell into desuetude. If we do not turn our masculine skills and methods into tools for female archaeology, we shall remain cut off from an important source of vitality. We may waste time re-inventing forms and formulations which already exist. We may also dishonor our mothers in the casual assumption that they have nothing to teach us. In the same way that feminist anthropologists have transformed their disci- pline, we too must reconstitute the literary landscape as composed of women as well as men, regardless of the fact that the men were always more conspicuous.

Clearly literature is only one of the faces at which this kind of excavation must be carried out, but it is one of the most important. The data we have to assemble is much more ambiguous than bone-fragments and pottery shards because the relationship of words to the external realities that they describe is itself not necessarily clear. The tools for correct interpretation of the data have themselves to be refined, but if the data itself is incomplete and arbitrarily assembled, no valid inferences can be made. [. . .]

It is not enough to take a text like the fifteenth-century 'English Trotula' and remark upon the fitful gleams of a pro-feminist attitude which may be discerned in it. The writing of women, however amateurish and unassuming, is not without structure, nor is it unmarked by influences literary and other; these are the considerations which make the whole question of whether a text like the 'English Trotula' is actually by women, as well as being for them and about them, so difficult to answer. It takes a trained sensitivity to discern what is genuinely creative and individual in a newly discovered text, even when the context is thoroughly understood. Only a truly creative critic can produce the kind of writing-about-writing which will modify sensibility so that a new public can respond to unfamiliar styles.

Scholars working in the field of women's literature have then to develop a formidable range of skills. The most basic of these are probably the bibliographic techniques by which texts are first located, then identified in their time and place, then deciphered and their internal references traced and explicated. As indispensable is the sense of history which confers the perspective in which the work must be seen as representative or eccentric, original or traditional, belonging to one school of thought or another, advancing a tendency in the development of, say, feminist thought or opposing it. Scholarly thoroughness and critical brilliance are not often found in the same person, but students of women's literature owe it to their subject to praise the works for the right reasons, that is, to identify the inner organizing principles in them, from which their vitality, if any, stems, together with the problems attendant on living in the shadow of male genius. [. . .]

1982

From: Germaine Greer, 'The Tulsa Center for the Study of Women's Literature: What We Are Doing and Why We Are Doing It', *Tulsa Studies In Women's Literature* (Tulsa, 1982), Spring, 1:1, pp. 5–26.

Anne K. Mellor takes up a similar line to Germaine Greer in an even more polemical manner:

In the future, a feminist as well as a new historical criticism of the Romantic period in England must challenge these traditional prejudices and undertake the intellectual enquiry already well underway in other fields of English and American literary criticism, the opening and reshaping of the literary canon. We must read with renewed attention and appreciation the hundreds of female and male writers working in the early nineteenth century, all those novelists, essayists, journalists, diarists, and letter-writers who had narratives to tell other than those plotted as 'natural supernaturalism' or 'the romantic sublime' or 'romantic irony'. In these forgotten or wrongly dismissed writings, we may find stories of equal or greater significance than those told by Blake, Wordsworth, Coleridge, Byron, Percy Shelley, and Keats, tales of parenting and motherhood, of male and female friendship, of sexual and racial and class oppression, of anger and desire and unrecompensed loss and jouissance, above all, tales of *shared* rather than solitary experience.

1988

From: Anne K. Mellor, ed., 'On Romanticism and Feminism', in *Romanticism and Feminism* (USA: Indiana University Press, 1988), p. 8.

Stuart Curran makes some general statements based on historical facts about women's writing specifically in the 1790s:

> [. . .] the burst of activity by women writers that marks the 1790s was not so much a novel cultural phenomenon as a logical development of forces already in place. In the 1770s and 1780s women had moved to the forefront of the publishing world. What is surprising – even to the extreme – is how little real threat men seem to have felt at this determined incursion into their realm. Boswell's propensity for recording every snippy remark uttered by Johnson leaves us with the memory that he compared women preachers to dogs walking on their hindfeet, but what should be emphasized is his constant presence among the Bluestockings and his general encouragement of Elizabeth Carter, Hester Thrale, and the young Helen Maria Williams. For Johnson the determining basis for judgment was likely to be politics not gender. It is certainly true that these years witnessed much satire upon scribbling ladies and a commonplace fear of the effects from their romantic novels on well-bred but innocent daughters. Yet, so stereotyped are these strictures that they appear mere ready-to-hand conventions: if a tone of condescension enters them, it seldom goes beyond the usual huff and puff of the patriarchy vaunting its institutionalized prerogatives. An objective chronicle of the 1780s would have to allow that there appeared ample room for women alike as readers and as writers in the rapidly expanding fortunes of the book trade and that no one strongly felt the need to stand in the way. By the end of the 1790s, however, as is indicated by Richard Polwhele's *Unsexed Females* (1798), which excoriated a series of prominent women writers as carrying out Mary Wollstonecraft's pernicious agenda and altogether constituting a serious menace to the existing state of things, the lines were drawn very differently. Perhaps the confrontation was inevitable and by nature could not be glossed over by the geniality of late Enlightenment manners. Still, the equation of writing women with demands for female equality and both together with all the excesses of the Terror in France, which was the product of, and the propaganda elicited by, the reactionary politics of the early

years of warfare, determined much subsequent history, including
the essential ideological control of the 'Angel in the House'
syndrome years after the Napoleonic Wars had receded into
history.

But even such pressures could only divert or attempt to channel
the essential flood of writing by women. The 1790s were heady
times – 'Bliss was it in that dawn to be alive' – for women as well
as men. There were a few casualties. The effortless and elegant
vers de société that Lady Sophia Burrell produced for her circle at
Tunbridge Wells or that Lady Anne Miller commissioned for
various charities and printed over the years in four volumes of
Poetical Recreations at a Villa near Bath, no more than Boucher
or Fragonard could survive the transition into the new realities of
a revolutionary age. But for every loss there were a dozen gains.
The 1790s in Britain form the arena for the first concerted
expression of feminist thought in modern European culture: the
terms of argument are heavily weighted by the conventional
(which is to say, now long since exploded) wisdom of the age,
which supported masculinist dominance by the twin pillars of
female intellectual inferiority and the woman's essential role in the
family. But Mary Wollstonecraft was by no means the only
prescient vindicator of women's rights, and the scope of agitation
and its underlying cultural dynamics during this decade have yet
to be fully understood. It is clear, however, that a wholly new
sense of empowerment impels women writers, whatever the
individual's political professions. Entire new genres dominated by
women writers entered publishers' lists: one certain aspect of the
feminist polemics of the 1790s was the intense debate that erupted
over the education of children, particularly daughters. Conduct
books tumbled forth, often assuming a newly polemical or adver-
sarial tone. In *Practical Education* (1798) Maria Edgeworth with
her father Richard initiated the rudiments of a modern, scientific
approach to child development. Children's literature flourished,
attaining with the new century and the verse productions of Ann
and Jane Taylor and Adelaide O'Keeffe a new level of psychologi-
cal and social realism and with the animal conclaves of Catherine
Anne Dorset (Charlotte Smith's sister) an assured hold on the
fantastic. Less innocent of ulterior purpose were Hannah More's
Cheap Repository Tracts, which started forth in 1795 as the first
concerted attempt to speak to the working poor in their own
language and terms: the intent was undoubtedly reactionary, but

paradoxically, the effect was revolutionary, embodying a new stylistic and social realism, stimulating a readership and a sense of cohesive identity among the working class.

Something of the same dynamic of unanticipated inversion attends the birth of another genre without precedent, journalism from behind enemy lines. The 1790s, which saw all of Europe swept up for the first time in ideological warfare, elicited much skirmishing by paper as well. But if the grand debate on ideology is recalled from the clash between Burke and Paine (though Wollstonecraft was Burke's prior antagonist) and if the economic and purely political commentary were monopolized by men, the on-the-scene reportage fell by chance into the hands of women. Helen Maria Williams, confident as a poet and novelist of sensibility, adopted the tone of transcendent observer to chronicle her experiences in eight volumes of *Letters from France* between 1792 and 1798. Arriving in Paris just in time for the celebration of the Federation on July 14, 1790, she reacts with transport to the spectacle of a half million celebrants in the Champ du Mars: 'it required but the common feelings of humanity, to become in that moment a citizen of the world' (*Letters*, 1, 14). Wollstonecraft's own account, *An Historical and Moral View of the Origin and Progress of the French Revolution and the Effect It Has Produced in Europe*, published in 1794 during the Terror, emphasizes her role as independent observer viewing events through the prism, thus from a distance, of history and morality. Like Williams, she casts herself as a citizen of the world, affirming against the debacle produced in France the certain necessity of representative government in modern Europe and refusing to throw any sop to Burke's argument for 'virtual representation.' Both women execrate Robespierre and exhibit something like pity for the reactionary fearfulness of Burke. Although they both were in danger, and Williams claimed her writings so infuriated Robespierre that she had to flee France for safety, the tone of absolute transcendence they adopt comes naturally, enforced by their having no personal stake beyond a moral one in the events unfolding before their eyes. Citizens of the world, like women in England, do not vote. Women doubtless will suffer the consequences (Williams is the foremost mythologizer of the heroic martyrdom of Madame Rolland), but they do not make the political decisions that bring on revolutions and plunge countries into wars of empire. The implicit claim of Williams and Wollstonecraft, then, is that in such a fraught time only a woman can afford to be honest. Their dual assumptions – that the sole power women can claim comes from the pen, and that only the disinterested can wield moral authority – were by no means, however, limited to the urgent historical conditions that prompted their accounts, but have informed the polemical stance of women well into the modern age. Given the hovering presence of war and its effects throughout the Romantic period, this assertion of privileged authority might well be expected to survive the reaction against the feminism of the 1790s. [. . .]   1993

From: Stuart Curran, 'Women readers, women writers', in *The Cambridge Companion to British Romanticism*, ed. Stuart Curran (Cambridge: CUP, 1993), pp. 177–95.

Marlon B. Ross discusses the writing modes of a small group of dissenting women from an historical point of view:

During the early Romantic period, women's political discourse – across the ideological spectrum – occupies a position of dissent. Simply to speak about politics is to place oneself *against* the political establishment, where women's role is normatively defined solely by silent obeisance. The woman who speaks out purposefully *not to dissent* but rather to reaffirm her total subordination to the political establishment inevitably finds herself in a problematic position of dissent. The only pure form of feminine action she can take in offering her (non) political support to the status quo is to be silent. The woman who desires to dissent, however, finds herself in an ironically fortuitous position, possessing a political voice without the drawback of belonging to the corrupt interests of established power. For her, to speak politics is automatically to assault the status quo. Her primary problem is how to speak politics without being contaminated by the moral compromises which characterize mainstream politics.

This is a formal dilemma even more than a question of ideology, morality, or politics. Without bounded forms which can construct the process of reading as a political rather than merely a 'literary' phenomenon, ideological, moral, and political meanings will be lost. This is especially the case when a female dissenter borrows a literary form that is explicitly and traditionally cued as political discourse because its formal structure is deeply embedded within status quo politics. Because politicized generic forms are notoriously conventional – requiring author and reader to identify already legitimated political discourses – the female dissenter may have both an advantage and an impasse in resorting to such forms. Although the conventionality of the form may tie her more closely to the status quo political structure from which the form gains its meaning and authority, the fact that she has no formal authority within that structure may help to unbalance the form's links to established power.

The intrinsic dissenting status of the political woman is further complicated by the fact that most *overtly* politicized women belonged to a long tradition of Nonconformist religious and civil dissent. Deprived of their civil liberties, the nonconforming religious sects of the late eighteenth century were compelled to make the connection between freedom of conscience and political liberty. Taking seriously the project of political 'protest' veiled within the religious label 'protestant,' they understood that the only way to have genuine freedom of conscience was to gain the fundamental civil liberties that were jealously guarded by the established church and government. Freedom of conscience translated easily into the obligation to stand firmly for what is perceived as morally right, even though such a stance risks disobedience to established authority. But the dissenting sects were also responsible middle-class citizens, who wanted nothing more than to be the paragon of *law-abiding* freedom. They desired not just political freedom, but also political power. They wanted the right, not just to participate in government, but to control the concept of what constitutes just government and thus to control government itself.

To be a woman within this movement was to possess equally with men the freedom of conscience valued so highly by the liberal dissenting tradition. Because it was woman's fate to learn how to balance a chaste conscience with faithful submission to the 'politic father,' she found that her feminine subordination gave her special knowledge which it became her obligation to spread as a voice of dissent. Her status of double dissent – as a political female and as a female within a nonconforming community deprived of civil liberties – presented obstacles equal to the opportunities it afforded, for it required her to articulate the insight peculiar to her dual position without having any access to sanctioned political forms (academic oratory, parliamentary debate, legal pleading, court and ministerial intrigue, and so forth). More tellingly, her access to formal political participation was limited even within her own nonconforming communities. Among the conventional modes of politics practiced by the dissenters in their fight for civil rights (the petition, the political sermon, the political association, the corresponding society, and so on), the only formal avenue open to the political female was the periodical, which welcomed her literary contributions, even though these contributions were easy targets for controversy and could be dismissed as the presumptions of a political female.

Unlike political men, women like Hannah More who hoped to influence the 'conduct' of the nation had to take an indirect route to political participation through *politic words* (words chosen with an eye to feminine caution and decorous conduct), written as literary composition. At best, a woman writer could attempt to duplicate in her politic words those more 'direct' means of active political exchange such as the dissenting sermon and the corresponding society, with their accompanying advantages of direct contact and mutual interchange in an oral or conversational situation. She could compose a sermon, which she could 'deliver' only as a written text, or she could compose a political dialogue (a favorite form in the liberal journals), imitating the conversations available to men within their political societies, and hope that it would influence the actual dialogue within these societies despite her banishment from them.

With literary composition being her only avenue to formal political participation, the dissenting female found herself contradicted yet again by the traditions of literary composition itself, for the topical literary modes overtly associated with political discourse were off limits to her, unless she could find ways, ironically, of seeming to depoliticize the topical nature of the modes themselves. It is not that she would be prevented from writing a political tract (some brave women did so), but that in writing it she jeopardized, in the eyes of her readers, the feminine purity of her position and thus the basis for her political advantage – becoming More's 'disgusting' and 'unnatural' female politician, a licentious or mannish woman (*Strictures* 364). Just as More's status quo political tract is veiled by the form of a female conduct book, so the dissenting women writers had to find ways of exploiting traditional topical forms to suit their double dissension. Because literary composition itself was being increasingly reconceived as a nonpolitical arena, at least partly due to the increasing visibility of women within it, political women had to steer a difficult course, between exploiting overtly politicized literary modes for seemingly nonpolitical ends of general moral conduct and exploiting the depoliticized mantle of 'the literary' in general to veil their passion for politics. They could choose to speak politics in nonpolitical modes, and thus risk greatly diminishing the clarity and pointedness of their political passion, or they could choose literary modes that were overtly political while trying to infuse them with a recognizable 'feminine' decorum, again risking a softening of their political agenda. The latter option also risked readers being blinded to the deeper ideological substance and political stance by their own disgust with the surface indecorousness of a female politician. [. . .]

1994

From: Marlon B. Ross, 'The Woman Writer and the Tradition of Dissent', in *Re-visioning Romanticism: British Women Writers, 1776–1837*, ed. Carol Shiner Wilson and Joel Haefner (Philadelphia: University of Pennsylvania Press, 1994), pp. 93–4.

Carol Shiner Wilson and Joel Haefner summarize the ways in which both traditional and avant-garde literary critics in their attempts to define Romanticism(s) have overlooked women writers. They also identify those critics of the 1990s who are 'restoring and examining women's writing' of the British Romantic period:

Romanticism has always been a tantalizingly slippery term, open to interpretation, reinterpretation, and debate by scholars and critics. Typically, critical perspectives reflect the concerns of the specific historical times out of which they grow. Meyer Abrams, for example, in years of crisis and promise after World War II, felt compelled to rescue the English Romantic poets from New Critical accusations of intellectual flabbiness, and to argue that they internalized and transformed the crises of the French Revolution into high art. Today, with society and the academy more aware of the historical exclusion of women and minorities from the dominant discourse, scholars are reexamining the late eighteenth and early nineteenth centuries to find what is missing from traditional literary histories: modes of literary production and consumption, the role of radical dissent, diversity of genres, women writers and their works. [. . .]

From the 1920s to 1950s, Anglo-American critics like Irving Babbitt, T. S. Eliot, Cleanth Brooks, I. A. Richards, and T. E. Hulme considered English Romantic poetry confused, excessive, and self-absorbed. New Critic Cleanth Brooks, in *Modern Poetry and the Tradition* (1939), charged the Romantics with being, in essence, unmanly, with a lack of irony and wit, a suspicion of the intellect, sloppy imagery, and a lack of verve. By the 1970s, when the New Critics seemed tiresomely monolithic, the very Romanticism they condemned was valued as anticipating modern sensibility.

René Wellek, writing in 1949, rebutted Lovejoy, claiming to find a 'unity of theories, philosophies, and style' in Romanticism across national borders ('The Concept of Romanticism' 129). Finding the English Romantics consistent with the French and German, Wellek identified three shared criteria: 'imagination for the view of poetry, nature for the view of the world, and symbol and myth for poetic style' (161). The only woman writer he considered was Mme de Staël, whom he found important for her 'intermediary role' in bringing the romantic theories of Schlegel to readers through her *De l'Allemagne* (138–9). Wellek's scheme excluded Byron. Morse Peckham, in a 1951 essay in *PMLA*, sought 'to reconcile Lovejoy and Wellek, and Lovejoy with himself' through what he called a 'dynamic organicism,' whose values included change, growth, imperfection, diversity, and the creative imagination ('Toward a Theory of Romanticism' 235, 241). Wellek was distressed to see Byron newly accommodated under the rubric 'negative romanticism' ('Romanticism Re-examined' 199–221). Although grappling with the complexity of voices in Romanticism(s), none of these male critics looked at the works of Charlotte Smith, Mary Robinson, or Jane Taylor to extract or test questions of the centrality of the imagination, dynamic organicism, negative romanticism, or irony.

Abrams, in his impressive *The Mirror and the Lamp* (1953) and *Natural Supernaturalism* (1971), argued that Romantic poetry and poetics are expressive rather than mimetic, a dramatic break from the eighteenth-century tradition of Pope or Johnson. In *Natural Supernaturalism*, strongly echoing Wordsworth and Shelley, Abrams claimed that true poets are philosophical. That philosophical role is, implicitly, public and male. Romantic writers, he argued, sought to secularize significant themes and values of Christianity in a post-Enlightenment age. Harold Bloom's *The Visionary Company* (1961; reprinted 1971) argued for the brilliance of Blake's secularized Christianity. Discussions of religion in Abrams, Bloom, and others overlooked the dissenting tradition of Anna Barbauld, Lucy Aikin, or Hannah More.

In the 1970s and early 1980s, critics including Paul de Man, Geoffrey Hartman, Anne K. Mellor, Tilottama Rajan, David Simpson, and Jerome J. McGann identified indeterminacy, or Romantic irony, as fundamental to Romantic poetry, reflecting a world that is dynamic, open-ended, fraught with dangers and possibilities. Within this context, Michael G. Cooke, in *Acts of Inclusion* (1979), claimed that Romanticism, resisting the male-vs-female orthodoxy, attempts the 'interpenetration and interpresence' of the masculine and feminine (xix). The title of a pivotal chapter in his book is 'The Feminine as the Crux of Value.'

In *The Romantic Ideology* (1983), a touchstone of new historicist writing, McGann argued that theories of Romanticism have been constructed by critics who, seduced by 'Romanticism's own self-representations,' have become 'priests and clerics' perpetuating rather than analyzing the absorbed premises of Romantic art (1). In this framework, the Romantic poet manifests the self-fictions of the canonical six: disillusioned by political, social, and religious upheavals; apart from society because of his disillusionment and poetic genius; visionary; and, although never explicitly stated, male. Although McGann does not discuss women writers, Paul Cantor has rightly argued that, once 'the Romantic idea of the artistic genius is discredited, we are free to reevaluate all the so-called lesser figures of the early nineteenth century, especially long-neglected female authors, often stigmatized as mere popular authors ... and thus forced to live in the shadow of the so-called High Romantics' ('Stoning the Romance' 715).

The paradigm is shifting yet again. Virtually no scholarly publication in the 1990s dealing in a serious way with British Romanticism can ignore the contributions of women writers, and virtually no survey of British Romanticism can leave out Charlotte Smith, Mary Robinson, or Joanna Baillie as part of the literary and cultural conversation. The major impetus for restoring and examining women's writing has come from feminist studies. Scholars like Sandra Gilbert and Susan Gubar, Mary Poovey, Margaret Homans, Mary Jacobus, Susan Wolfson, Anne K.

Mellor, Susan Levin, Jane Aaron, and others have written about authors, including Mary Shelley, Dorothy Wordsworth, and Mary Lamb, who have been marginally canonized primarily because of their association with husband or brother. [. . .]

Texts by women writers from the Romantic period are now making small inroads into the standard undergraduate Romanticism class, but the underrepresentation of women writers persists. Harriet Kramer Linkin's recent survey ('The Current Canon') of Romanticism syllabi indicates that, while the Big Six are still taught in over 90 percent of courses, there are some inroads by women writers. Mary Shelley is taught in 56 percent of the courses, Dorothy Wordsworth in 49 percent. As Linkin points out, Mary Shelley and Dorothy Wordsworth are 'safe' additions because of their connections with already canonized figures. Maria Edgeworth, Anna Barbauld, Felicia Hemans, and Charlotte Brontë are read in only 4 percent of the courses; Jane Taylor, Anna Seward, Mary Hays, and Mary Robinson at least have been taught in a few courses. These are small numbers. But the fact that these women are being read at all is a sign of hope.

1994

From: Carol Shiner Wilson and Joel Haefner, eds, 'Introduction', in *Re-visioning Romanticism: British Women Writers, 1776–1837* (Philadelphia: University of Pennsylvania Press, 1994), pp. 1–14.

SUGGESTIONS FOR FURTHER READING

Primary Works

Baillie, Joanna, *The Dramatic and Poetical Works* (London: Longman, Brown, Green & Longmans, 1851).

—, *A Series of Plays*, 1798 facsimile edn (Spelsbury: Woodstock Books, 1990).

Barbauld, Anna Letitia (née Aikin), *The Works of Anna Letitia Barbauld*, 2 vols, with a Memoir by Lucy Aikin (London: Longman, Brown, Green & Longmans, 1825).

Burney, Fanny, *Diary*, ed. Christopher Lloyd (London: Roger Ingram, 1948).

—, *The Journals and Letters*, ed. Joyce Hemlow (London: Oxford University Press, 1972).

Clairmont, Claire, *The Journals of Claire Clairmont*, ed. Marion Kingston Stocking (Cambridge, Massachusetts: Harvard University Press, 1968).

Hays, Mary, *Letters and Essays, Moral and Miscellaneous* (London: T. Knott, 1793).

Lamb, Mary and Charles, *The Works of Charles and Mary Lamb*, 7 vols, ed. E. V. Lucas, vol. 6, *Letters, 1796–1820* (London: Methuen & Co., 1905).

—, *The Works in Prose and Verse of Charles and Mary Lamb*, 2 vols, ed. Thomas Hutchinson (Oxford: Oxford University Press, 1908).

Macaulay, Catherine, *Letters on Education* (London: T. Cadell, 1790).

Mitford, Mary Russell, *Our Village: Sketches of Rural Character and Scenery*, 5th edn, vol. 1 (London: Whittaker, Treacher & Co., 1830).

—, *The Letters of Mary Russell Mitford*, ed. and introd. R. Brimley Johnson (London: John Lane The Bodley Head, 1925).

More, Hannah, *Moral Sketches of Prevailing Opinions and Manners, Foreign and Domestic: with Reflections on Prayer* (London: T. Cadell & W. Davies, 1819).

—, *The Works of Hannah More*, new edn, vol. 5 (London: T. Cadell, 1830).

—, *The Letters of Hannah More*, ed. and introd. R. Brimley Johnson (London: John Lane The Bodley Head, 1925).

Randall, Anne Frances [*pseud.*], *Letter to the Women of England on the Injustice of Subordination* (London, 1799).

Robinson, Mary, *Memoirs*, 1801, ed. and introd. J. Fitzgerald Molloy (London: Gibbings & Co.; Philadelphia: J. B. Lippincott & Co., 1895).

Seward, Anna, *The Letters of Anna Seward: Written Between the Years 1784 and 1807*, 6 vols (Edinburgh: Archibald Constable & Co.; London: Longman, Hurst, Rees, Orme & Brown, William Miller & John Murray, 1811).

—, *The Poetical Works of Anna Seward with Extracts from her Literary Correspondence*, 3 vols, ed. Sir Walter Scott (Edinburgh: Ballantyne & Co., and London: Hurst, Rees & Orme, 1810).

Shelley, Mary and P. B., *History of a Six Weeks' Tour*, 1817 facsimile edn (Spelsbury: Woodstock Books, 1989).

Shelley, Mary, *The Letters of Mary Wollstonecraft [Godwin] Shelley*, vol. 1, ed. Betty T. Bennett (Baltimore & London: The Johns Hopkins University Press, 1980).

Taylor, Jane, *Prose and Poetry*, with an Introduction by F. V. Barry (London: Humphrey Milford [OUP], 1925).

Trollope, Frances, *Domestic Manners of the Americans* (Gloucester: Alan Sutton Publishing, 1832, new edn, 1984).

Williams, Helen Maria, *Letters from France, 1792–6*, facsimile edn, introd. Janet Todd, Scholars' Facsimiles and Reprints (New York: Delaware, 1975).

Wollstonecraft, Mary, *The Works of Mary Wollstonecraft*, 7 vols, ed. Janet Todd & Marilyn Butler (London: Pickering & Chatto, 1989).

Wordsworth, Dorothy, *Journals of Dorothy Wordsworth*, ed. Mary Moorman (London: Oxford University Press, 1971).

—, *Letters of Dorothy Wordsworth*, ed. Alan G. Hill (Oxford: Oxford University Press, 1981).

—, *The Grasmere Journals*, ed. Pamela Woof (Oxford: Oxford University Press, 1991).

Dorothy and William Wordsworth, *The Letters of William and Dorothy Wordsworth: II. The Middle Years*, ed. Ernest de Selincourt, rev. Mary Moorman, 2 vols (Oxford: Clarendon Press, 1969).

Secondary Works

Checklists and Dictionaries

Alston, R. C., *A Checklist of Women Writers, 1801–1900: Fiction, Verse, Drama* (London: The British Library, 1990).

* Blain, Virginia, Patricia Clements, and Isobel Grundy, eds, *The Feminist Companion to Literature in English: Women Writers from the Middle Ages to the Present* (London: B. T. Batsford, 1990).

Hammond, N. G. L. and H. H. Scullard, eds, *The Oxford Classical Dictionary* (Oxford: Oxford University Press, 1970, reprinted 1979).

Rose, H. J., *A Handbook of Greek Mythology* (London: Methuen & Co., 1928, 6th edn, 1958, reprinted 1960).

Thorne, J. O. and T. L. Collocott, eds, *Chambers Biographical Dictionary* (Edinburgh: Chambers, revised 1984).

* Todd, Janet, ed. *A Dictionary of British and American Women Writers: 1660–1800* (USA: Rowman & Littlefield, 1984, pbk edn, 1985).

—, *A Dictionary of Women Writers* (London: Routledge, 1989).

Warrack, Alexander, comp., *Chamber's Scots Dictionary* (Edinburgh: W. & R. Chambers, 1911; reprinted 1968).

Dictionary of National Biography.

Biographies, Memoirs, Essays, Criticism

Ashmun, Margaret, *The Singing Swan: An Account of Anna Seward* (New Haven: Yale University Press and London: Oxford University Press, 1931).

Blunden, Edmund, *Charles Lamb and His Contemporaries* (Cambridge: Cambridge University Press, 1934).

* Butler, Marilyn, *Romantics, Rebels and Reactionaries: English Literature and Its Background* (Oxford: Oxford University Press, 1981).

Cambridge History of English Literature, vol. 9 (Cambridge: Cambridge University Press, 1966).

* Curran, Stuart, ed., *The Cambridge Companion to British Romanticism* (Cambridge: Cambridge University Press, 1993).

Carhart, Margaret S., *The Life and Work of Joanna Baillie* (New Haven: Yale University Press and London: Oxford University Press, 1923).

Courtney, Winifred F., *Young Charles Lamb: 1795–1802* (London: Macmillan, 1982).

* Favret, Mary A. and Nicola J. Watson, eds, *At the Limits of Romanticism* (Bloomington: Indiana University Press, 1994).

* Ferguson, Moira, *Subject to Others: British Women Writers and Colonial Slavery, 1670–1834* (London & New York: Routledge, 1993).

* George, M. Dorothy, *London Life in the Eighteenth Century* (London: Kegan Paul, Trench, Trubner & Co., 1925, reissued Penguin, 1966, reprinted 1987).

Gittings, Robert, and Jo Manton, *Dorothy Wordsworth* (Oxford: Oxford University Press, 1985).

Hill, Bridget, *The Republican Virago: The Life and Times of Catherine Macaulay, Historian* (Oxford: Oxford University Press, 1992).

Homans, Margaret, *Bearing the Word: Language and Female Experience in Nineteenth-Century Women's Writing* (Chicago: University of Chicago Press, 1986).

Hopkins, Mary Alden, *Hannah More and Her Circle* (New York & Toronto: Longmans Green & Co., 1947).

Jones, M. G., *Hannah More* (Cambridge: Cambridge University Press, 1952).

Kelly, Gary, *Women, Writing, and Revolution, 1790–1827* (Oxford: Oxford University Press, 1993).

Lane, Maggie, *Literary Daughters* (London: Robert Hale, 1989).

Levin, Susan M., *Dorothy Wordsworth and Romanticism* (USA: Rutgers, The State University, 1987).

* Mellor, Anne K., ed., *Romanticism and Feminism* (Bloomington: Indiana University Press, 1988).

—, *Romanticism & Gender* (London & New York: Routledge, 1993).

Myers, Sylvia Harcstark, *The Bluestocking Circle: Women, Friendship, and the Life of the Mind in Eighteenth-Century England* (Oxford: Oxford University Press, 1991).

Plumb, J. H., *England in the Eighteenth Century* (London: Penguin, 1950, revised 1963, reprinted 1987).

Roberts, William, ed., *Memoirs of the Life and Correspondence of Mrs Hannah More*, 3 vols (London: R. B. Seeley and W. Burnside, 3rd edn, 1835).

Rodgers, Betsy, *Georgian Chronicle: Mrs Barbauld and Her Family* (London: Methuen, 1958).

Rogers, Katharine M., *Feminism in Eighteenth-Century England* (Urbana: University of Illinois Press, 1982).

Sales, Roger, *English Literature in History: 1780–1830, Pastoral and Politics* (London: Hutchinson, 1983).

—, *Jane Austen and Representations of Regency England* (London & New York: Routledge, 1994).

Showalter, Elaine, *The New Feminist Criticism: Essays on Women, Literature and Theory* (New York: Pantheon, 1985, reprinted London: Virago, 1986).

Thompson, E. P., *The Making of the English Working Class* (London: Victor Gollancz, 1963, revised Pelican, 1968, reprinted 1980).

Thompson, William, *Appeal of One Half of the Human Race, Women, Against the Pretensions of the Other Half, Men, to Retain Them in Political, and Thence in Civil and Domestic Slavery* (London: Longman, 1825).

* Todd, Janet, *The Sign of Angellica: Women, Writing and Fiction, 1660–1800* (London: Virago, 1989).

Tompkins, J. M. S., *The Polite Marriage* (Cambridge: Cambridge University Press, 1938).

Williams, Jane, *Literary Women of England* (London: Saunders, Otley, 1861).

* Wilson, Carol Shiner and Joel Haefner, eds, *Re-visioning Romanticism: British Women Writers, 1776–1837*, (Philadelphia: University of Pennsylvania Press, 1994).

Woof, Pamela, 'Dorothy Wordsworth and Mary Lamb, Writers', *Charles Lamb Bulletin* (Tyne & Wear, 1989), July, 67, 69–82.

* The asterisked works are recommended to students.

ACKNOWLEDGEMENTS

I am grateful to R. W. Noble for his literary advice, and I also wish to thank the staff of the British Library, the London Library, the Senate House Library and the University of North London Learning Centre for their courteous assistance.

The editor and publishers wish to thank the following for permission to use copyright material:

The British Library for Mary Shelley's letter to Maria Gisborne (mss Ashley 5022);

Cambridge University Press for material from Stuart Curran, 'Women readers, women writers' in *The Cambridge Companion to British Romanticism*, ed. Stuart Curran, 1993, pp. 177–95;

Harvard University Press for material from *The Journals of Claire Clairmont*, ed. Marion Kingston Stocking, 1968, pp. 182–4;

Macmillan Ltd for material from *Journals of Dorothy Wordsworth*, ed. Ernest de Selincourt, 1947, pp. 7–31;

Oxford University Press for material from *The Letters of William and Dorothy Wordsworth, Vol. 2, The Middle Years*, ed. Ernest de Selincourt, revised by Mary Moorman, 1969, pp. 23–4, 85–6.

Tulsa Studies in Women's Literature for material from Germaine Greer, 'The Tulsa Center for the Study of Women's Literature: What We Are Doing and Why We Are Doing It', *Tulsa Studies in Women's Literature*, 1, 1, Spring 1992;

University of Pennsylvania Press for material from Carol Ann Shiner and Joel Haefner, 'Introduction' and Marlon B. Ross, 'The Woman Writer and the Tradition of Dissent' in *Re-Visioning Romanticism:*

British Women Writers, 1776–1837, eds Carol Shiner Wilson and Joel Haefner, 1994, pp. 1–14, 93–6.

Every effort has been made to trace all the copyright holders but if any have been inadvertently overlooked the publishers will be pleased to make the necessary arrangement at the first opportunity.

INDEX OF AUTHORS' NAMES

Joanna Baillie, pp. 97–103
Anna Letitia Barbauld (née Aikin), pp. 87–96
Fanny Burney (afterwards Madame d'Arblay), pp. 137–48
Claire Clairmont, pp. 237–40
Mary Hays, pp. 75–85
Mary Lamb, pp. 191–8
Catherine Macaulay (afterwards Graham), pp. 55–67
Mary Russell Mitford, pp. 199–211
Hannah More, pp. 105–19
Mary Robinson (née Darby), pp. 121–35
Anna Seward, pp. 45–54
Mary Wollstonecraft Shelley, pp. 213–35
Frances Trollope (née Milton), pp. 241–9
Jane Taylor, pp. 149–59
Helen Maria Williams, pp. 69–74
Mary Wollstonecraft, pp. 3–43
Dorothy Wordsworth, pp. 161–89

WOMEN'S WRITING
IN EVERYMAN

Poems and Prose
CHRISTINA ROSSETTI
*A collection of her writings, poetry
and prose, published to mark the
centenary of her death*
£5.99

Women Philosophers
edited by Mary Warnock
*The great subjects of philosophy
handled by women spanning four
centuries, including Simone de
Beauvoir and Iris Murdoch*
£6.99

Glenarvon
LADY CAROLINE LAMB
*A novel which throws light on the
greatest scandal of the early nine-
teenth century – the infatuation of
Caroline Lamb with Lord Byron*
£6.99

Women Romantic Poets
1780–1830: **An Anthology**
edited by Jennifer Breen
*Hidden talent from the Romantic
era rediscovered*
£5.99

**Memoirs of the Life of Colonel
Hutchinson**
LUCY HUTCHINSON
*One of the earliest pieces of
women's biographical writing, of
great historic and feminist interest*
£6.99

**The Secret Self 1: Short Stories
by Women**
edited by Hermione Lee
'A superb collection' The Guardian
£4.99

The Age of Innocence
EDITH WHARTON
*A tale of the conflict between love
and tradition by one of America's
finest women novelists*
£4.99

Frankenstein
MARY SHELLEY
*A masterpiece of Gothic terror
in its original 1818 version*
£3.99

The Life of Charlotte Brontë
ELIZABETH GASKELL
*A moving and perceptive tribute
by one writer to another*
£4.99

Victorian Women Poets
1830–1900
edited by Jennifer Breen
*A superb anthology of the era's
finest female poets*
£5.99

**Female Playwrights of the
Restoration: Five Comedies**
edited by Paddy Lyons
*Rediscovered literary treasure
in a unique selection*
£5.99

All books are available from your local bookshop or direct from:
Littlehampton Book Services Cash Sales, 14 Eldon Way, Lineside Estate,
Littlehampton, West Sussex BN17 7HE (*prices are subject to change*)

To order any of the books, please enclose a cheque (in sterling) made payable to
Littlehampton Book Services, or phone your order through with credit card details (Access,
Visa or Mastercard) on 01903 721596 (24 hour answering service) stating card number
and expiry date. (*Please add £1.25 for package and postage to the total of your order.*)

In the USA, for further information and a complete catalogue call 1-800-526-2778